Exploring *Atlas Shrugged*

Exploring *Atlas Shrugged*

Ayn Rand's Magnum Opus

Edward W. Younkins

LEXINGTON BOOKS

Lanham • Boulder • New York • London

Published by Lexington Books
An imprint of The Rowman & Littlefield Publishing Group, Inc.
4501 Forbes Boulevard, Suite 200, Lanham, Maryland 20706
www.rowman.com

6 Tinworth Street, London SE11 5AL, United Kingdom

British Library Cataloguing in Publication Information Available

Library of Congress Cataloging-in-Publication Data

ISBN: 978-1-7936-3642-3 (cloth)
ISBN: 978-1-7936-3644-7 (pbk.)
ISBN: 978-1-7936-3643-0 (electronic)

Contents

Introduction

When I first read *Atlas Shrugged*, I was immediately captivated by Ayn Rand's striking narrative power and by her remarkable philosophical insights. The plot of this great novel was a model of integration among theme, story, and characters. All elements were logically connected, tied to the whole, and integrated with the novel's unifying theme. Even the philosophical speeches were integrated with the events of the story. The brilliantly constructed, intricate, and interwoven plot was a miracle of organization including multiple layers or tiers of depth.

Here was a novel about the great minds of the world going on strike while the world is heading toward destruction. The heroes are giants of intellect and productivity who make the villains' evil possible through their own assistance and support (i.e., their moral sanction). Early in the novel, we see a society and a culture in which producers are not valued, appreciated, or rewarded. They lack the freedom to start companies, to develop new products, to compete, to make profits, and to keep their wealth. Although their minds have been constrained by government intervention and regulation, their persecution is made possible by their acceptance of the prevailing morality of altruism. Irrational and/or immoral people and schemes can only succeed when they are not opposed by rational people. It takes the voluntary withdrawal of the sanction and the talents of the best and the brightest to begin the transformation of the world.

This book is an exploration and a celebration of Rand's monumental work of philosophy and literature that is the culmination of her literary life and the product of her many years of thinking and hard work. The chapters herein analyze her novel's integrating elements of theme, plot, and characters from many perspectives and on various levels of meaning. Although these chapters address the philosophical, literary, and other aspects of *Atlas Shrugged* and are geared to general readers who are fans of this great novel, it is hoped that scholars will also enjoy them and benefit from reading them. Such a rich and complex novel of ideas warrants and rewards additional study and critical analysis.

Ayn Rand was born in 1905 in Russia where she experienced the Bolshevik Revolution, the Communist takeover of Russia, and the political persecutions that resulted from those events. In 1926, she escaped the brutal oppression of Communist despotism by going alone to the United States where she became a screenwriter in Hollywood and the author of two powerful and popular novels in the 1940s and 1950s—*The Fountainhead* and *Atlas Shrugged*.

Written between 1945 and 1956, *Atlas Shrugged* went through numerous changes and revisions. This novel about the men of the mind going on strike retained the working title, "The Strike," for nearly a decade. During this period, socialism was a popular political philosophy among American intellectuals, professors, politicians, journalists, and labor leaders. Many American citizens believed that government should have the power to tax heavily, to coercively redistribute wealth and income, and to regulate private businesses. Capitalism was under attack by socialists and supporters of the welfare state. Although Rand's primary goal in writing *Atlas Shrugged* was to dramatize how life could be and ought to be, it also aided in her efforts to defeat the reigning cultural climate of collectivism in politics, economics, and morality and to present her radical new philosophy (later to be named Objectivism) in a dramatized form.

This alternative-reality allegory is both dystopian and utopian in nature. As a dystopian novel, *Atlas Shrugged* depicts the United States experiencing a period of social and economic collapse. Rand projected a dystopian future of what the world's People's States, and America in particular, could become if current trends toward collectivism and altruism escalate. Abstracting from the present (i.e., when she was writing the novel), Rand constructs a future world of omnipresent and intrusive government in which language is corrupted by government officials and crony capitalists who declare that the public good is their goal rather than to benefit themselves. *Atlas Shrugged* portrays a future in which America's movement toward statism has accelerated. Whereas the dystopian side dominates the novel, the utopian aspect is reflected in Galt's Gulch (or Mulligan's Valley), an ideal society that provides a model of what a future world based on reason, science, and individualism could be like.

Since its publication in 1957, *Atlas Shrugged* has sold over eight million copies. Respondents to a joint Library of Congress—Book of the Month Club survey in 1991 hailed the book as second only to the Bible in its significant impact on their lives. A 1998 Random House/Modern Library readers' poll placed it at the top of their list of the greatest novels of the twentieth century.

In addition, in 2018, *Atlas Shrugged* came in at number twenty in Public Broadcasting Services' (PBS) *The Great American Read* poll.

Appealing on many levels, *Atlas Shrugged* is a moral defense of capitalism, political parable, social commentary, science fiction tale, mystery story, love story, fantasy tale, adventure saga, boardroom drama, chronicle, realistic fiction in the romantic tradition, mythological saga, epic, and more. The further and deeper that I studied *Atlas Shrugged*, the more I was able to appreciate how these multiple facets enrich one another. In addition, Rand effectively included several tiers, levels, or layers of exposition, meaning, suggestive descriptions, themes, and plot elements.

Atlas Shrugged is a great story that helps people to understand the nature of the world in which they live. It illustrates that only a free society is compatible with the nature of man and the world and that capitalism works because it is in accordance with reality. Capitalism is shown to be the only moral social system because it protects man's mind, his primary means of survival and flourishing. *Atlas Shrugged* is a powerful tool to educate, persuade, and convert people to a just and proper political and economic order that is a true reflection of the nature of man and the world properly understood.

Atlas Shrugged portrays capitalism as the only system that is objective, just, and compatible with individual freedom. The reader is shown that individual freedom, private property, free markets, voluntary exchange, and a limited government produce a society that meets the needs and preferences of, and is in accordance with the nature of, imperfect but rational beings in a finite world.

Atlas Shrugged has inspired both passionate admiration and violent antagonism. Over the years, it has reached a large audience despite mainly negative initial attitudes of critics and intellectuals who wrote reviews savagely attacking it. Denounced by many reviewers and scholars, *Atlas Shrugged* generated enormous controversy upon its publication. Nevertheless, since its release, innumerable readers have affirmed and attested to its importance to their lives. For many individuals open to her ideas, her masterpiece has served as a mythical foundation that concretizes the essence of Objectivism through the actions of its characters.

SYNOPSIS

Rand's prophetic masterpiece, *Atlas Shrugged* (1957), takes place at a time when the government is seeking ever more control and where the men of commerce are mysteriously disappearing. The United States is the only nation that has not become a People's State (i.e., a socialist country). This novel depicts the businessman's role as heroic and the business hero as a persistent independent thinker. It also presents an integrated conceptual and moral case for freedom and against collectivism. *Atlas Shrugged* tells the story of the last stages of conflict between productive businessmen and looter politicians and bureaucratic rent-seeking businessmen who use government edicts to gain favorable treatment for their companies. The theme of the novel is the role of the mind in human existence. It illustrates this theme by showing what the world would be like if the rationally purposeful creators stopped producing by going on strike. Chapter 1 provides an overview and synopsis of Rand's epic story of heroic businessmen.

The story takes place in a slightly modified United States. The country has a head of state rather than a president and National Legislature instead of a Congress. The time is ostensibly the not-too-distant future in which American society is crumbling under the impact of the welfare state and creeping socialism (most other nations have already become Communist People's States). The story may be described as simultaneously anachronistic and timeless. The pattern of industrial organization appears to be that of the late 1800s with large capital-intensive corporations being owned and run by individual entrepreneurs. The mood seems to be close to that of the Depression era of the 1930s. Both the social customs and the level of technical knowledge are reminiscent of the 1950s. The degree of government interference and political corruption is similar to that of the 1970s.

The story is about a revolution brought about by the heroes of *Atlas Shrugged*. It is about the fall that occurs in the world when the thinkers and creators go on strike. Led by the mysterious John Galt, this small group of heroic prime movers voluntarily withdraws from society, hastening the collapse of the economy. Galt said that he would stop the motor of the world and, through his ingenious strategy of a strike of the men of the mind, does just that. Through the use of persuasion, Galt and his college friend, Francisco d'Anconia, recruit a band of heroic men whose actions impact an entire nation. These men of the mind strike in support of individual freedom and individual rights, including the right to think for oneself and to act upon that thinking. The strike illustrates the role of the mind in human existence and brings about the fall of the American economy and the end of the country's movement toward socialism. Galt's speech on the radio informs the masses of the existence and reason for the strike and urges the common man and woman to join it.

The section titles of *Atlas Shrugged* have Aristotelian significance. The titles are related to the Aristotelian laws of logic: Non-Contradiction (the Law of Non-Contradiction), Either-Or (the Law of Excluded Middle), and A is A (the Law of Identity). In Part One, there are a series of paradoxes and apparent contradictions with no apparent logical solution. Part Two is concerned with fundamental dichotomous choices. In Part Three, all the apparent contradictions are resolved and the true nature of the events is identified.

Atlas Shrugged opens with the country in a state of worsening economic conditions and Dagny Taggart, vice-president of operations at Taggart Transcontinental Railroad, trying to keep her company going by working to repair and rebuild the crumbling Rio Norte Line that serves Ellis Wyatt's oil fields in Colorado, the last prosperous industrial area in the country. Talented and productive entrepreneurs are retiring and disappearing. People's sense of pessimism, despair, and hopelessness is embodied in the expression, "Who is John Galt?."

The Mexican government nationalizes Taggart's San Sebastian Line built to serve Francisco d'Anconia's copper mines. Now viewed as a worthless playboy, but still the world's richest copper industrialist, Francisco was Dagny's lover during their teenage years. James Taggart, Dagny's incompetent brother and president of the company, had invested heavily in a railroad for that territory. The mines are discovered to be worthless and James Taggart takes credit for Dagny's decision to remove valuable assets from that region before the nationalization takes place.

In order to make up for the losses sustained from the San Sebastian take-over, James Taggart uses his political influence to get the National Alliance of Railroads to pass the Anti-dog-eat-dog Rule to destroy Taggart's only competitor in Colorado, Dan Conway's Phoenix-Durango Railroad.

Ellis Wyatt demands that Dagny do whatever it takes to supply adequate rail service to his oil wells before the rule takes effect. To do so, she must rebuild the Rio Norte Line quickly and decides to use Rearden Metal for the rails for this line. In a meeting with her brother, Jim, she informs him that she canceled the order that he had placed with Associated Steel owned by his undependable friend, Orren Boyle. It took Hank Rearden ten years to develop Rearden Metal, an alloy stronger and lighter than steel.

Francisco had deliberately misled investors leading to their losses. He informs Dagny that he intentionally built worthless mines in order to harm d'Anconia Copper and Taggart Transcontinental. Then at the Reardens' wedding anniversary party, Francisco tells Rearden that his dependent family members have a weapon that they are using against him and that he needs to defend himself.

The State Science Institute (SSI), under Dr. Robert Stadler, denounces Rearden Metal and issues a report condemning it as potentially unsafe. Because of this denunciation, some businesses boycott Taggart Transcontinental and its stock price plummets. In order to shield the firm, Dagny decides to start her own company to rebuild the line, agreeing to return it when it succeeds. She defiantly chooses to name her railroad the John Galt Line.

The legislature passes the Equalization of Opportunity Bill, which prevents an individual from owning companies in different fields. In compliance with this bill, Rearden's ore mines are turned over to Paul Larkin and his coal mines are transferred to Ken Danagger.

The first train runs successfully on the John Galt Line. Dagny and Hank become lovers, travel together, discover the remnants of a revolutionary motor in an abandoned factory that runs on static electricity, and attempt to find the inventor of the motor.

Crippling new legislation forces successful Colorado firms to share their profits with their poor, competitor neighbors. As a response, Ellis Wyatt sets fire to his oil wells and disappears. This is followed by the progressive disappearance of other industrialists.

Dagny continues her attempts to find the inventor of the motor or someone who can rebuild it. Dr. Stadler recommends Quentin Daniels as a young scientist who may be able to reconstruct the motor. Dagny believes that there is a destroyer who is removing the men of the mind. As she suspects, Ken Danagger is the next conquest of the destroyer.

Hank Rearden refuses to sell Rearden Metal to SSI. Knowing that Hank had sold an illegal amount of Rearden Metal to Ken Danagger, Dr. Floyd Ferris threatens that he will take Rearden to court if he doesn't sell to SSI. Francisco visits Hank at his mills to introduce key ideas about moral codes and moral sanctions to him. When a fire breaks out, they work together to extinguish it, Hank saves Francisco's life, and Francisco comes to understand Hank's love of his mills. Charges are brought against Rearden and Danagger, and at his trial, Hank refuses to participate in the proceedings or to recognize the right of the court to try him. The judges levy a fine on him and then suspend the sentence.

Because of the cascading consequences of crippling regulations in Colorado, Taggart Transcontinental is forced to close the Rio Norte Line. Directive 10-289 is passed and includes a new set of laws that puts the government in charge of all business operations. These laws require that all workers remain at their current jobs, all businesses stay open, all patents be turned over to the government, and much more. Dagny resigns over the new directives and goes to her family's cabin in the mountains. Ferris blackmails Hank to sign a "Gift Certificate," turning his patent on Rearden Metal over to the government. He signs because he wants to avoid exposure of his affair with Dagny, thereby protecting her reputation. After hearing of a major accident at the Taggart Tunnel, Dagny returns to her job in New York.

Dagny receives a letter from Quentin Daniels, the scientist she had hired to rebuild the motor, saying that he may be the next person to quit and disappear. After phoning him, she rushes to Utah to persuade him not to leave. Attempting to stop him, she learns more about John Galt on her train trip.

According to a hobo she encounters, Galt was an engineer at the Twentieth Century Motor Company where the owners had put a socialist program into practice. He was the first person to quit the company. The train stops and the crew abandons it. After locating a private plane, she spots another plane leaving with Daniels and the "destroyer," pursues them, and crashes into a remote valley where she learns the secret behind the disappearance of the "men of the mind."

There Dagny meets John Galt, who is both the destroyer and the inventor of the motor, and falls in love with him. She also finds all the great minds who have disappeared and learns why each one went on strike. She is asked to join the strike and remain in the valley but turns down the invitation because she can't give up her railroad and her values while she thinks that they are still possible to achieve. Dagny chooses to return to the outside world and Galt also goes so that he can watch over her.

When Dagny returns, she learns that the government has nationalized the railroad industry. The government wants her to make a speech on the radio reassuring the public about the new laws. Instead, she announces that she had been Hank Rearden's lover and that he had turned over his patent because of a blackmail threat.

With the economy on the brink of collapse, Francisco destroys the rest of his assets and disappears. Dagny is called to the Taggart Tunnel to deal with a switch system failure. She spots John Galt among the track workers. He follows her into an empty tunnel and they make love for the first time. They talk and he warns her about inadvertently leading the looters to him.

When Hank Rearden refuses to participate in the Steel Unification Plan, the government smuggles thugs into Rearden's mills, and they start a riot in which the Wet Nurse is killed. Rearden is rescued by Francisco, who had been working there. After they talk, Hank retires and joins the strike.

The head of state is scheduled to deliver a radio address regarding the economic situation of the country. John Galt interrupts the address and takes over the airwaves to deliver a three-hour speech explaining the nature and reasons for the strike, the morality of life, the morality of death, and the need to choose between them. This speech constitutes Rand's presentation of the essentials of her philosophy of Objectivism.

The leaders of the government want to make Galt the country's economic dictator. Dagny unintentionally leads them to him. They capture and arrest him and try to convince him to become the economic dictator. He refuses their offer and is tortured in a vain attempt to force his cooperation. James Taggart ceases to be able to evade his own evil when he realizes that he wants to kill John Galt. He collapses, suffering a total mental breakdown. The strikers rescue Galt and they go back to the valley to prepare to return to the world to rebuild the economy.

PHILOSOPHY AND LITERATURE

Chapter 2 draws on the views of scholars who have written about *Atlas Shrugged* in order to make a case that it is a highly integrated work of imaginative literature. The chapter focuses on the ways in which integration is manifested in *Atlas Shrugged*. Part 1 examines the philosophical structure of the novel. Part 2 addresses the literary structure. This is followed by a discussion of Rand's techniques of characterization. An analysis of the speeches and the theme of mind-body integration concludes the discussion.

Atlas Shrugged introduces Rand's groundbreaking philosophical ideas and revolutionary moral vision in the form of an epic novel. It is the philosophical and artistic capstone of her novels and the demarcation work and turning point that culminated her career as a novelist and propelled her into a new career as a popular philosopher. This remarkable intellectual achievement has become one of the most influential books ever published, impacting a variety of disciplines including philosophy, literature, economics, business, and political science, among others.

In *Atlas Shrugged*, Rand presents her original, brilliant, and controversial philosophy of Objectivism in a dramatized form. More than a great novel, it expounds a radical new philosophy with amazing clarity. *Atlas Shrugged* presents an integrated and all-embracing perspective of man and man's relationship to the world and manifests the essentials of an entire philosophical system—metaphysics, epistemology, ethics, and politics. This philosophical system is embodied in the actions of the story's heroes. Although dramatization is paramount in *Atlas Shrugged*, Rand also effectively uses dialogue and narration along with the less frequently used supplemental techniques of symbolism and the re-adaptation and recasting of Greek myths to tell them from an Objectivist perspective.

The most extraordinary characteristic of *Atlas Shrugged* is its integration. Everything in the novel is connected to the unifying theme of "the role of the mind in human existence." The unity of a novel depends upon necessary causal and logical connections among its various features. Every event, action, and character serve both dramatic and philosophical purposes. Rand included no random elements or events.

Atlas Shrugged is a story of human actions on a monumental level. In it, Rand skillfully ties physical actions to fundamental human values. Although she also deals with the mental portraiture and analysis of her characters, her main concern is with human action. She selects and integrates actions and events that dramatize the theme of the novel, which is "the role of the mind in human existence." Rand portrays man as a volitional being who needs a rational moral code to guide his actions. She shows that the concept of value is a crucial element in a man's life.

Rand thinks in essentials in uniting all the issues and the actions of the characters in her story. Her chief concern is with values and issues that can be expressed in action. The story's plot action is based on the integration of values and actions and of mind and body. Rand thereby shows actions supporting wide abstract principles. She uses the story of *Atlas Shrugged* as a vehicle for manifesting her ideas, bringing philosophy to life through character and plot.

Clearly Rand's evocative writing has huge emotional impact because of the sense of life, or implicit outlook on life, that she portrays in *Atlas Shrugged*. Rand's novel provides a moral sense of life involving the emotional experience of admiration for man's highest potential. Her powerful mythical work elicits extraordinarily strong positive and negative emotional responses depending upon each particular reader's sense of life and view of man and the world. Its mythic stature, in part at least, may also be related to the huge time and emotional investment necessary to read Rand's nearly 1,200-page *magnum opus*.

Rand not only illustrates the dramatic conflict between the good and the bad (e.g., Dagny and Rearden versus the looters), she also shows the conflict between the good and the good (e.g., Galt and the strikers versus Dagny and Rearden). Galt drives the conflict in order to dramatize the martyrdom of the men of the mind whose own victimhood is made possible only by their own error. It is through that conflict that Dagny, Rearden, and the other scabs come to understand the nature of their mistake. Rand's fascinating story tells how Dagny and Rearden discover the secret of the strike and are ultimately led to join it.

The heroes of *Atlas Shrugged* are giants of intellect and productivity who make the evil of the villains possible through their own support and assistance (i.e., their sanction). These great minds were partly to blame because they acceded to the altruist claims of the would-be destroyers of capitalism. Under the altruist moral code, the highest moral value is self-sacrifice rather than one's flourishing and happiness. Although Rand had great admiration for the producers and entrepreneurs as heroic, she also displayed her disdain for their unwillingness to defend themselves against a moral code of self-sacrifice that holds that an individual's life should be devoted to serving the needs of others. Altruism (literally otherism) sees business profitability, proficiency, and success as being in opposition to the moral tradition of duty, which says that we must sacrifice selflessly and serve others. Of course, the altruist creed is unable to explain why it is moral to serve the interests and happiness of other people, but not to serve one's own interests and happiness.

Rand defines altruism the same way as it was originally defined by Auguste Comte, the nineteenth-century sociologist who invented the term. The basic principle of altruism (or otherism) is that service to others is the only justification of a person's existence. Self-sacrifice to others is an individual's highest moral duty. Rather than having the right to exist for his own sake, a person lives for the benefit of others. The identity of the beneficiary of an action, rather than the morality of the action itself, is deemed to be the standard of morality. Altruism says that others must be the beneficiaries. When defined in this manner, altruism should not be confused with kindness, compassion, goodwill, or respect for other people. Altruism requires self-sacrifice. This involves the surrender of a more important value for a lesser value. Sacrifice is therefore the essence of morality. In *Atlas Shrugged*, Rand illustrates the destructive effects of a moral code based on self-sacrifice.

Altruism can be voluntary or it can be enforced by the government, but there is an inextricable relationship between the two. In *Atlas Shrugged*, John Galt and the other strikers oppose the ideology of sacrifice that underpins the expanding government that is leading the country toward destruction through the redistribution of wealth and power. The novel illustrates that central planning and government intervention in the economy disturb the rational planning of individuals, productivity, and trade relationships. It dramatizes the martyrdom of the men of the mind whose victimhood is made possible by their own error in accepting the prevailing moral code of altruism that punishes them for their virtues. Rand refers to this error as the "sanction of the victim." The strike is John Galt's ingenious strategy to solve society's problems. Galt creates a band of heroic men to implement this strategy. In order to do this, he must first teach the producers that they have no duty to live for others and that they do have a right to their own lives. As a result, the independent minds withdraw from society to live in Galt's Gulch, an ideal community that illustrates what the world could be like.

By including only that which is essential, Rand illustrates the connection between metaphysical abstractions and concrete expressions. *Atlas Shrugged* is a feat of complex structural integration. The author carefully selected the details with no event, character, line of dialogue, or description included that does not further and reinforce the theme of the importance of reason. Nothing is thrown in arbitrarily.

The construction of the John Galt Line most directly depicts the mind's role in human existence. Much of the balance of the novel demonstrates the effects of the absence of the men of the mind. *Atlas Shrugged* teaches that prosperity and productivity depend upon the mind by showing both the presence and the absence of the producers in the world.

Atlas Shrugged dramatizes and explains that what is primary in studying human action is the nature of man and that man's distinctive mode of action includes rationality and free will. Rand portrays men as rational beings with free will who have the ability to form their own purposes and aims. She shows that human action involves purposeful, intentional, and normative behavior.

A Romantic novel like *Atlas Shrugged* presumes man's free will, his freedom to choose, and his ability to attain a purpose. A rational being can select a goal, act to achieve it, and discover or create the means to accomplish it. A human being can make choices about what he will do. A person's free will choice is the cause and the cause generates the effects.

The characters and events of *Atlas Shrugged* portray the philosophical principles that affect the actual existence of men in the world. The conflict between the looters and the creators dramatizes the struggle between contradictory values and moralities. Because objective human values can be identified through conceptual (i.e., abstract) thinking based on the observation of reality, the reader is given concretes in the novel in order for the abstract values to become real for him.

Atlas Shrugged is the systematic dramatization of a rational philosophy that includes a view of life as exaltation and the universe as benevolent. It depicts conflict in action between whim-worshipping looters who seek power over man and the creators who accept, learn, and deal with the absolute laws of nature and existence. The secondhanders are concerned with "who makes it possible," meaning both whom they should enslave and whom they should get to enslave them.

Rand, like Aristotle in his *Nicomachean Ethics*, holds an agent-centered approach to morality and concentrates on the character traits that constitute a good person. Rand's heroes are shown to hold proper principles and to develop appropriate character traits. The villains in the novel provide examples of what happens to people when they hold faulty principles (or compromise certain important principles) and fail to develop essential virtues.

Rand presents her characters in a stylized form according to their essential characteristics. Rand explained that her characters are individuals in whom certain attributes are focused more sharply and consistently than in the average human being. Having removed incidental and irrelevant attributes, she explores each character's personal traits and motives and connects those traits and motivations to their actions. Issues in the story emerge from particular actions taken by the characters. Actions reveal essential aspects of a character. Rand understood that what a character does portrays the character better than what he says and vastly better than what other characters and the author say about him.

Together, actions and dialogue (i.e., words in the context of a character's actions) aid in grasping the motives of a character. A character's consistent actions, words, decisions, concerns, motives, premises, and values reveal what is at the philosophical root of his character. In addition, the name and physical appearance of a Randian character point toward whether that character is virtuous or evil. Not only are her characters personified in their names, their morals (good or bad) are reflected in their physical appearances, as well.

Rand presents her characters as parallels and contrasts. Her purposeful characters face different problems and choices. She puts characters with intensely held contrasting worldviews and motivations into circumstances that place them into conflict with each other.

Although Rand wrote *Atlas Shrugged* to portray her ideal this-worldly man, John Galt, the novel is populated by more than 100 characters, most of whom can be placed in the easily identifiable categories of heroes and villains. Supplying her own judgment, Rand leaves little or no leeway for the reader's interpretations of a character's classification.

Galt is the hero of *Atlas Shrugged* whose principles drive the action and conflict of the story. Although he doesn't make an actual appearance until two-thirds of the way through the novel, he is mentioned in the very first and last sentences of chapter 1 in the slang expression "Who is John Galt?" that is meant to connote a sense of hopeless futility and resignation. His influence is omnipresent as he was the inventor of the motor, the destroyer removing the men of the mind, a student of both Robert Stadler and Hugh Akston, the first employee to quit the Twentieth Century Motor Company, a supposed legendary character, the worker whom Eddie Willers talks with in the Taggart cafeteria, the man leaving Ken Danagger's office just before Danagger tells Dagny that he has decided to retire, and more. Dagny even renames the Rio Norte Line the John Galt Line as an act of defiance.

Galt is the prime mover who leads the thinkers and creators on strike on behalf of individual rights, the morality of rational self-interest, and political freedom and against an enforced moral code of altruism. Galt and the other boundary-crossing heroes walk away and stand up for what they believe in. Galt, the embodiment of Rand's most deeply held values, always faces reality, never avoids the truth, is not sidetracked by his emotions, and respects that other people have to freely make their own decisions and choices. The motivation and purpose of his crusade and his evolution and maturation as a character are not revealed directly via narration, but instead through dialogue involving other characters.

Dagny Taggart is the protagonist-heroine of the novel. The narrative path of the novel follows Dagny's account more than that of any other character. Her character is developed in detail from childhood until the present. She is both Galt's most threatening enemy and the woman that he loves. He is both the inventor of the motor whom she seeks and the destroyer whom she has vowed to kill. Dagny is the brilliant woman who runs a transcontinental railroad, who struggles to save her company from government coercion and from the incompetence of her brother, James, the firm's president (in name only). Until later in the novel, Dagny believes that the looters must be open to reason, are persuadable, and that they want to live.

Hank Rearden is an industrialist who, through ten years of Herculean effort, invented Rearden Metal, a substance stronger and lighter than steel. He is a martyred industrialist whose quest to understand and resolve his emotional and moral conflicts is essential to the plot. Through much of the story, he holds the mistaken premise of the mind-body split or dichotomy both in economics and in sex. Once he abandons the idea that the body is low and base, he is able to understand and appreciate his own greatness and value. By the time he departs for Galt's Gulch, Hank has discarded the weaknesses of guilt and self-sacrifice. He no longer accepts the moral premise that an individual has an unchosen obligation to serve others. He has freed himself from the chains of the morality of self-sacrifice.

Much of *Atlas Shrugged* is the story of how Dagny and Hank learn about the secret of the strike and are led to join it. Dagny and Hank were overly optimistic and overly confident and were not rebellious enough. Business colleagues and lovers throughout a great deal of the story, they unintentionally supported the looters' program.

Francisco d'Anconia is Galt's friend and ally, the first man to join Galt's strike, and a recruiter for the strike. A superb copper industrialist, he masquerades as a worthless playboy in order to hide his real purposes. A childhood friend and eventually a lover of Dagny in their teens, he gives her up in order to work for the strike. Francisco sabotages his own mines and works to undermine its structure of looter-invested capital, thereby accelerating the country's financial and economic collapse. Deceiving Dagny about his true character, he joins with her in helping to free Hank from the shackles of the self-sacrifice ethics in both material production and in sex. Although Francisco and Dagny share the same values, they pursue them with different premises in mind—he goes on strike and she continues to battle the looters in the outside world. Francisco battles the looters as well, but in a different and more effective way.

Like Francisco, Ragnar Danneskjöld is a friend of Galt who joins the strike at its very beginning. A philosopher and a man of justice, he becomes a pirate who robs and sinks government relief ships and returns the wealth to those who produced it.

Dagny encounters a number of men who later become strikers including Owen Kellogg (an employee of Taggart Transcontinental), Ken Danagger of Danagger Coal, Ellis Wyatt of Wyatt Oil, and Quentin Daniels (the physicist she hired to attempt to reconstruct the motor). She also meets a former philosophy professor at Patrick Henry University, Hugh Akston, while he was working as a short-order cook. In addition, she also comes across some notable and virtuous individuals who do not join the strike such as Dan Conway of the Phoenix-Durango Railroad, Mr. Ward of Ward Harvester, and contractor Dick McNamara, among others.

While in Mulligan's Valley, she meets a number of other heroic strikers including, but not limited to, Calvin Atwood of Atwood Light and Power, composer Richard Halley, Lawrence Hammond of Hammond Car Company, Dr. Thomas Hendricks, Roger Marsh of Marsh Electric, Judge Narragansett, Ted Nielsen of Nielsen Motors, Dwight Sanders of Sanders Aircraft, and Andrew Stockton of Stockton Foundry. The inhabitants of Galt's Gulch live and work there while awaiting the collapse of the collectivist state.

Jeff Allen is the tramp and former skilled lathe operator at the Twentieth Century Motor Company. He tells Dagny the story of the collapse of that company under the socialist plan of the Starnes heirs (Eric, Gerald, and Ivy) and of the engineer named John Galt, who promised to stop the motor of the world. She leaves Allen in charge when she departs the frozen train in order to seek help.

Three of the most likable and good characters suffer bad ends in the novel. Cherryl (Brooks) Taggart is a hero worshipper who wrongly idolizes and marries James Taggart and later discovers that it is Dagny who embodies what she thought Jim was. The Wet Nurse (Tony) is a young bureaucrat and moral relativist just out of college who is sent to Rearden's mills to enforce government policies and to spy on Rearden. Transformed by his contact with Rearden and his mills, he comes to admire Rearden, to develop objective moral principles, and to seek a real job at the mills. He gives his life to protect Rearden's mills when he is shot by government thugs rioting at the mills. Eddie Willers is Dagny's childhood friend and her fiercely loyal and competent assistant who always wants to do what is right. The last that we hear about him is that he is left on a stranded train. Eddie represents the vulnerable common man with limited ability to fight or to escape.

Atlas Shrugged is filled with villainous characters. James Taggart, a major scoundrel in the novel, is an espoused altruist who seeks power over other people. He wants to be known as a humanitarian and philanthropist, but he doesn't care about other people. He is a whim-worshipper who thinks that all he has to do is to "want" something. Although he does not realize it until late in the novel, his goal is destruction and he is a nihilist and spiritual killer. He is motivated by his hatred of the good. He does not want to be held responsible for anything and he uses his government connections in order to destroy his competitors. Jim marries Cherryl, attempts to shatter her spirit, and wants unearned love and adoration from her. Cherryl discovers that he is a looter and that he married her to keep her from rising. He evades his true motives until he realizes that he wants Galt to die. Recognizing the full depth of his own moral depravity, he loses his mind and suffers a mental breakdown.

Like James Taggart, Lillian Rearden is a nihilist. She is more evil than Taggart, however, in that she is conscious of her hatred of the good. She has no illusions that the one goal of her life is to destroy the husband she hates.

Her destructiveness is intentional. She deviously manipulates Hank in order to diminish his sense of self-worth. Lillian uses his virtues against him in order to evoke feelings of guilt and to reduce his greatness.

Wesley Mouch began his political career as Rearden's "Washington man." After selling Rearden out with regard to the Equalization of Opportunity Bill, this mediocre influence peddler obtains a job heading up the Bureau of Economic Planning and Natural Resources. He strives to pass the state's Directive 10-289 and becomes the country's economic dictator.

Robert Stadler is the world's greatest physicist who once taught Galt, Francisco, and Ragnar at Patrick Henry University. Holding a theoretical versus applied science split, he is committed to reason and truth in pure science but is dismissive of applied science and material production. Believing that most people are irrational beings who would not voluntarily support theoretical science, he endorses and becomes the head of SSI, thereby using government force to finance his theoretical noncommercial ventures. This brilliant man chooses to renounce the mind by throwing in with the force-wielders. He is doomed once he turns his mind over to the brutes.

Floyd Ferris, top coordinator of SSI, is a manipulative and murderous bureaucrat with a desire for political power. He attacks the mind in his book *Why Do You Think You Think?*. Stadler knows that this book is trash, but he does nothing to condemn it. It contains many of the same ideas as those espoused by Simon Pritchett at the Reardens' wedding anniversary party. Dr. Pritchett had taken Hugh Akston's place in the philosophy department at Patrick Henry University. Ferris's book is filled with "ideas" of "thinkers" such as Hume, Kant, Hegel, and Marx. Advancing the notion of skepticism, Ferris says that, because knowledge is impossible, man should act according to his instincts and feelings. He defends materialism and says that the brain is an instrument of distortion. Ferris goes on to say that only contradictions exist—reality is contradictory and unknowable. He attempts to give people a reason not to think. He wants them to accept, adjust, and obey. Ferris is a power-luster who wants to be a dictator. He wants to attack and destroy men's minds, thus paving the way for him to control them. Ferris uses technology to create deadly Project X and the Ferris Persuader that is used to torture John Galt.

The philosophical speeches are integrated elements of the plot, make explicit the principles dramatized throughout the story, and move the action forward. For example, Galt's speech is given on the radio at the right point of time to the American people. Galt says that he is the man who removed the men of the mind from the world. He explains the reasons for the strike to the masses and that the strike is against the morality of self-sacrifice and unreason. His speech sums up the meaning of what has occurred in the novel up to this point—it ties together key ideas previously presented. Galt explains the importance of reason and abstract principles to gain knowledge, to produce, and to live. Individuals need to reject the doctrine of self-sacrifice and to create a society of rights, freedom, and reason. After a brief explanation of the reasons for the strike, Galt's speech is broken down into three sections: (1) The Morality of Life (Code of the Producers), (2) The Morality of Death (Code of the Looters), and (3) The Need to Choose between those two codes. Galt proposes a course of action for individuals who want to live.

ECONOMICS

Chapter 3 provides a summary of economic issues found in *Atlas Shrugged*. It discusses the role of individual initiative, creativity, and productivity in economic progress as illustrated in this novel. It also shows the novel's depiction of the benefits of trade and the destruction of exchange relationships and production that results from government intervention in the economy. Rand included a great many valuable insights about money in the novel's famous "money speech." In addition, the chapter analyzes Galt's Gulch as a free-market economy. The novel is, in part, a treatise on economics providing a literary treatment of proper economic principles.

Atlas Shrugged can be used to teach the basic principles of economic reasoning, to explore the nature of entrepreneurship, and to analyze the character of money. It provides a solid grounding for issues such as supply, demand, exchange, price, value, and so on. This novel provides a defense of an unregulated market system and dramatizes the operations of both proper and improper economic laws, principles, concepts, issues, and themes. It illustrates the validity of proper economic laws and the invalidity of improper economic laws. Rand's economic ideas in *Atlas Shrugged* can be successfully integrated into college-level economics classes. Reading *Atlas Shrugged* can provide a stimulating springboard for economic debates and can broaden students' understanding of fundamental economic issues.

Rand's masterwork is a prime example of how an economically literate author can construct meaningful stories that portray valid principles of economics and political economy. *Atlas Shrugged* is well-suited to animate discussions on a variety of topics including, but not limited to: the mind as the source of wealth; the role of the entrepreneur; the role of initiative, creativity, and productivity in economic progress; the essence of competition; the nature of profit; the role of money; the benefits of trade; rewards for innovation and efficiency; the destructive results of government intervention; taxation; public choice economics; too-big-to-fail industries or institutions; labor contracts; comparative economic systems; and how private property and the price system work to coordinate mutually beneficial exchanges.

Atlas Shrugged illustrates how crony capitalists like James Taggart and his friends attain "success" by currying favor with Washington politicians. The "aristocracy of pull" involves the exchange of favors between politically connected rent-seeking businessmen and cooperative government bureaucrats. It shows how people with political pull make it harder for those with ability and talent to succeed. Each of the laws passed in *Atlas Shrugged* involves a rationale that says that it is in the public interest or perhaps aimed at saving a particular industry "as a whole" or to stop the economic decline of the entire country. The real agenda is to benefit advocating interest groups or individuals (i.e., businessmen and political officials) with financial rewards and/or gains in political power. The ultimate results of these laws are negative consequences for specific individuals or businesses, consumers, or the general public.

Rand depicts the heroes of *Atlas Shrugged* overcoming obstacles. They (especially Dagny and Hank) are shown to be self-starters and the motive power of their own happiness. The producers are dramatized as self-initiated valuers who go by their own judgment and seek their own well-being. It is the self-actuating rational valuers who propel the world and sustain it. Rand's heroes are extraordinary characters who represent people as they could be and should be. *Atlas Shrugged* is a study of the great producers who have the ability to see, make connections, and create what has not been seen before. It shows that the mind is at the root of the creation and maintenance of wealth and that the passionate producer is the prime mover and visible hand in markets.

Production, like existence, is primary and rests on the laws of identity and causality. Consumption comes after, and depends upon, production. According to Rand, if human life is the standard, then productive work is a major virtue, and entrepreneurs and industrialists can be viewed as potentially heroic. Recognizing the integration of mind and body, Rand contended that the rational, purposeful, and creative character of human action is manifested in the act of material production.

Government intervention discourages innovation and risk-taking and obstructs the process of wealth creation. In *Atlas Shrugged*, the producers' minds are shackled by government policies. Lacking the freedom to create, compete, and earn wealth, the independent thinkers withdraw from society. This is Rand's dramatization of the proper moral response to the bureaucratic assault on the entrepreneurial spirit.

Atlas Shrugged identifies government intervention as the great enemy of the businessman. Rand details how government intervention into private markets produces costs and unintended consequences that are more harmful than the targeted problem itself. Socialistic bureaucrats attempt to protect men from their own minds and tend to think only of intended, primary, and immediate results while ignoring unintended, ancillary, and long-term ones. Government-produced impediments to a free society include taxation, protectionism, antitrust laws, regulation, welfare programs, inflation, and more.

An example of the above is the Anti-dog-eat-dog Rule passed by a private body, the National Alliance of Railroads, under which every member pledges to subordinate his own interests to those of the industry as a whole. Blaming transportation shortages on vicious competition, the rule states that a given region can only have one railroad to be decided by seniority (i.e., historical priority). The real goal was to help James Taggart put Dan Conway's superb Phoenix-Durango Railroad out of business. Orren Boyle had worked to get this rule passed and, in return, Taggart then used his political influence in Washington to pass the Equalization of Opportunity Bill that benefited Boyle's Associated Steel by forbidding any person or corporation from owning more than one type of business. The stated rationale was that it is unfair to permit one person or corporation to have several business enterprises while others have none. The real goal and result was that Hank Rearden's coal mines and ore mines be divested, delivering the latter to Paul Larkin, who would give Boyle the first chance to acquire the ore.

Then there were the Colorado Directives that were ostensibly intended to deal with the national emergency by forcing Colorado to share the pain of the rest of the country. This package of new directives killed the boom in Colorado and redistributed the earnings of that state's profitable firms to crony capitalists like James Taggart, who supported and lobbied for the passage of these directives. These directives led to the retirement and disappearance of many competent and productive Colorado industrialists such as Ellis Wyatt. Adding to the impact of these directives were the Fair Share Law, the Preservation of Livelihood Law, and the Public Utility Law, all passed through the efforts of lobbying interest groups.

The espoused purpose of Directive 10-289 is to stop the country's economic decline by freezing the economy in its current state. In the name of the general welfare, eight radical changes are decreed. Point 1 requires all workers to stay at their jobs and not quit or be fired. Point 2 forbids business closings and owners from leaving or retiring. Point 3 abolishes all patents and copyrights and orders that they must be turned over to the government by means of Gift Certificates. Point 4 prohibits the introduction or sale of new inventions. Point 5 states that every business or person engaged in production must not produce more or less than they did in the Basic Year. Point 6 requires that everyone spends the same amount of money as spent in the previous year. Point 7 freezes all forms of income (prices, salaries, dividends, profits, interest rates, etc.) at their current levels. Point 8 makes the Unification Board the final arbiter and interpreter of the directive. Whereas the supposed purposes of Directive 10-289 are to protect the people's security and to achieve full equality and total security, the real purpose is to permit the writers of the directives and the members of the Unification Board to retain and enhance their power.

The Railroad Unification Act results in the Railroad Unification Plan under which all of the railroads use each other's tracks and equipment without being charged. At the end of the year, all of the profits are put into a "pool" and are distributed based on the number of miles of track each owns and maintains rather than on the number of miles traveled, the number of trains run, or the number of tons of freight carried. Because Taggart Transcontinental owns by far the most miles of track (much of which is currently unused), James Taggart's company will be allocated the largest proportion of the railroad income. The Steel Unification Plan is modeled after the Railroad Unification Plan. Under it, all of the steel companies' earnings are to be allocated based on the number of furnaces that each company owns. Boyle's Associated Steel has a great many idle furnaces and would be paid a great deal more than its actual output would warrant. On the other hand, Rearden Steel would be paid a lot less than its actual output would dictate. Both of these acts are based on the Marxist principle of redistribution of wealth: "from each according to his ability . . . to each according to his need."

Francisco d'Anconia's "money speech" at James Taggart and Cherryl Brooks's wedding reception contains a number of valuable insights about money, wealth, and production. Francisco's ideas on money are primarily directed to Hank Rearden. Francisco explains that money is a tool of exchange that presumes the existence of productive individuals and the results of their efforts. He also points out that money is made possible only by people who produce and that wealth is the source of money. Money is the effect, rather than the cause, of wealth. Money symbolizes production that has already taken place and that has been judged as valuable by other people. Man's mind is at the root of production and productiveness is a virtue. Francisco explains that money is, or should be, an objective standard of value tied to reality in order to act as an integrator and proper measure of economic value and that such a standard requires an objective commodity such as gold. Money earned by a person is a moral symbol of his productive ability. The essence of Francisco's speech is that money makes life possible and is, therefore, "the root of all good" and certainly not the "root of all evil."

BUSINESS

Atlas Shrugged is a novel about business and the people who create businesses. Chapter 4 describes Rand's treatment of business and entrepreneurs in the novel. It begins with an explanation of how *Atlas Shrugged* demonstrates that wealth and profit are creations of the human mind. The next section compares the worldviews of the novel's business heroes and villains. This is followed by an in-depth analysis of the novel's main business protagonists—Dagny Taggart and Hank Rearden. The next part provides summaries of other business characters. The last section examines how the novel is used in college-level business courses.

Throughout the years, businesspeople have been among *Atlas Shrugged*'s most devoted admirers. In this great novel, Rand wrote about business, people who create businesses, and individuals located in the world of business. She championed industrial processes and producers and also embraced the potential of future new technologies. Rand also distinguished between authentic businesspeople (producers) and inauthentic businesspeople (looters) and between money-makers and money-appropriators.

Atlas Shrugged is very much a novel about business and entrepreneurs. The novel clearly demonstrates that wealth and profit are creations of the human mind. Wealth, in the form of goods and services, is created when individuals recombine and rearrange the resources that comprise the world. The human mind, through discovery, ingenuity, and creativity, is able to continually increase the wealth of the world. Profits are a person's reward for wealth creation. Entrepreneurs create wealth by offering what is perceived to be a more valuable combination of resources than the combined value of the resources that existed previously. The entrepreneur does not profit at the expense of others. Exchange in a free market is a positive-sum game involving win-win relationships.

Human life is maintained by the rational thought, values, and actions of the thinkers and producers. *Atlas Shrugged* illustrates how business improves the world and leads to human flourishing by creating positive-sum relationships of exchange in a free market. By its very nature, business is consistent with human nature and, when properly (i.e., ethically) practiced, helps to create a better world and to contribute to human flourishing and personal happiness. One's productive work is an important ingredient of a successful and fulfilling life.

Legitimate profit making is moral because it requires businessmen to form normative abstractions of objective values based on reality and to develop a virtuous character. *Atlas Shrugged* showcases the difference between ethical and unethical business practices and demonstrates the breadth and depth of Rand's thinking about commerce. It explores the nature of entrepreneurship and differentiates between business activities in a free market and those in what today could be called a mixed economy or a welfare state. Rand shows us the difficulties encountered in building an enterprise; the burden of dealing with regulations, cronyism, political pull, and rent-seeking; and the ethical challenges of life in the business world.

The heroes of the story are giants of ability, moral character, and achievement. Some of them are productive geniuses who create futuristic inventions. There is a sharp contrast in worldviews and a clash of purposes and actions between these heroes and the villains of the story who are crooked politicians, government bureaucrats, and politically connected businessmen such as James Taggart and Orren Boyle. Both the heroes and the villains are larger than life. Rand's philosophy of Objectivism is embodied in the actions and lives of the story's heroes. Rather than being presented naturalistically, these characters are depicted as logical embodiments of elemental concepts concretized in human action.

Rand's version of virtue ethics can supply a powerful foundation for operating a successful business. Rand's Objectivist values can provide an underpinning for a firm's long-term sustainable success, as well as for the flourishing and happiness of its employees. *Atlas Shrugged's* heroic wealth creators are independent individuals of superior ability and confidence who pursue their goals relentlessly in the face of obstacles, setbacks, and failures. Business heroes such as Dagny Taggart, Hank Rearden, Ellis Wyatt, Ken Danagger, and others focus on reality; are visionary; are purposeful and moral; are enthusiastic lovers of wealth creation; and are committed to the motive power of their own happiness, justice, and the profit motive, properly understood. They possess all of the Objectivist virtues including rationality (the primary virtue), independence, honesty, integrity, justice, productivity, and pride—the total of the preceding virtues that can also be thought of as moral ambitiousness. These virtues can supply an integrated framework for managers' and employees' decisions and actions. The Objectivist virtues can be linked to the survival and success of firms and their employees. In order to attain a company's goals, values, and purposes, these virtues need to be integrated within a firm's culture and climate of achievement.

Atlas Shrugged's business protagonists, Dagny Taggart, Hank Rearden, Francisco d'Anconia, Ken Danagger, Ellis Wyatt, and others, build and understand their businesses from the ground up. Possessing talent, ambition, and integrity, they are focused and purposeful prime movers in the market who understand that human intelligence is the source of wealth and that wealth is not causeless. They realize that reality is absolute and is not to be faked. As managers, they earn respect from their employees and from others in the business community by treating them as traders making mutually acceptable voluntary agreements. They embody the virtue of justice by judging and rewarding their workers objectively based on their merit. In addition, they are constantly seeking to hire and promote the most rational, competent, and talented individuals. Understanding that innovation is the fuel of business success, they set an innovative long-term vision and strive to innovate constantly. These successful leaders make mutually beneficial (positive-sum or win-win) deals. They assume ultimate responsibility for the success of their organizations and expect their employees to take responsibility for their actions and performance.

Under the "leadership" of James Taggart, Taggart Transcontinental's misguided corporate strategy is to attain "success" through mutual favors among his scheming, pragmatic, and parasitic cronies such as Orren Boyle. Taggart, the main villain in *Atlas Shrugged* and heir to a railroad fortune, is ambitious and starved for power and approval. Lacking the ability or energy to actually run and build the railroad, he defaulted those responsibilities to his sister, instead developing connections in government, and using these connections to secure subsidies and privileges for his company and to destroy his competition. Taggart does not understand that political entrepreneurship does not lead to legitimate business success. Improperly obtained wealth does not make one important or virtuous.

Atlas Shrugged is currently being taught in colleges and universities in a variety of courses. It provides an excellent vehicle for teaching issues in business, business ethics, economics, and political and economic philosophy. The use of *Atlas Shrugged* aids students in moving between abstract principles and applied realistic business examples. The novel serves as a link between philosophical concepts and the technical and practical aspects of business and illustrates that philosophy is accessible and important to people in general and to businesspeople in particular. The only way for man to survive in society is through reason and voluntary trade. *Atlas Shrugged* focuses on the positive and shows readers what it takes to achieve genuine business success and how to create value. Reading and studying *Atlas Shrugged* helps students to better understand the philosophical, moral, and economic concepts underpinning business and capitalism.

SOCIAL CHANGE

The purpose of chapter 5 is to discuss several ways in which *Atlas Shrugged* is related to social change. It explains how characters such as entrepreneurs and strikers introduce change in the novel as well as how *Atlas Shrugged* itself can be employed as a tool for bringing about change in the real world. The potential effects of the novel on readers are examined, as are the efforts of social movements that have embraced and incorporated the ideas found therein into their own philosophy.

A template for social change is exhibited in *Atlas Shrugged* both as a literary work and as a philosophical and educational treatise. The most pertinent and radical social change that this novel can be used to dramatize and explain is free-market capitalism. It illustrates the relative advantages of capitalism over other political-economic systems with respect to productivity, morality, and its compatibility with the nature of man and the world.

Within the novel itself, the entrepreneurs and strikers act as change agents. The entrepreneurs in *Atlas Shrugged* are moral agents of economic changes that can lead to social and cultural changes. They obtain wealth by discovering or creating new and innovative products that further flourishing on earth. As prudent practitioners in their areas of specialization, they apply their talents to the goal of living well. These virtuous individuals create new organizations, increase employment, and develop new production processes, thereby contributing to the idea and reality of capitalism. Not only do they inspire others with their vision, leadership, and achievements, they also encourage new patterns through which society changes.

The strikers take direct action by withdrawing the "sanctions of the victims" in order to speed up the collapse of society. John Galt and Francisco d'Anconia are the strike's main recruiters; Ragnar Danneskjöld raids state-owned cargo ships in order to return rightly owned property to the producers; and various entrepreneurs, industrialists, inventors, and engineers withdraw from society. They leave the outside world and abandon their businesses and wealth in their efforts to attain independence and to create a free society.

Atlas Shrugged itself can be a means for change in the real world. It can be used to illustrate the conceptual and moral foundations of a free society and as a tool to educate, persuade, and convert people to support a social system based on those foundations. Also, on a more emotional level, people are affected by stories and *Atlas Shrugged* has the potential to have transformative effects on many individuals who read it and are excited by the actions and speeches of its heroes.

Atlas Shrugged has the potential to bring about change if the novel's philosophic meaning is grasped by enough individuals. This novel illustrates the dynamic interactions between the personal, psychological, ethical, economic, cultural, structural, and other dimensions of society. Social change must take effect within and between each of these levels and dimensions.

Some social movements and organizations have already adopted or adapted ideas demonstrated in *Atlas Shrugged* into, or as, their own philosophy. To some degree, it motivated the Tea Party movement. In addition, both the Ayn Rand Institute and The Atlas Society are confident that *Atlas Shrugged* can help in changing the world and work to promote Rand's ideas.

Often referred to as the "Bible of Objectivism," *Atlas Shrugged* has been hailed as a "blueprint for the future" and as a potential source for social change. It succeeds as a brilliant novel of ideas, is destined to be a force in the world, and will be discussed and analyzed by thinkers in a variety of fields for a long time to come.

THE PHILOSOPHY OF OBJECTIVISM

I have included an Appendix at the end of this book that provides an overview of Rand's philosophy of Objectivism as embodied in *Atlas Shrugged*. It will be of interest to readers who are not familiar with her ideas and will provide a background for readers who wish to study specialized aspects of Rand's philosophy in greater detail.

Ayn Rand (1905–1982) constructed an entire integrated and coherent philosophy to underpin her ethics and politics, which stress the virtue of acting in one's rational self-interest, individual happiness, and natural rights. In her normative argument for laissez-faire capitalism, Rand places freedom as a precondition for virtue. She derives an objective ethics based on the nature of man as a goal-seeking entity with the end goal of life as man *qua* man. According to Rand, happiness relates to a person's success as a unique, rational human being possessing free will.

Rand's rational epistemology holds that knowledge is based on the observation of reality and that it is possible to gain objective knowledge of both facts and values. She explains that a concept is a mental integration of factual or perceptual data and that properly formed concepts are objective and contextual. Her epistemology transcends both apriorism and empiricism. Although she refers to essences or concepts as epistemological rather than metaphysical, she actually also means relational and contextual (i.e., based on the interrelationships among all of the relevant information in a given context of knowledge).

Rand says that at the root of the concept of value is the conditional characteristic of life and that ethics is an objective metaphysical necessity. Morality is a means to the end of life and ethics deals with concepts that Rand sees as rational and objective. Viewing reason as man's means of survival, she maintains that man's primary choice is to focus his consciousness. Rand saw the virtues as inextricably linked and as the means to obtaining the values which, along with the virtues, enable people to attain their happiness.

Rand's philosophy is a systematic and integrated unity that is founded on the axioms of existence, identity, and consciousness. Rand explains that knowledge is based on the observation of reality and that to attain knowledge, a person employs the processes of induction, deduction, and integration. She contends that it is possible to obtain objective knowledge of both facts and values. Rand says that the essential characteristics of a concept are epistemological (she also means contextual and relational) rather than metaphysical.

Rand maintains that values are epistemologically objective when they are discovered through objective conceptual processes and that they are metaphysically objective when their achievement requires conforming to reality. She argues that man's life is the ultimate value and that the individual human life is the standard of value for a human being—a creature possessing volitional consciousness. Her naturalistic value theory holds that it is the concept of life that makes the concept of value possible and that reason is a man's only judge of value. Rand states that it is possible for a person to pursue objective values that are consonant with his own rational self-interest. It's just not only possible for objective values to be in agreement with a person's rational self-interest, also one must pursue objective values in order to act in his rational self-interest. According to Rand, ethics is rational, objective, and personal. Her rational egoism is based on the Aristotelian idea that the objective and rational end of a human being is his flourishing and happiness—egoism is a virtue because nature requires it. A person has the natural right to initiate his own conduct in line with his own judgment. She views rights as the link between a person's moral code and society's legal code.

A FEW FINAL WORDS

I would like to thank Lexington Books and *The Journal of Ayn Rand Studies* for granting permission to have my previously published chapters and articles republished in this book. I would also like to acknowledge that work on this book was assisted by the BB&T Charitable Foundation. The BB&T Charitable Foundation provided a gift in 2006 that resulted in the founding of Wheeling University's Institute for the Study of Capitalism and Morality. As is the case with all of my books, I am enormously grateful to Carla Cash for her most capable and conscientious work in bringing this book to print. Individuals who have provided suggestions for improving this book are acknowledged at the end of each specific chapter. At the end of this Introduction, I have provided a list of recommended resources for individuals who want to learn more about *Atlas Shrugged*. In addition to these resources, I suggest that interested individuals read some of the many articles on *Atlas Shrugged* that have appeared in *The Journal of Ayn Rand Studies* since its founding. Also, I want to recognize the great work done by the Ayn Rand Institute and The Atlas Society in promoting the ideas espoused by Ayn Rand in *Atlas Shrugged* and her other writings. Finally, I want to dedicate this book to all admirers of *Atlas Shrugged* past, present, and future.

ACKNOWLEDGMENTS

I would like to thank the following individuals for their useful comments and suggestions for improving the Introduction: Winton Bates, Roger Bissell, Mimi Gladstein, Jerry Kirkpatrick, Jomana Papillo, Chris Sciabarra, Brian

Simpson, Kathleen Touchstone, Michelle Vachris, Robert White, and Gary Wolfram.

RECOMMENDED RESOURCES

Bernstein, Andrew. 1995. *Philosophic and Literary Integration in Ayn Rand's 'Atlas Shrugged.'* Seven Audio Lectures. New Milford, CT: Second Renaissance Books.
————. 2000. *CliffsNotes on Rand's "Atlas Shrugged."* Foster, City, CA: IDG Books Worldwide.
Curry, Timothy, and Anthony Trifiletti. 2013. *Who Is John Galt? A Navigational Guide to Ayn Rand's "Atlas Shrugged."* CreateSpace.
Ghate, Onkar. *A Teacher's Guide to the Signet Edition of "Atlas Shrugged."* Irvine, CA: The Ayn Rand Institute.
Gladstein, Mimi Reisel. 2000. *"Atlas Shrugged": Manifesto of the Mind.* New York: Twayne.
Hsieh, Diana. 2015. *Explore "Atlas Shrugged": A Study Guide for Ayn Rand's Epic Novel.* Sedalia, CO: Philosophy in Action.
Kelley, David, ed. 2014. *"Atlas Shrugged": The Novel, the Films, the Philosophy.* Washington, D.C.: The Atlas Society.
Mayhew, Robert, ed. 2009. *Essays on Ayn Rand's "Atlas Shrugged."* Lanham, MD: Lexington Books.
Salmieri, Gregory. 2007. *"Atlas Shrugged" as a Work of Philosophy.* Four Audio Lectures. New Milford, CT: Second Renaissance Books.
Salmieri, Gregory, and Ben Bayer. 2017. *The Atlas Project: A Chapter-by-Chapter Discussion of "Atlas Shrugged."* https://campus.aynrand.org/Atlas-project-resources-and-policies/#miscellaneousresources.
Salsman, Richard. 1997. *The Invisible Hand Comes to Life: Economics in "Atlas Shrugged."* Two Audio Lectures. New Milford, CT: Second Renaissance Books.
Tracinski, Robert. 2019. *So Who Is John Galt, Anyway?: A Reader's Guide to Ayn Rand's "Atlas Shrugged."* Charlottesville, VA: TPC Books.
Wright, Darryl. 2007. *Ayn Rand's Ethics from "The Fountainhead" to "Atlas Shrugged."* Two Audio Lectures. New Milford, CT: Second Renaissance Books.
Younkins, Edward W., ed. 2007. *Ayn Rand's "Atlas Shrugged": A Philosophical and Literary Companion.* Aldershot, England: Ashgate.

Chapter 1

Synopsis of *Atlas Shrugged*

In *Atlas Shrugged* (1957) Ayn Rand presents her original, brilliant, and controversial philosophy of Objectivism in a dramatized form. This novel articulates a theoretically consistent, systematic, and intellectually sound defense of capitalism; expounds the principles of traditional liberalism, voluntary cooperation, and individual freedom; and exposes the errors of collectivism and coercion. *Atlas Shrugged* is the philosophical and artistic capstone of Ayn Rand's novels.

Atlas Shrugged characterizes business and businessmen in a favorable light by emphasizing: the possibilities of life in a free society; the inherent ethical nature of capitalism and the good businessman; the strength, courage, integrity, and self-sufficiency of the hardworking businessman; and the entrepreneur as a wealth creator and promotor of human progress. Teachers can use this great novel to promulgate the conceptual and moral foundations of a free society to their students. *Atlas Shrugged* is a powerful tool to educate people with respect to a just and proper political and economic order that is a true reflection of man and the world properly understood. This novel has a strong emotional impact, portrays a positive sense of life, and serves as a blueprint for the future and potential source for social change.

Atlas Shrugged shows the businessman's role as potentially heroic by celebrating the energy and opportunity of life for men of talent and ambition to make something of themselves. This superb novel teaches that acts of courage and creativity consist in having integrity rather than in blind obedience and in inspiring others instead of following them. *Atlas Shrugged* portrays the business hero as a persistent, original, and independent thinker who pursues an idea to its fruition. Rand's masterpiece dramatizes the positive qualities of the businessman by showing the triumph of individualism over collectivism; depicting business heroes as noble, appealing, and larger than life; and by characterizing business careers as at least as, if not more, honorable as careers in medicine, law, or education.

Atlas Shrugged is beginning to be taught in colleges and universities in a variety of courses. It is being used in the classroom to study the moral foundations of capitalism and commerce and related topics in philosophy, economics, free enterprise, management, business, and other areas. This novel provides an excellent base for teaching issues in business, business ethics, economics, and political and economic philosophy. The use of *Atlas Shrugged* aids in moving between abstract principles and realistic business examples. The novel serves as a link between philosophical concepts and the practical aspects of business and illustrates that philosophy is accessible and important to people in general and to businesspeople in particular.

Atlas Shrugged fosters a spirited exchange of ideas among students in the classroom as many students respond strongly and positively to this novel and its heroes. The novel presents the pursuit of profit as thoroughly moral, makes the discussion of capitalism intellectually legitimate, provides a powerful critique of socialism, and challenges the prevailing beliefs of our culture. Students are impressed with *Atlas Shrugged*'s prophetic nature. It portrays the U.S. economy collapsing due to government intervention and regulation, politicians placing the blame on capitalism and the free market, and the government countering with ever more controls that further the crisis. Government intervention is shown to discourage innovation and risk-taking, and the novel portrays how regulations in a mixed economy are made with political interest groups lobbying the government which grants favors to those who have the most votes, political pull, or influence.

Atlas Shrugged possesses striking narrative power and manifests the essentials of an entire philosophical system. It is a model of integration among theme, story, and characters. Its most extraordinary quality is its integration with every event, action, and character serving both dramatic and philosophical purposes. *Atlas Shrugged* is a very intentional novel with every detail designed to mean something by the author. Even the philosophical speeches are integrated with the events of the story. The lengthy philosophical speeches are integrated components of the plot, make explicit the principles dramatized throughout the actions of the novel, and move the story forward.

Ayn Rand formulated her characters in *Atlas Shrugged* with reference to philosophical principles and premises. She presents no random details and focuses on the essentials to understanding each character. Each character serves a purpose and the author skillfully matches characters against each other. Rand presents her characters as parallels and contrasts. In this story of human action, the author ties physical actions to the values of her characters.

The actions of the novel support philosophical moral principles through the purposeful progression of events. The reader sees values embodied in a concrete form in the world. The most crucial events are dramatized. Rand also effectively uses flashbacks and symbolism as supplementary techniques. There are no "floating symbols" as the author typically illustrates an idea in action and then uses a symbol to bring abstract subject matter down to the observational level. In her strongly ironic novel, Rand also effectively alters and adapts some famous Greek myths in order to tell these from an Objectivist viewpoint. By changing them, she challenges their traditional meanings and infuses them with new meanings reflecting her revolutionary worldview. Another one of her techniques is to contrast the universe of the men of reason and the men of unreason in consecutive scenes.

This both anachronistic and timeless story takes place in the not-too-distant future in a slightly modified United States where there is a head of state instead of a president and a National Legislature rather than a Congress. American society is crumbling under the impact of the welfare state and creeping socialism, and most other nations have already become Communist People's States. Most companies are owned and run by individual entrepreneurs. A somber mood and sense of dread permeate a society that is filled with government interference and political corruption.

The story is an apocalyptic vision of the last stages of a conflict between two classes of humanity—the looters (noncreators) and the nonlooters (creators). The looters are proponents of high taxation, big labor, government ownership, government spending, government planning, regulation, and redistribution. They include politicians and their supporters, intellectuals, government bureaucrats, scientists who sell their minds to the bureaucrats, and liberal businessmen, who, afraid of honest competition, sell out their initiative, creative powers, and independence for the security of government regulation. The looters are impervious to reason and believe that the prime movers will always come to their aid and save them. The looters believe that by expropriating the wealth of the creators they will gain an unearned moral status and self-esteem.

The nonlooters—the thinkers and doers—are the competent and daring individualists who innovate and create new enterprises. These prime movers love their work, are dedicated to achievement through their thought and effort, and abhor the forces of collectivism and mediocrity. The battle is thus between the nonearners who deal by force and "profit" through political power and earners who deal by trade and profit through productive ability. *Atlas Shrugged* is a story of the struggle between people with contradictory visions, values, and moralities.

Atlas Shrugged illustrates that there are good and bad businessmen and that businessmen don't always act virtuously. There are two kinds of businessmen—those who lobby government for special privileges, make deals, as well as engage in fraud and corrupt activities and the real producers who succeed or fail on their own. Rand's business heroes are independent, rational, and committed to the facts of reality, to the judgment of their own minds, and to their own happiness. Each of them thinks for himself, actualizes his potential, and views himself as competent to deal with the challenges of life and as worthy of success and happiness. *Atlas Shrugged* makes a great case that the businessman is the appropriate and best symbol of a free society.

Production is the means to the fulfillment of men's material needs. *Atlas Shrugged* masterfully illustrates that the production of goods, services, and wealth metaphysically precedes their distribution and exchange. The primacy of production means that we must produce before we can consume. Production (i.e., supply) is the source of demand. This means that products are ultimately paid for with other products. Rand shows that, because life requires the production of values, people in business are heroic. The heroes of *Atlas Shrugged* find joy in taking risks and bringing men and materials together to produce what people value.

Atlas Shrugged chronicles the rise of corrupt businessmen who profit by dealing with dishonest politicians. They avoid rationality and productivity by using their political pull and pressure groups to loot the producers. The looters exploit the creators in both physical and spiritual concerns. They attack the self-esteem of the producers by advocating the morality of altruism, which holds that the pursuit of happiness is a source of guilt. The looters employ need, weakness, and incompetence as a demand on the creators. They deem it to be acceptable to receive altruistic "gifts" if a person is weak, suffering, or incompetent. Rand is scathing in her indictment of these villains who would rob the creative thinkers who are responsible for human progress and prosperity.

Government intervention discourages innovation and risk-taking and obstructs the process of wealth-creation. In *Atlas Shrugged* the producers' minds are shackled by government policies. Lacking the freedom to create, compete, and earn wealth, the independent thinkers withdraw from society. This is Rand's recommended response to the bureaucratic assault of the entrepreneurial spirit. Whereas the theme of *Atlas Shrugged* is the role of the mind in human existence, the plot-theme is the men of the mind going on strike against an altruist-collectivist society.

Atlas Shrugged delineates government intervention as the great enemy of the businessman. Rand details how government intervention into private markets produces costs and unintended consequences more harmful than the targeted problem itself. Socialistic bureaucrats attempt to protect men from their own minds and tend to think only of intended, primary, and immediate results while ignoring unintended, ancillary, and long-term ones. Government-produced impediments to a free society are shown to include taxation, protectionism, antitrust laws, regulation, welfare programs, inflation, and more.

The plot is built around several business and industrial executives. The beautiful Dagny Taggart, perhaps the most heroic female protagonist in American fiction, is the operating genius who efficiently runs Taggart Transcontinental Railroad, which was founded by her grandfather. Her brother James, president in title only, is an indecisive, incompetent, liberal businessman who takes all the credit for his sister's achievements. Dagny optimistically and confidently performs Herculean labors to keep the railroad running despite destructive government edicts, her brother's weaknesses, the incompetence of many of her associates, and the silent and inexplicable disappearance of society's competent industrialists. Free of inner conflict, Dagny is passionately creative and comfortable with respect to her fundamental relationship to existence. She is a model of synthesis, unity, and mind-body integration. Dagny is an engineer and the operating vice-president of a transcontinental railroad who deals with every industry and every policy of the looters. Because of her integrating context, she has contact with every industry, thus permitting the reader to see the total collapse of modern industrial civilization.

As both society and her railroad are disintegrating, Dagny attempts to rebuild an old Taggart rail line. In the process, she contacts Hank Rearden, a self-made steel tycoon and inventor of an alloy stronger and lighter than steel. Rearden, Dagny's equal in intelligence, determination, and sense of responsibility, becomes her ally and eventually her lover. They struggle to keep the economy running and ultimately discover the secret of the continuing disappearance of the men of ability.

John Galt, a messiah of free enterprise, is secretly persuading thinkers and doers to vanish mysteriously one after the other—deserting and sometimes sabotaging their factories before they depart. Galt explains how desperately the world needs productive individuals, but how viciously it treats them. The greater a person's productive ability, the greater are the penalties he endures in the form of regulations, controls, and the expropriation and redistribution of his earned wealth. This evil, however, is only made possible by the sanction of the victims. By accepting an underserved guilt—not for their vices but for their virtues—the achievers have acquiesced in the political theft of their minds' products. Galt masterminds his plan to stop the motor of the world by convincing many of the giants of intellect and productivity to refuse to be exploited any longer by the looters and the moochers, to strike by withdrawing their talents from the world by escaping to a secret hideout in the Colorado Rockies, thus leaving the welfare state to destroy itself. The hero-conspirators will then return to lay the groundwork for a healthy new social order based on the principles of laissez-faire capitalism.

Galt, the mysterious physicist who is also a philosopher, teacher, and leader of an intellectual movement, has invented a motor that can convert static electricity into useful but inexpensive kinetic energy. He chooses to keep his invention a secret until it is time for him and the other heroes to reclaim the world. For two-thirds of the novel, Galt exists only as a plaintive expressive—Who is John Galt?. He has been in hiding, working underground as a laborer in the Taggart Tunnels, while recruiting the strikers.

One of the key hero-characters is Francisco d'Anconia, an aristocrat, a copper baron, and former lover of Dagny, who prefers to destroy his mines systematically rather than to let them fall into the hands of the looters. Another is Ragnar Danneskjöld, a philosopher-turned-pirate, who raids only public, nonprofit, commerce ships in order to return to the productive individuals what is rightly theirs.

The men of ability fade out of the picture and are labeled traitors and deserters by Dagny and Hank, who remain fighting at their desks. Ironically, because they have not been told of the conspiracy, Dagny and Hank are even battling their natural allies—the ex-leaders of the business world who have gone on strike. The result is that not only is there a dramatic conflict between the good and the bad, there is also a conflict between the good and the good. Dagny and Hank, the primary creators, are philosophically against the looters, but in action they support them. Also, existentially Dagny and Rearden oppose Galt and the other strikers, but philosophically they agree with them.

Dagny pursues one of the deserters by a plane to a valley deep in the Rockies, crashes, and accidentally discovers John Galt's headquarters—the Utopian free-enterprise community created by the former business leaders along with several academicians, artists, and artisans. They have set up Galt's Gulch (also known as Mulligan's Valley) as a refuge from the looters and moochers of the outside world.

Galt's Gulch is the hidden valley that is the Atlantis of *Atlas Shrugged*. This paradigm and microcosm of a free society consists of a voluntary association of men held together by nothing but every man's self-interest. Here, productive men who have gone on strike are free to produce and trade as long as they observe the valley's customs. In this secret free society, enshrouded by the crumbling interventionist one, each individual is unencumbered in the pursuit of his own flourishing and happiness.

Dagny is the last hero, except for Hank, to reach Galt's outpost. While there, she listens to the logic of Galt and his associates and falls in love with Galt, who represents all that she values. Inspired by the vision of Rearden, who continues to search for her and to battle the looters, she decides to return to a world in shambles. Dagny and Hank refuse almost to the end to accept Galt's plan and stubbornly fight to save the economy. John Galt returns as well so that he can look out for her and be there when she decides she has had enough.

Mr. Thompson, head of state, is scheduled to address the nation regarding economic conditions when he is cut off the air and preempted by John Galt, who, in a three-hour speech, spells out the tenets of his rational philosophy. He tells the citizens that the men of the mind have gone on strike, that human beings require freedom of thought and action, and that they must reject the code of self-sacrifice.

Dagny inadvertently leads the looter-politicians to Galt. They capture him and, in an attempt to save the crumbling economy, they offer him the position of economic dictator, which he promptly refuses. They take him prisoner and torture him but the torture machine breaks down. Then, in a melodramatic confrontation, Galt is rescued by the Utopian entrepreneurs, and the looters are vanquished. Galt, Dagny, and the other men of the mind return to the valley, rewrite the Constitution, and add a clause stating that Congress shall make no law abridging the freedom of production and trade. At the end of the novel, just before going back to rebuild the world, Galt symbolically traces the sign of the dollar in the air.

Atlas Shrugged is an achievement of intricate structural composition and integration. The titles of its three major sections pay tribute to Aristotle, correspond to his basic philosophical axioms, and accomplish a thematic goal by implying something regarding the meaning of the events and actions in the respective sections of the novel. In Part One, called Non-Contradiction, there is a numerous series of strange and apparently contradictory events and paradoxes with no discernible logical solutions. In Part Two, Either-Or, based on Aristotle's Law of Excluded Middle, Dagny faces a fundamental choice with no middle road—to continue to battle to save her business or to give it up. Part Three, A is A, is based on Aristotle's Law of Identity. In it, Dagny and Rearden (along with the readers) learn the true nature of the events, and all of the apparent contradictions are identified and resolved. The Aristotelian laws of thought are not simply how we must think in order to gain knowledge. They are also ontological laws that pertain to the fundamental nature of reality. All that exists must comply with these principles.

The major plot of *Atlas Shrugged* is the story of the strike. Rand provides clues throughout Parts One and Two regarding the existence of the strike and, through the use and emphasis of subsidiary surface plots, she is able to keep the major plot hidden and to reveal the strike only in a step-by-step retrospective manner. The secondary plots include (1) Dagny Taggart and Hank Rearden's struggles to save their respective companies and industries primarily through the construction of the John Galt Line, and (2) Dagny's quests to find the inventor of the revolutionary motor and to find and stop the destroyer who is draining the brains of the world. There are observable and unobservable lines of action in the novel. We see our heroes striving to construct the John Galt Line and searching for the inventor of the motor. We also see the looters, their policies, and the effects of their policies. What is not discernible is John Galt removing the men of the mind from the world and relocating them to Mulligan's Valley. The link between these two spheres of action is Eddie Willers, who unknowingly feeds information to John Galt, disguised as a low-level worker with whom Eddie has lunch.

Until this point, we have discussed *Atlas Shrugged* from a big picture perspective. We now turn to a more detailed look at the purposeful progression of events of this long and complex novel.

The story begins in a devastated New York City with empty stores, closed businesses, crumbling buildings, and the disappearance of capable workers. Feeling a sense of dread and doom, Eddie Willers, assistant to Dagny Taggart, vice-president of operations of Taggart Transcontinental Railroad, walks the streets of this city in decay. As he approaches the Taggart Transcontinental Building, a beggar asks him, "Who is John Galt?." Eddie confronts the company's president, James Taggart, regarding the replacement of the crumbling tracks of the Rio Norte Line which serves the Wyatt oil fields and the other industrialized areas of Colorado, America's last booming industrial center. Wyatt has devised a method for extracting oil from shale. Dagny runs things and carries Jim, who is preoccupied with evading responsibility.

While on a Taggart train named the Comet, Dagny hears a young brakeman whistling a tune which he describes as Richard Halley's Fifth Piano Concerto. He becomes evasive when Dagny points out that Halley only wrote four concertos before his mysterious disappearance. A faulty signal stops the Comet and Dagny gives orders with respect to the stopped train. Realizing that good men are becoming hard to find, Dagny plans on promoting Owen Kellogg, a promising young engineer.

Dagny meets with Jim regarding the ordering of new metal rails for the Rio Norte Line. James wants to use rails supplied by his friend Orren Boyle, a liberal businessman who runs Associated Steel and who is constantly delaying delivery of the rails. Dagny prefers to use Rearden Metal, a revolutionary alloy stronger and lighter than steel. Denounced by metallurgists, the metal that took industrialist, Henry (Hank) Rearden, ten years to develop had not yet been tried commercially. Dagny, who has studied the metal, accepts responsibility and tells Jim that the Boyle order has been canceled and that Rearden is to supply the rail.

When Dagny meets with Owen Kellogg, he unexpectedly resigns. Dagny calls Halley's publisher and discovers that, indeed, he had only written four concertos. These events are the first of many mysterious and seeming contradictions that confront the heroes of *Atlas Shrugged*.

Hank Rearden pours the first heat of Rearden Metal and reflects on his accomplishment and his life as he walks home from his mills. When he arrives at his home, he finds a gathering that includes his wife, Lillian, his brother, Philip, his mother, and family friend, Paul Larkin. His family members berate him and attempt to make him feel guilty because of his work. Hank has feelings of obligation to his manipulative wife and mother and to his ungrateful brother. Hank gives his wife a bracelet made from the first pouring of Rearden Metal for which his family members reproach him as egotistical. Lillian ironically refers to it as the chain by which Hank holds them all in bondage. Hank agrees to have an anniversary party and he gives Philip a huge amount of money for one of his liberal causes. Hank discusses the political situation with Larkin, who warns him about the loyalty of Wesley Mouch, Rearden's Washington man.

In a meeting at the top of a skyscraper in a cellar-like, windowless, bar room, James Taggart conspires with Wesley Mouch, Orren Boyle, and Paul Larkin to sacrifice Dan Conway and Hank Rearden. They agree to use their political power and connections to crush Taggart Transcontinental's only competition in Colorado, Dan Conway's superb Phoenix-Durango Railroad, and to strip Hank Rearden of his ore mines. They also discuss Mexico and the San Sebastián Line built by Taggart Transcontinental to serve the San Sebastián Mines. The novel then discusses the careers and history of Dagny and James Taggart. Dagny rises because of her productivity and James because of his Washington ability. Eddie Willers is then shown in the underground employee cafeteria talking with a nameless worker. At this point in the novel neither Eddie nor the reader knows that the worker is John Galt, the ultimate hero of the story.

Eddie tells Dagny that McNarama, Taggart Transcontinental's and the country's best contractor, has quit and vanished. The San Sebastián Mines and Line are nationalized and James Taggart takes credit before the board of directors for the decision to strip the lines of any valuable assets. As a part of the deal agreed to in the cellar-like bar room, the National Alliance of Railroads passes the Anti-dog-eat-dog Rule which ostensibly places a ban on "destructive competition" by granting seniority to the oldest railroad company in a given region of the country. Its real purpose is to put Dan Conway's Phoenix-Durango Railroad out of business. Dagny encourages Conway to fight the rule but Conway gives up.

Ellis Wyatt and the other Colorado industrialists are now forced to use Taggart Transcontinental for their transportation needs. In order to handle this business, Dagny must quickly rebuild the Rio Norte Line. Wyatt confronts Dagny with an ultimatum. Dagny and Hank then discuss their plans to rebuild the line using Rearden Metal.

The San Sebastián Mines are revealed to be worthless and a fraud. Dagny makes an appointment to confront Francisco. While Dagny walks over to see Francisco at the Wayne-Falkland Hotel, she recalls her childhood friendship and later romance with Francisco and the d'Anconia family history. She remembers his purposefulness and ability and how he unexpectedly turned into a playboy. Dagny is bewildered because she knew that Francisco had been brilliant and productive just two years earlier. Dagny asks Francisco about his motives, and he tells her that he intentionally wanted to ruin his investors like James Taggart, Orren Boyle, and others who attempted to ride on Francisco's coattails. He deliberately caused the San Sebastián disaster knowing that it would harm Wyatt Oil, Taggart Transcontinental Railroad, d'Anconia Copper (his own company), and other companies.

At the Reardens' anniversary party, a variety of intellectuals all support the pending Equalization of Opportunity Bill. The guests reduce men to instinct and are against free will, logic, melody, plot, and property rights. They damn the values and virtues that Hank Rearden embodies. Francisco arrives at the party, approaches Hank, and thanks him for his values and virtues. He also warns Hank that his freeloading family members have a weapon that they are using against him. Hank is grateful to Francisco but still is suspicious of him. Dagny trades her diamond bracelet to Lillian for the one made with Rearden Metal.

The reader is shown that the exploiters are men like James Taggart, Wesley Mouch, and Robert Stadler, whereas the exploited are individuals like Hank Rearden, Dagny Taggart, and Ellis Wyatt, who fail to understand the nature of the evil looters whom they face. Dagny and Hank endeavor to rebuild the Rio Norte Line, and Hank designs an innovative bridge of Rearden Metal that combines a truss with an arch. Dagny refuses to debate Bertram Scudder on his radio show regarding the safety of Rearden Metal. Her brother James had tried to talk her into appearing on Scudder's program.

Dr. Potter of the State Science Institute (SSI) attempts to obtain the rights of Rearden Metal but Hank refuses. Potter offers Hank a great deal of government money. The SSI attempts to bribe and threaten Rearden to keep his new metal off the market because of the "social damage" it will cause to steel producers (like Orren Boyle) who can't compete with him. The SSI alleges potential weaknesses in the metal and, as a result, the public begins questioning its safety. Dagny reads about SSI's denunciation of Rearden Metal and makes an appointment to see Robert Stadler, the head of the institute, to see if he will retract SSI's damaging and unproven allegations. Stadler refuses because he does not want SSI to look bad. Stadler, the theoretical physicist, has contempt for practical technology. He tells Dagny about the failure of the three most promising students that he had taught at Patrick Henry University. Two are Francisco d'Anconia and Ragnar Danneskjöld, the pirate, and the third is probably now some "second assistant bookkeeper."

The railroad union forbids its employees to work on the Rio Norte Line and the stock price of Taggart Transcontinental plummets. Dagny decides to take a leave of absence to construct the Rio Norte Line on her own. As a result, the "John Galt Line" is born. This is the name that the defiant Dagny gives to her new railroad. If her efforts are successful, then she will turn the line back over to Taggart Transcontinental. Dagny seeks investors for her new company, asks Francisco to purchase John Galt Line bonds, and he refuses.

James Taggart had previously used his political friendship with steel producer Orren Boyle to influence the National Alliance of Railroads to pass the Anti-dog-eat-dog Rule. In turn, Boyle employs Taggart to use his influence in Washington in order to strip Hank Rearden of his ore mines, delivering them to Paul Larkin, who would provide Boyle with the first chance to obtain the ore. Taggart uses his Washington connections to pass the Equalization of Opportunity Bill, which forbids any one person or corporation from owning more than one type of business concern. Although the stated rationale for this antitrust legislation is that it is unfair to permit one individual or corporation to own several types of business enterprises, the hidden agenda is to allow Boyle's Associated Steel to compete with Rearden Steel. This new antitrust law forces Rearden to surrender his subsidiary coal and iron ore mines. The law prohibits Hank from using the mines that supply raw materials to make Rearden Metal.

Rearden and the other Colorado businessmen invest in the John Galt Line. Dagny and Hank are becoming strongly attracted to one another. Hank complies with the Equalization of Opportunity Bill and sells his ore mines to Paul Larkin and his coal mines to Ken Danagger, a Pennsylvania coal producer and friend of Hank. Rearden gives an extension to Taggart Transcontinental on its rail payments. The John Galt Line is completed before its deadline. The John Galt Line is denunciated as unsafe and the union attempts to stop the first run of the line. Every Taggart engineer volunteers for its first run. Dagny and Hank ride in the locomotive on the first run to Colorado which is a resounding success. They have dinner at Ellis Wyatt's home to celebrate. They make love for the first time that night and their romance begins.

The morning following Hank and Dagny's night of passion, Rearden condemns them both for their low urges, but Dagny is happy for what happened. She regards having sex with Rearden as being noble, whereas he considers it to be low and base. She realizes that sexual attraction is based on the mutual admiration for each other's values and other qualities. Despite his condemnation, Hank resolves to continue what he considers to be their depraved affair. James Taggart meets Cherryl Brooks, an innocent shop girl and hero-worshipper, who admires achievement and thinks that Jim is one of the people responsible for the John Galt Line's success. Dagny returns ownership of the John Galt Line to Taggart Transcontinental. Wesley Mouch is appointed to head up the Bureau of Economic Planning and National Resources.

Hank and Dagny decide to take a vacation together. They drive around the country looking at abandoned factories. At the Twentieth Century Motor

Company in Wisconsin, they discover the remnants of a motor that is capable of extracting static electricity from the atmosphere and converting it into usable kinetic energy. They are shocked to find such a revolutionary invention on a scrap heap in an abandoned factory. Dagny and Hank vow to find the inventor of the motor.

Dagny searches for the inventor of the motor in Rome, Wisconsin, where she speaks with Mayor Bascom and other city officials about the Twentieth Century Motor Company. When she speaks to Eddie Willers, he tells her that politicians want to pass laws that would destroy industrial production in Colorado. Through the proposed legislation others would be able to cash in on Colorado's success perhaps crippling many Colorado enterprises in the process. Paul Larkin betrays Rearden by shipping the ore to Orren Boyle in compliance with the crooked deal arranged in the skyscraper-cellar-bar room some time ago.

Dagny's search for the inventor of the motor leads her to the widow of a former chief engineer of the Twentieth Century Motor Company's research department. Mrs. Hastings tells Dagny that her husband's young assistant had invented the motor. She doesn't know him but provides a clue that leads Dagny to a remote local diner in Wyoming. The cook there knows who the inventor is but will not tell Dagny who he is. Dagny is surprised to learn that the cook making hamburgers is the great philosopher, Hugh Akston, a former professor at Patrick Henry University, who had retired many years before. Akston talks about his three star pupils. He will not explain why he left the teaching profession and tells her that "contradictions do not exist" and that if she encounters a paradox, she should check her premises because one of them is wrong.

When Dagny returns to Cheyenne, she finds that a new series of directives and taxes have been placed on the Colorado industrialists. The Colorado Directives were intended (at least officially) to help with the national emergency by forcing Colorado to share the suffering. The directive was actually due to the efforts of economic interest groups who wanted the industrially successful state of Colorado to force its profitable firms to redistribute their earnings. Dagny rushed to see Ellis Wyatt in Colorado, but she is too late. The defiant Ellis Wyatt has set fire to his wells and has disappeared. As the Colorado situation worsens, other industrialists will retire and vanish. Mouch's Colorado Directives will hasten the retirement and disappearance of many Colorado industrialists who had created productive enterprises and who are forced to carry less competent businessmen with them. The Colorado Directives put Wyatt Oil and other companies out of business and will ultimately wipe out the Rio Norte Line.

Colorado's economy continues to collapse as many of the state's industrialists are vanishing. Dagny has therefore been forced to cut trains on the

Colorado schedule. In her attempt to either find the inventor of the motor or a person who can reconstruct it, Dagny has another meeting with Robert Stadler. She shows him the fragmentary notes left by the inventor. Looking at the motor and the remaining pages of notes, Stadler realizes the extraordinary accomplishment in the field of theoretical physics that the inventor had made. He is also baffled as to why a man with such a great mind would waste his time making a practical motor. Stadler recommends a young scientist at the Utah Institute of Technology to work on reconstructing the motor. The physicist, Quentin Daniels, has refused to work for the government. Stadler tells Dagny that he once knew a John Galt.

The government passes a ruling with respect to the amount of Rearden Metal that can be sold to each customer, and the government bureaucrats send a young college graduate to monitor Rearden's activities as deputy director of distribution. His name is Tony, but the workers dub him the "Wet Nurse." Hank is approached and ordered to supply 10,000 tons of Rearden Metal for the mysterious Project X without telling him what the project is. Hank refuses and tells the agent from the SSI, the "Traffic Cop," that the government has the guns and could use them to seize his metal if it wanted it. Hank understands that his "voluntary cooperation" is needed in order to give the appearance of a moral transaction. The government needs Rearden to pretend that he is not being coerced. The agent's shocked reaction makes Hank realize that the looters require his sanction and that he should continue to refuse to grant his sanction in the future. Later Hank and Dagny discuss the nature of sanction.

Dagny begins to believe that there is a destroyer who is systematically eliminating the men of the mind. Hank secretly sells more Rearden Metal than legally permitted to Ken Danagger. Jim Taggart marries Cheryl Brooks, and Hank Rearden accompanies his wife, Lillian, to the wedding reception. Francisco arrives and announces that the new order of the world is the "aristocracy of pull." It is replacing the aristocracy of money. He later makes a speech praising the virtue and morality of money and production.

In his "Money Speech," Francisco says that money is made possible only by men who produce. Money is a tool of exchange which presumes productive men and the results of their activities. He explains that wealth is the source of money and that money is the effect, rather than the cause, of wealth. He points out that production initiates the demand for other products and services—production is the source of demand. Francisco notes that money should be an objective standard of value tied to reality in order to act as an integrator of economic value. An objective standard requires an objective commodity such as gold.

Francisco approaches Hank at the reception and says that he wants to morally equip him for his self-defense. Rearden is attracted to Francisco's ideas despite having contempt for the apparent manner in which he is living. Francisco warns Hank not to deal with d'Anconia Copper. He then loudly announces that his company is having problems. This incites panic among the crooked investors in d'Anconia stock who realize that they will be losing money.

Hank takes Lillian to the train station after the wedding celebration and he then spends the evening with Dagny. Lillian confronts Hank about where he slept that night. She has discovered that he is having an affair, but she does not know who the woman is. Hank admits to the affair but will not divulge the woman's identity. Lillian plans on her knowledge of the affair and on Hank's sense of guilt to control him.

Hank is visited by Floyd Ferris of the SSI, who attempts to blackmail Rearden into agreeing to sell Rearden Metal to the institute. He says that Hank Rearden and Ken Danagger will be put on trial for the illegal sale of Rearden Metal if Hank does not sell his metal to the SSI. Hank refuses and the government brings charges against them.

Eddie Willers and the unnamed worker (i.e., John Galt) discuss in the Taggart Cafeteria Dagny's suspicion about the existence of a destroyer and how she is afraid that Ken Danagger will be the next industrialist to disappear. Dagny makes an appointment to see Danagger and travels to Pittsburgh to talk to him. Dagny waits for several hours in the outer office while Danagger is speaking to someone else. Dagny attempts to convince Danagger to stay but he tells her that he is quitting and that he will not give her the reason for his doing so.

Francisco visits Rearden at his mills and asks why Hank puts up with all of the suffering. He wants to know what is so worthwhile to remain in business under such crippling conditions. Francisco talks about the ideas of moral sanction and opposing moral codes. There is a furnace breakout and the two magnificently fight the fire side by side. Francisco helps to save Rearden's furnace and during the ordeal Rearden saves Francisco's life. Rearden asks Francisco to finish the question he had been asking. Francisco understands that this is not the right time to continue that discussion. He knows the answer—it is Hank's love for his mills.

At Thanksgiving dinner, the night before Rearden's trial, Hank confronts his brother Philip and frees himself of the guilt that he has felt toward his family. At his trial, Hank says that he does not accept the court's authority or their moral and legal premises. He says that he will offer no defense because he does not perceive his sale to Danagger to be a crime. Using Francisco's words, he states that he has the right to produce and sell any quantity of his metal to whomever he wants as he sees fit to do so. Rearden explains that the government does not have the right to compel and that the trial is simply an institutionalized attempt to seize his metal. The judge fines him and suspends the sentence as the crowd applauds and cheers.

Rearden visits Francisco at his hotel suite. He tells Francisco that he admires his intellect but deplores his depraved playboy lifestyle. Francisco says that his playboy image is a façade or camouflage. He says that in his entire life he has only loved and slept with one woman. Francisco then leads a discussion of the nature and meaning of sex and money.

Hank tells Francisco that he has placed an important order with d'Anconia Copper. Francisco is taken aback, goes to the phone, but stops. In that moment of indecision, Francisco had the power to prevent some disaster affecting Rearden to occur. He tells Hank, by taking an oath to the only woman he has ever loved, that he is Rearden's friend despite what might happen in the future. A few days later, Ragnar Danneskjöld sinks d'Anconia ships carrying Rearden's supply of copper. The angry Rearden feels a sense of great betrayal.

The ships of the world's last copper producer, d'Anconia Copper, continue to be sunk by Ragnar Danneskjöld. Because no copper arrives in America, electrical appliances cease to be produced there. In addition, Hank Rearden fails to deliver Rearden Metal rail needed to replace Taggart Transcontinental's disintegrating mainline track. The Atlantic Southern Bridge collapses leaving Taggart Transcontinental as the only path across America. Because of the copper shortage, Taggart's track continues to deteriorate, train wrecks take place, and companies using Taggart Transcontinental to transport their goods go out of business. The Taggart Board meets to formally close the John Galt Line (i.e., the Rio Norte Line), and Francisco is waiting to talk to Dagny after the meeting. Dagny and Hank go to Colorado for the closing of the line that had been so important to them.

James Taggart is at the mercy of the government, the railroad unions that are demanding wage increases, and his customers demanding rate reductions. Jim desperately needs information that he can trade to the government so that he will be able to keep his shipping rates at their current levels. He conspires with Lillian Rearden and appeals to her for help. He knows that she wants to destroy her husband. She discovers that Hank is traveling by train under a phony name and concludes that he must be traveling with his mistress. She goes to confront Hank, realizes that her husband's lover is Dagny, and is devastated and terrified. Hank refuses when Lillian demands that he give Dagny up.

The government enacts Directive 10-289 that has the purported purpose of stopping the country's decline by freezing the economy in its present state. Comprehensive central government planning is to be used to maintain the status quo. This directive will allow top government officials and politically connected businessmen to retain their power and to enhance their control over the economy. Directive 10-289 mandates that all workers remain at their current jobs, that no business is permitted to close, and that all patents and copyrights be "voluntarily" turned over to the government. It also forbids the introduction of new products and innovations and requires firms to annually produce a number of goods identical to the number produced during the preceding year. In addition, the directive freezes all wages, prices, and profits and requires every person to spend the same amount of money as he did in the preceding year. This directive prevents businesses from adjusting expenses and making other strategic and tactical decisions. The directive also establishes a Unification Board to hear all disagreements stemming from the new laws. The Board's decision on any issues that emerge will be final. Because appeals for exceptions can be made to the Unification Board, the buying and selling of economic favors are the logical result. In response to the directive, more people each day fail to show up at work.

Dagny resigns in response to Directive 10-289 and retreats to a family cabin in Woodstock when she reflects on the nature of purpose and on her conflict with respect to going back to work or not. Dagny confides her whereabouts to Eddie. Hank does not resign. He knows that he has two weeks to sign the Gift Certificate turning the rights to Rearden Metal over to the government and he wants to be there to refuse to do so. The Wet Nurse offers to look the other way and to cover up anything that Rearden does to break the new laws.

Floyd Ferris visits Hank and tells him that Lillian had told him about Hank's affair with Dagny. Ferris says that the government has evidence of the affair and will make it public if Hank does not sign the Gift Certificate. Hank thinks about morality, his love for Dagny, and his guilt for not divorcing Lillian immediately and making public his love for Dagny. In order to save Dagny's reputation, he signs the Gift Certificate. He will not let her suffer for his errors.

Eddie tells the worker in the Taggart cafeteria that Dagny has quit and that she is staying in a mountain lodge in the Berkshires. Furious at his wife for disclosing his relationship with Dagny to the looters, Hank moves out of his house and into an apartment. He instructs his lawyers that Lillian is to receive no alimony or property settlement. Walking home one evening he is approached by the pirate Ragnar Danneskjöld, who attempts to give him a number of bars of gold in partial repayment for the unjust income taxes he has paid over the years. The pirate explains his purpose as a man of justice. Rearden rejects the gold but later saves Ragnar from the police.

Taggart Comet, full of passengers, breaks down and a replacement diesel engine cannot be found. Politician Kip Chalmers demands a nonexistent engine. All that can be found is a coal-burning engine that is unsafe to go through a long tunnel. Many Taggart employees evade responsibility for the decision to use the coal burner and disaster occurs. All those aboard the train are asphyxiated in the tunnel and an army munitions train runs into the stalled Comet resulting in an immense explosion.

Francisco shows up at the cabin where Dagny is staying. He tells her that he was one of the first men to quit, that for twelve years he has deliberately, systematically, and slowly been destroying d'Anconia Copper, and that she too has a right to quit. Francisco introduces the notion to Dagny that she is enabling her enemies, the looters. While they talk, the radio announces news of the Taggart Tunnel train wreck disaster in the heart of the Rocky Mountains making transcontinental traffic impossible. Dagny rushes back to New York, resumes her duties, and reroutes trains utilizing the tracks of other railroad firms. She finds that her brother, James, has his letter of resignation ready (just in case).

Dagny goes home to her apartment and that evening Francisco visits her to try to convince her to leave her railroad. Hank shows up and is enraged to see Francisco who he thinks has betrayed him. Francisco realizes that Dagny is Hank Rearden's mistress and tells Rearden that Dagny is the woman he loves. Hank slaps Francisco who, exercising great self-restraint, does not retaliate. Dagny fears that Francisco might break and kill Hank. After Hank slaps Francisco, she says that Francisco was her first lover.

Quentin Daniels sends a letter to Dagny telling her that he is resigning. He refuses to work under Directive 10-289. Dagny calls him and he agrees to wait for her to visit him. Eddie arrives at Dagny's apartment, sees Rearden's initialed robe, and realizes that she is sleeping with him. Later Eddie eats dinner with the worker (John Galt) in the cafeteria. He tells the worker about Daniels who has been working on the motor and that Dagny is going to Utah to talk with him before the destroyer takes him away. Eddie also reveals to the worker that Dagny and Hank Rearden are having an affair.

Dagny is traveling cross country to Utah when she sees a hobo hitching a ride in her car. She rescues the tramp and invites him to have dinner with her. During their conversation, he tells her that he used to work at the Twentieth Century Motor Company and that he and other employees there had come up with the phrase "Who is John Galt?" some twelve years ago. The hobo, Jeff Allen, then relates the story of the Starnes heirs' small-scale socialist experiment in which the employees as a group voted to decide the needs of each worker as well as the expected production of each laborer based on an assessment of his ability. The result was predictably that, when earnings are not based on productivity, incentives diminish, production plummets, and bankruptcy results. The tramp tells Dagny that the first man to quit was a young engineer named John Galt who vowed that he would stop the motor of the world.

The train stops suddenly and the crew deserts in the middle of nowhere. A "frozen train" such as this is becoming common because men have no legal way to leave their jobs. Dagny spots Owen Kellogg, the young engineer who quit early on in the story, who tells her that he is going on a month's vacation with his friends. Dagny leaves with Owen Kellogg to walk down the track to phone for help and leaves Jeff Allen in charge. She gives instructions to Kellogg, walks to a small airfield, rents a plane, and flies to Utah, where the airfield attendant informs her that Quentin Daniels had just left with a man in another plane. Dagny realizes that this man must be the destroyer. She races after that plane in hers and crashes in the mountains.

Dagny's injuries are not serious but she does lose consciousness. When she awakens and opens her eyes, she sees John Galt, who is both the inventor of the motor and the man who is removing the men of the mind from the outside world. All of the great men who have disappeared are there. They are on a strike of the mind against an oppressive code that worships incompetence and altruism. She is taken to Galt's home where she could be considered to be a guest and/or a prisoner. She is taken on a tour of the valley where Galt's motor supplies the power for the residents' appliances and for a ray source that hides the valley from detection. Ragnar and Galt are concerned about Francisco who is late in arriving. When Quentin Daniels shows up he says that a great many people in the outside world, including Hank Rearden, are looking for the wreckage of Dagny's plane. Francisco finally arrives, sees Dagny, and is relieved.

Dagny stays at Galt's home where she works as a servant in order to pay her debts due in gold for the expenses that she has incurred in the valley. Dagny and Galt are strongly attracted to one another but they stay in separate rooms because she is still a scab. Although she falls in love with Galt who has watched her and loved her for years, she is still his enemy until she decides to join the strike.

Dagny has dinner at the home of Midas Mulligan where she meets the industrialists, scientists, philosophers, inventors, artists, and so on who reside in what is called "Galt's Gulch," "Mulligan's Valley," or "Atlantis." At that dinner the purpose of the valley's residents is formally revealed along with the history of the valley that was established by Mulligan. Each resident in turn proclaims his reasons for joining the strike. Dagny realizes that she will need to make a choice with respect to becoming a striker and staying in the valley or returning to the outside world to continue battling the looters.

For a month Dagny voluntarily works as Galt's housekeeper and cook. Hank Rearden is continuing to search for Dagny, and Francisco wants to contact him to let him know that she is alright but John Galt refuses. Most of the strikers live in the outside world for much of each year but they all spend the month of June together in Galt's Gulch. Dagny accompanies Hugh Akston's three students to their annual reunion at Akston's home.

Francisco believes that he has lost Dagny to Hank Rearden not realizing that John Galt is the man whom she has sought for her entire life. Galt knows about Dagny and Francisco's history together and that Francisco is still in love with Dagny. Francisco invites Dagny to stay at his home during her last week in the valley. Dagny asks Galt to decide and he says no because he realizes that such an action is against the self-interest of all three of them. At the end of the month Dagny decides to return to the world because she still thinks there is a chance to defeat the looters. She cannot give up her railroad. She believes that her values are still possible to achieve in the outside world, that she can save the railroad, that the looters love their lives, and that she can persuade them to see the truth. John Galt returns as well so that he can watch over Dagny and be there when she decides to join the strike. Galt drops Dagny off in the outside world.

Robert Stadler is called by Floyd Ferris to attend a public demonstration of the previously top-secret Project X, a new weapon that uses sound waves to cause terrible destruction over a radius of 100 miles. Its purported purpose is to provide public security. Project X is revealed and demonstrated. Stadler is horrified by its effects yet he still goes along and sanctions it by delivering a speech that Ferris had prepared for him.

Dagny returns to New York and phones Hank, who is totally surprised by her call. She finds out that the railroad industry has been nationalized under the Railroad Unification Plan. The director of Unification is looter-politician Cuffy Meigs. The plan is actually James Taggart's desperate scheme to keep Taggart Transcontinental from going out of business by means of existing off its competition. The plan provides that the total profits of all railroad companies be allocated according to the number of miles of track each owns instead of according to the amount of service that each supplies.

James Taggart attempts to get his sister to appear on Bertram Scudder's radio program to make a speech reassuring the public that the railroad industry is not failing. She refuses but Lillian Rearden tells Dagny that the government bureaucrats know about her affair with Hank and that they will announce it to the public if she fails to appear on Scudder's show. In response to this blackmail attempt, Dagny appears on the show and proudly proclaims that she had been Hank Rearden's lover and that Rearden had been black-mailed into signing the Gift Certificate turning over the rights to Rearden Metal to the government.

Dagny goes to her apartment and finds Hank waiting there for her. Rearden realizes that she has met her true love during her absence because during her speech she spoke of their affair only in the past tense. They discuss their plans to fight the looters. Hank wants to talk to Francisco, the man that is helping him to escape from the looters' altruist ethics.

Eddie Willers tells Cherryl Taggart the truth about who it is that runs Taggart Transcontinental—she finds out that it is Dagny rather than her husband. Over the years of their marriage, she had already formed doubts with respect to his moral character and his role in the railroad. Jim brags and wants to celebrate his "achievement" of a crooked political deal in which the nationalization of d'Anconia Copper will make him a great deal of money. Recalling the details of their marriage, Cherryl confronts James and asks him why he married her. She wants to know what motivates him. They argue and she leaves. Cherryl visits Dagny and apologizes.

Lillian Rearden arrives and appeals to James Taggart to use his political power to stop her forthcoming divorce from Hank, which will leave her penniless. He tells her that he does not have the power to prevent the divorce. Lillian then has sex with James in an effort to hurt her husband one final time while she is still his wife. Cherryl returns, hears a woman's voice, and knows that her husband has been unfaithful. James tells Cherryl that he will not grant her a divorce. He says that he married her because she was worthless and he felt sorry for her. She does not believe him. Cherryl now understands that James is a nihilistic killer of the good. He sought to destroy her because of her ambition and virtues. Unable to destroy the men of the mind, James turned his hatred of the good on the poor shop girl and hero-worshipper. Cherryl runs out of the house and commits suicide by jumping into the river where she drowns. Cherryl's fatal error was that she thought that James was Dagny.

The unreason of the looters is exemplified by James Taggart who is anti-effort and has the need to feel superior. He is on the death premise. He evades, rationalizes, and disregards his responsibility to think. He wants his consciousness to control reality. James thinks that all he has to do is to "want" something. He wants to be rich without earning wealth and to be loved and admired without earning the right to be loved and admired. Jim is motivated by his hatred of good men and his desire to kill them.

A copper shortage drastically affects Taggart Transcontinental and other companies. At the very moment Chilean legislation nationalizes d'Anconia Copper, Francisco simultaneously destroys every property belonging to his company. There is nothing left for the looters to take. Francisco disappears after destroying his holdings. The Washington planners attempt to placate Rearden, his divorce trial goes through smoothly, and the Wet Nurse warns him that something is up. He says that the Washington bureaucrats are planning to impose a new restrictive policy on Rearden Steel but he does not know what it is. The politicians are sneaking their men into Rearden's factories. Both Philip, Hank's brother, and Tony, the Wet Nurse, appeal to Hank for a job. He turns Philip down because he is not competent and tells Tony that he would hire him gladly and at once but the Unification Board won't allow him to do that.

Politicians no longer even pretend that they are working for the public good. Instead they use their political power to create their own personal fortunes. They even divert freight trains as political favors. Cuffy Meigs sends freight cars necessary for the Minnesota wheat house to Ma Chalmers's

soybean project in Louisiana. She is the mother of the Washington politician Kip Chalmers. The result is the rotting of the much-needed Minnesota
crops.

A copper wire breaks in the Taggart Terminal causing its signal system
to go down. Dagny rushes to the tunnel, calls for help from another railroad,
and decides to improvise a lantern scheme to signal and move the trains
manually using her track workers. During the emergency, Dagny spots John
Galt in the middle of a group of unskilled workers. After she issues orders to
the workers, she goes into the tunnels and Galt follows her there. There they
make love for the first time. Afterward, they talk and he tells her that he will
be killed if she unintentionally leads the politicians to him.

The steelworker's union asks for a raise but the Unification Board refuses
making it sound like the rejection came from Hank Rearden. The government
"accidentally" attaches all of Rearden's money making it unavailable to him.
His property is seized on trumped-up tax charges. His family does not want
him to quit and vanish, so his mother visits him and beseeches him to stay
(and to sacrificially provide them with financial help).

Hank goes to New York to meet with the looters, including Mouch,
Holoway, Lawson, Ferris, and Jim Taggart. They tell Rearden that they are
prepared to launch a new Steel Unification Plan that is patterned after the
Railroad Unification Plan. Under the plan, all of the steel companies' earnings are to be rewarded according to the number of furnaces each owns.
Because Orren Boyle has a great many idle furnaces, he would be paid for
almost double his actual output. In turn, Rearden would be paid for less than
half of his actual output. Both the Railroad Unification Plan and the Steel
Unification Plan require companies to produce according to each one's ability
with the profits allocated according to each firm's needs.

Rearden tells them that, no matter what his output is, he will go broke
under that plan. They tell him that "you'll do something." They expect him
to make the irrational work. He now understands their nature and the fact that
he has been supporting them—he has sanctioned their view of existence. He
rejects their plan and drives back to his mills in Philadelphia.

As he approaches his mills, he hears gunfire and sees a mob. His mills are
under attack. He comforts the dying Wet Nurse who was attempting to defend
the mills against the government thugs who had infiltrated his workforce.
Rearden is attacked and is hit in the head with a pipe but an unknown worker
saves him. The worker is Francisco who had been working undercover as
"Frank Adams" in Rearden's mills. It was Francisco who successfully organized the workers' resistance and defense of the mills. When Hank regains
consciousness in the infirmary, he is reunited with Francisco who finishes
telling him what he needed to hear. Rearden retires, vanishes, and joins the
strike. At long last, Hank is freed from the grasp of the looters.

The people of America learn that Hank Rearden has quit and the country falls into even greater chaos and is near collapse. The government has announced that Mr. Thompson will speak to the country over the radio on November 22 to discuss the crisis and his plan to remedy it. Instead John Galt overwhelms the radio signals and takes over the airwaves.

A scheduled national broadcast by the head of state is interrupted by Galt, who, in a three-hour speech, spells out the tenets of his philosophy. Among his many provocative ideas is the notion that the doctrine of Original Sin, which holds man's nature as his sin, is absurd—a sin that is outside the possibility of choice is outside the realm of morality. Another provocative idea is that both forced and voluntary altruism are evil. Placing the welfare of others above an individual's own interests is wrong. The desire to give charity, compassion, and pleasure unconditionally to the undeserving is wrong.

Galt explains that reality is objective, absolute, and comprehensible, and that man is a rational being who relies upon his mind as his only means to obtain objectively valid knowledge and as his "basic tool of survival." The concept of value presupposes an entity capable of acting to attain a goal in the face of an alternative. The one basic alternative in the world is existence versus nonexistence. A is A—existence exists. "It is only the concept of 'Life' that makes the concept of 'Value' possible." An organism's life is its standard of value. Whatever furthers its life is good and that which threatens it is evil. It is therefore the nature of a living entity that determines what it ought to do.

Galt identifies man's life as the proper standard of man's values and morality as the principle defining the actions necessary to maintain life as a man. If life as a man is one's purpose, he has "a right to live as a rational being." To live, man must think, act, and create the values his life requires. Because a man's life is sustained through thought and action, the individual must have the right to think and act and to keep the product of his thinking and acting (i.e., the right to life, liberty, and property).

He asserts that because men are creatures who think and act according to principles, a doctrine of rights ensures that an individual's choice to live by those principles is not violated by other human beings. All individuals possess the same rights to freely pursue their own goals. These rights are innate and can be logically derived from man's nature and needs—the state is not involved in the creation of rights and merely exists to protect an individual's natural rights. Because force is the means by which one's rights are violated, it follows that freedom is a basic good. Therefore, it follows that the role of government is to "protect man's rights" through the use of force but "only in retaliation and only against those who initiate its use."

Galt's speech explicitly ties together all of the ideas previously dramatized in the actions, descriptions, and dialogues in the novel, leads to Galt's eventual capture and the story's climax, hastens the collapse, and makes the rebuilding of society easier. Galt's speech is necessary in order to understand the climax of the novel. When the looters hear his speech, they realize that he is the best thinker in the world and thus search for him in order to enlist his help in saving the deteriorating economy. It is the speech that moves Galt from mythical to concrete status in the novel. The events and actions prior to the speech provide the inductive evidence needed to derive the principle that "the mind is man's tool of survival." By then the reader and the American people in the novel have seen the men of the mind in the world, their gradual disappearance, the effects of the looters' policies, and the resulting crumbling of the world. It is through this speech that Galt demonstrates the value of the men of the mind. Galt's long speech is warranted because the detailed and complex events previously presented concretize the message given in his speech. The knowledge contained in Galt's speech is what convinced the strikers earlier in the novel to abandon their firms and to retreat to Galt's Gulch.

The philosophy of the morality of life embodied in the speech is what the producers needed to hear and accept in order for them to realize their own greatness and to stand up against the looters. It is the right moment for the speech as the strike has served its purpose. It was not delivered until the American people were ready to hear it. In large part, Galt's Objectivist statement is addressed to the common but rational listeners in an effort to gain their support by going on strike themselves. Galt tells them that the world is perishing from the morality of death (i.e., sacrifice), which requires the renunciation of the mind, about the existence of, and reasons for, the strike; about the existence of a proper, rational morality of life and reason; and that they need to withdraw their moral approval (i.e., sanction) of the morality of death.

After hearing Galt's speech, Mr. Thompson wants to negotiate a deal with him. When Thompson asks what to do, Dagny tells him to have the looters give up power but they will not do that. Stadler suggests that Dagny will lead them to Galt. The desperate government officials seek John Galt. They want him to become the country's economic dictator so that the men of the mind will return and rescue the government. The looters broadcast repeated appeals in their attempts to reach Galt. Fearing for Galt's safety, Dagny looks up his address on Taggart's payroll records and goes to his apartment. He tells her that it is extremely likely that the government officials had her followed. He says that they will torture her in order to force her to go along with their wishes if they discover what they mean to one another. He tells her to "betray" him and to take the side of the police when they arrive which she does. They arrest Galt, take him to the Wayne-Falkland hotel, and attempt to convince him to take charge. He, of course, refuses. Stadler is summoned and meets with Galt. Stadler wants to have Galt killed!

There are riots in California, and one of the warring groups has taken over a rail station there with the result that Taggart Transcontinental is unable to provide cross-country transportation. Eddie Willers goes there to see if he can restore order. While he is in California, the looters announce that they will reveal the details of the "John Galt Plan" to save the economy. Galt is ordered to the ballroom to make a speech at a televised press conference. When they parade him before the TV cameras, he turns sideways to reveal a hidden gun that was pointed at him and exclaims, "Get the hell out of my way."

Robert Stadler hears the press conference over the radio and realizes that, caught between the looters and the men of the mind, he has nowhere to go. If the looters win, he will be under their control, and if Galt wins, he will be turned away as a traitor to the mind. Stadler decides to establish his own domain and drives to the Project X site in Iowa, hoping to use that weapon to create his own kingdom. He gets past the guards and spots the drunken Cuffy Meigs at the controls of Project X. Meigs had the same idea and had beaten Stadler to it. They struggle and the weapon goes off creating mass destruction for hundreds of square miles and killing everyone at the facility, including Stadler.

Robert Stadler, a man of great intelligence and the director of the State Science Institute, is the novels' Plato-like character who holds a theoretical-versus-applied-science split. He is a cynical and brilliant theoretical physicist and intellectual elitist who believes that most people are corrupt, stupid, and incapable of virtuous behavior and that only a rare handful of men are open to reason. Stadler is contemptuous of applied science and material production. He is a thoroughgoing Platonist who thinks that the human mind, reason, and science exist on a higher realm that has nothing to do with life on earth.

Stadler resorts to the extortion of citizens to finance his theoretical noncommercial projects. Why would a man with such a great mind tragically turn to the use of brute force to get the funding he desires? The answer is that Stadler concludes that his work must be sustained through government force because he thinks that reason is impotent in the world. Because he wants unearned material wealth for his laboratory, he aligns himself with the statist brutes and looters and their barbarous methods. Stadler thinks that the role of the mind is to deal with a higher realm of reality that is divorced from this world and that, therefore, the mind is inefficacious in dealing with this world. He deduces that brute bodily power is dominant in a world in which most people are irrational, emotional, and impervious to reason. Because most individuals can't appreciate science, he needs a state-backed science institute to force people to finance his research. John Galt recognizes that Stadler, his former professor at Patrick Henry University, is a traitor to the mind and breaks with him when he endorses and joins the State Science Institute. At one time, Stadler would say that the phrase 'free scientific inquiry' was redundant. He later insists that government is necessary to conduct scientific inquiry.

Stadler, a man once with a great mind, chooses to renounce the mind by throwing in with the force-wielders and, in the end, is destroyed by his own power-lust. Stadler is doomed once he turns his mind over to the brutes. He is destroyed because he mistakenly thinks that he can survive by joining the power-lusters. At that point, the men of the mind become his enemy alongside the looters who always were his enemy given that Stadler, at least in the beginning, was one of the thinkers. Ultimately, Stadler has nowhere to go. Toward the end of the novel, he realizes that, if Galt and the other men of the mind are victorious, he will be repudiated as a traitor to the mind and that, if the looters win, he will be shackled to the irrational brutes.

The looters take Galt to a small concrete structure in the SSI where they torture him with a series of electrical shocks provided by the Ferris Persuader. The generator breaks down and Galt tells them how to fix it. Dagny has called Francisco who left a phone number to call in case such an event occurred. While Dagny is getting ready to look for Galt, she receives a call telling her that Taggart Bridge crossing the Mississippi River was destroyed by the explosion of Project X. She tells the caller that she does not know what to do and goes to join Francisco. Dagny has finally decided to join the strikers.

James Taggart, while attempting to break John Galt, realizes that his life has been devoted to destroying the good. Trying to evade his own evil, he breaks down and collapses. Taggart always desired the unearned regarding both physical and spiritual concerns. He does not have any positive ambitions or purpose. He only wants political influence and the opportunity to destroy. He seeks to destroy value because it is value. Although he wants unearned money, he does not view money as a value. Being on the death premise, his goal is to destroy the values required by life. Taggart desires a world in which reason and purpose are not required to survive and flourish in it. Rebelling against life and existence, he conceals his nihilism even from himself. He fabricates and simulates concern with values that promote life. He is under the illusion that obtaining wealth and "success," without effort or rational thought, will give him moral status and self-esteem. Ultimately, the self-deceived Taggart's desire to steal became a desire to destroy values even though such destruction will result in the loss of his own life.

Upon entering the SSI, Dagny shoots a guard who refused to decide what he should do. She along with Francisco, Ragnar, and Rearden invade the premises and free Galt from his torturers. With the rescued John Galt they travel by plane to Galt's Gulch. As they pass over New York City, the lights of the city go out. Having saved the Taggart station in California, Eddie Willers is heading back home on the Comet when it breaks down in Arizona and the members of the crew cannot fix the engine. The passengers and the crew, except for Eddie, leave with a passing covered wagon. Eddie refuses to give up and stays with the marooned train. He cannot let go of the railroad. Eddie's fate is bleak but uncertain. He cannot repair the train but he does have great friends like Dagny and the other heroes who will certainly do their best in attempting to find him. Back in the valley John Galt declares an end to the strike and announces that it is now time for the men of the mind to return and rebuild society.

Atlas Shrugged concretizes through hierarchical, progressive, and inductive demonstration Rand's systematic philosophy of Objectivism. In her great novel, she dramatizes grand themes and presents an entire and integrated view of how a man should live his life. She primarily does this by illustrating the steady growth in knowledge, understanding, and appreciation of the strikers' motives on the parts of Dagny Taggart and Hank Rearden. As they form successively higher abstractions and conceptualizations and draw conclusions, the alert reader is able to concurrently gain a wider and deeper perspective on the novel's events.

Part One tells the story of Dagny Taggart's greatest accomplishment, the construction of the John Galt Line, and of its paradoxical consequences. Part Two contrasts two opposite moral codes and the effects of each, tells of Hank Rearden's progressive liberation from guilt, and explains Dagny's conflict stemming from her mistaken premises regarding the looters and the strikers. In Part Three, Rearden and Dagny grasp more abstractly, fully, and deeply the state of the world and how they should act in it. Let's take a closer look at these two characters.

Dagny, like Hank, is a self-initiator who goes by her own judgments and is the motive power of her own happiness. Unlike Rearden, she does not feel guilty for her achievements. She understands that the world lives because of the work of the prime movers and then hates them for it. Dagny recognizes that the creators are expected to feel guilty for their virtues. Of course, the creators are guilty only of not claiming their moral virtues and values.

Dagny does not fully understand the world's situation and is conflicted because of this lack of knowledge. From her perspective, the strikers are giving up and she sees that as dishonorable and as a form of capitulation. Of course, at one point of the novel, Dagny is on a "mini-strike" of her own when Directive 10-289 is passed. For most of the story, Dagny is on the "wrong track" by believing that the looters love their lives and that they want to live. She thinks that she can persuade them to see the truth and that she can win the war. Throughout Part Three, she progressively comes to realize that the looters are irrational and do not value their lives. This begins to become apparent to her when she meets with Mr. Thompson and the other looter-politicians.

Throughout most of the novel, Dagny believed that she was right to go on. She needed to check her premises. She ultimately realizes that the looters do not value her products or those of the other producers. By the end of the story, she understands what motivates the looters. By then she understands the contradictions in her principles and the need to go on strike. She realizes that there is no chance of winning in the world of the looters.

Dagny has a fuller and more explicit conception of morality than Rearden does and is more morally consistent than he is. Her error is that she does not fully understand the looters' moral code and motives. Their motives become fully clear to her when they want to torture and/or kill Galt rather than to switch course and rescue themselves. Prior to this point, she believed that the looters would eventually comprehend the uselessness of their policies and would concede.

Hank Rearden, a great industrialist who accepts the mind-body dichotomy, is the primary human instantiation of Atlas in the novel. He is a master of reality whose erroneous surface ideas do not corrupt his essential character and subconsciousness in terms of his psycho-epistemology. Although Rearden's words and ideas sanction an unearned guilt, his actions belie his words. Down deep he does not believe the notion of the mind-body split.

Hank and the other industrialists are the worst victims of the conventionally accepted altruist-collectivist philosophy. It is the mistaken sanction of the men of ability that paves the way for the parasites and statist looters who want the creators to produce for the world and then to suffer for doing so. A moral code based on altruism and the idea of a mind-body split holds the creators guilty because of their greatest virtues. Once Rearden and the other producers gain an understanding of the looters' evil and of the importance of their own morality, they will obtain the sense that life is about accomplishment and joy rather than about suffering and disaster.

It is under the tutelage of Francisco and Dagny that Rearden slowly awakens to the truth; comprehends the nature, causes, and interrelationships between his personal and work-related problems; understands the motives of the looters and his family; and realizes his own virtues and values. They are able to provide Hank with a moral sanction and lead him to realize that he has been guilty in accepting a wrong moral code and of giving the looters and his family a moral sanction based on the wrong code of morality. Throughout much of the novel, he needed to attain a belief in his own morality and in his right to self-esteem.

Hank's decision to go on strike takes a long time to develop. Until his discussion with the looters regarding the proposed Steel Unification Plan, he thought that the looters would ultimately be rational. After the confrontation, Rearden drives back to his mills, happens upon the dying Wet Nurse, is saved by Francisco (disguised as worker "Frank Adams"), and listens to Galt's logic as delivered to him by Francisco. In the next chapter he disappears to Mulligan's Valley. Now seeing the truth, he recognizes that he must give up the world in order to save it.

For much of the novel Dagny and Hank considered the looters' evil policies to be self-defeating. They did not understand that they are not impotent
if they are empowered by the good. It was only the producers' toleration
and tacit acceptance of the looters' moral code that made the devastating
results possible. In order to be able to effectively battle their enemies, Dagny
and Hank had to come to understand how they were complicit in their own
victimization. The moral code of self-sacrifice had been used against, and
accepted by, the creators who had been made to feel guilty for their achievement and wealth. This is the "sanction of the victim" moral principle.

Rearden's exploitation is more extreme than Dagny's. She has an explicit
awareness of morality that he does not have. Rearden questions his right to
his own happiness and self-esteem and she does not. He partially accepts
altruism and does not explicitly understand that he goes by a moral code in
his work life. He does so implicitly because his work life exemplifies morality
as it leads to production, life, and life-enhancing values.

There have been many good philosophical novels and good business novels but none have been as brilliantly integrated and unified as *Atlas Shrugged*.
Atlas Shrugged is arguably the greatest combination of philosophy, business,
and literature written to date. Ayn Rand's presentation of businessmen as
heroes makes this novel virtually unparalleled in the history of literature.
This great novel has been brought to the big screen in the form of a trilogy of
films. Part One was released in the Spring of 2011, Part Two was released in
the Fall of 2012, and Part Three was released in 2015.

NOTE

This chapter previously appeared as "Atlas Shrugged," in *Exploring Capitalist Fiction* by Edward Younkins (Lanham, MD: Lexington Books, 2014). All rights reserved and reprinted with permissions.

Chapter 2

Atlas Shrugged as Philosophy and Literature

In *Atlas Shrugged* (1957), Ayn Rand presents her original and controversial philosophy of Objectivism in a dramatized form. More than a great novel, it expounds a radical new philosophy with amazing clarity. *Atlas Shrugged* presents an integrated and all-embracing perspective of man and man's relationship to the world and manifests the essentials of an entire philosophical system—metaphysics, epistemology, politics, and ethics. *Atlas Shrugged* embodies Objectivism in the actions of the story's heroes.

Leonard Peikoff (2004) explains that the most extraordinary quality of *Atlas Shrugged* is its integration. Ayn Rand understood that everything that is included in a novel affects that novel. She realized that the unity of a literary work depends upon the necessary causal and logical connections among its many aspects. It follows that she included no random elements or events. Rand tied everything to *Atlas Shrugged's* unifying theme of "the role of the mind in human existence" (Rand [1971] 1975, 81).

Atlas Shrugged is a model of integration among theme, story, and characters. All elements are logically connected, tied to the whole, and synthesized with the novel's unifying theme. In *Atlas Shrugged*, every character, event, line of dialogue, or description is related to its theme. Even the philosophical speeches are integrated with the events of the story.

According to Chris Matthew Sciabarra (2007):

As a novel, *Atlas Shrugged* is a remarkable achievement of integration. Rand had always seen the plot of a novel, its story, as a structured totality: "a story is an end in itself," she wrote to one correspondent. "It is written as a man is born—an organic whole, dictated only by its own laws and its own necessity—an end in itself . . ." (Letter to Gerald Loeb, 5 August 1944, in Rand 1995, 157). And so, it is no coincidence that *Atlas Shrugged* itself is a superbly integrated "organic whole," one that fused action, adventure and sensuality with philosophy, contemplation and spirituality, incorporating elements of science fiction and fantasy, symbolism and realism. It launched a philosophical movement that has been nothing less than revolutionary in its implications. (31)

Atlas Shrugged is appealing on many levels. It is a moral defense of capitalism, political parable, social commentary, science fiction tale, mystery story, love story, and more. The longer and more deeply a person studies *Atlas Shrugged*, the more he or she will be able to appreciate how these multiple approaches to plot enrich one another. Taken together, these manifold perspectives impart a moral sense of life that inspires admiration for each individual person's highest potential (i.e., as he or she can be and ought to be).

Peikoff observes that *Atlas Shrugged*'s marvelously constructed and interwoven plot is a miracle of organization encompassing multiple layers or tiers of depth. Every event, action, and character serve both dramatic and philosophical purposes. Every line is important. Rand's emblematic characters have all irrelevancies and accidents removed. Rand probes each character's motives, connects a set of personal traits to each character's motivation, and integrates the actions of the characters with their motivation and character traits.

Rand selects and integrates actions and events that dramatize the theme of the novel. *Atlas Shrugged* is a "story about human beings in action" (Rand 2000a, 17). Rand thinks in essentials in uniting all of the issues of the actions in the novel. Her concern is with values and issues that can be expressed in action. The story's plot action is based on the integration of values and actions and of mind and body. Rand thereby shows actions supporting wide abstract principles.

The events and characters of *Atlas Shrugged* portray the philosophical principles that affect the actual existence of men in the world. The conflict between the looters and the creators dramatizes the struggle between contradictory visions, values, and moralities. Because human values are abstractions made from observations, the reader is given concretes in the novel in order for the abstract values to become real for him or her.

By including only that which is essential, Rand illustrates the connections between metaphysical abstractions and their concrete expressions. *Atlas Shrugged* is a feat of complex structural integration. The author carefully selected the details with no event, character, line of dialogue, or description included that does not further and reinforce the theme of the importance of reason. Nothing is thrown in arbitrarily. Rand was aware of the specific purpose of every chapter, paragraph, and sentence and could state a reason for every word and punctuation mark in the novel (4).

This chapter is a "summary of the literature" that frequently relies on the views of people writing about *Atlas Shrugged* to make a case for *Atlas Shrugged* as a highly integrated novel. All of the parts of this chapter explain, in one way or another, how integration and unity are represented in *Atlas Shrugged*. The first section examines the philosophical structure and integration of this great philosophical novel. The next part deals with issues of literary structure and integration. This is followed by an examination of Rand's techniques of characterization and character development as displayed in *Atlas Shrugged*. The subsequent section takes a look at the philosophical speeches. Mind-body integration is the subject of the last major section. The conclusion discusses *Atlas Shrugged* as the embodiment of a fully integrated philosophical novel.

PHILOSOPHICAL INTEGRATION

Atlas Shrugged is an achievement of intricate structural composition and integration. The titles of its three major sections pay tribute to Aristotle, correspond to his basic laws of thought, and accomplish a thematic goal by implying something regarding the meaning of the events and actions in the respective sections of the novel. In Part One, called "Non-Contradiction," there is a long series of strange and apparently contradictory events and paradoxes with no discernible logical solution. In Part Two, "Either-Or," based on Aristotle's Law of Excluded Middle, Dagny faces a fundamental choice with no middle road—to continue to battle to save her business or to give it up. Part Two also focuses on the conflict between two classes of humanity—the looters and the creators. Part Three, "A is A," is based on Aristotle's Law of Identity. In it, Dagny and Rearden (along with the reader) learn the true nature of the events, and all the apparent contradictions are identified and resolved (Minsaas 1994; Bernstein 1995). By Part Three, both the characters and the readers are able to see the story as an interrelated network of events. In addition, there are multiple and integrated layers and levels of meaning and implications for each of *Atlas Shrugged's* thirty chapters. Rand's chapter titles are meaningful at the literal level in addition to being significant at deeper philosophical and symbolic levels (Bernstein 1995; Seddon 2007, 47–56).

Douglas B. Rasmussen (2007, 33–45) explains that Rand's reality-is-intelligible thesis is vividly expressed in the section titles of *Atlas Shrugged*. The basic meaning of this thesis is that the things of existence have an identity and that these things can be known. As he explains,

These titles correspond to the Aristotelian laws of thought: Non-Contradiction (the Law of Non-Contradiction [also sometimes called The Law of Contradiction];

Either-Or (the Law of Excluded Middle); and A is A (the Law of Identity). For Rand, as for Aristotle, these laws of thought are not merely how we must think in order to obtain knowledge; they also describe the fundamental character of reality. These laws are thus ontological and pertain to the very nature of being. Nothing can ultimately exist or be that fails to comply with these principles. The nature of reality is such that (1) something cannot be and not-be at the same time and in the same respect; (2) something either exists or does not exist at a given time and in a given respect; and (3) something is what it is at a given time and in a given respect. (34)

Rasmussen notes that for Rand, the laws of thought are not a priori mental categories that people impose on sense perceptions to make them intelligible. Rather, they are laws of reality. It follows that the method of logic is defined by the laws of reality. There is a difference between something as it exists in a man's cognition and as it exists independently of that cognition.

According to Greg Salmieri (2007), the messages of Part One are relatively concrete compared to the lessons of Parts Two and Three.[1] Part One sets the context of the novel and tells the story of Dagny Taggart's greatest accomplishment, the construction of the John Galt Line, and its paradoxical consequences. It illustrates that rationality is the cause of the construction of the John Galt Line. Part Two is essentially moral and is more abstract than Part One. It contrasts two opposite moral codes (the morality of life and the morality of death) and the effects of each. Part Two also portrays Hank Rearden's progressive liberation from guilt and Dagny's conflict stemming from her mistaken premises regarding the looters and the strikers. Part Two also demonstrates the redounding sequence of events and consequences of the actions of the strikers and the looters and introduces the idea of the "destroyer." Part Three can be viewed as metaphysical or as moral/metaphysical. This part recasts moral issues in terms of opposite attitudes toward existence. It follows Rearden and Dagny as they grasp more abstractly, fully, and deeply the state of the world and how they should act in it. The whole truth becomes apparent to them when they hear Galt's speech, every point of which is a structured restatement of a progressive reasoning process that has taken place throughout the novel. They ultimately come to understand the relevant principles, thereby realizing the need to go on strike.

Salmieri explains that *Atlas Shrugged* is epistemologically progressive and hierarchically inductive as its characters draw abstractions concurrently as the readers are intended to draw them. The characters perform successive inductions and abstractions throughout the novel, ending in extremely wide and abstract principles as expressed in Galt's speech. As the characters operate at successively higher levels of abstraction, they see ever more remote and complex causal connections. Rand's characters first comprehend narrow truths about alternative moral codes and then go broader and deeper with respect to the philosophical significance, meaning, and connection of these truths. Throughout the novel, new realizations lead to more questions.

Atlas Shrugged becomes progressively more abstract as Dagny and Rearden come to understand increasingly broader abstractions and larger causal connections. By grasping more abstract and sophisticated concepts, these characters, along with the alert reader, gain a wider contextual perspective on the novel's events. Both Dagny and Rearden steadily but gradually gain further realizations about what motivates the looters. They comprehend more deeply and abstractly the nature of two alternative moral codes and what happens if one chooses the wrong moral code. The climactic results are a way of thinking and capping integration that is expounded in Galt's speech and evidenced in Dagny and Rearden's decisions to go on strike. *Atlas Shrugged's* plot-theme, the mind on strike, is the essential line of its events. It is the central means of presenting the theme and the main conflict and of linking the theme to the action (Rand 2000a, 40–44; [1971] 1975, 82–86). More specifically, the plot-theme is the "men of the mind going on strike against an altruist-collectivist society" (Rand [1971] 1975, 85). This is the central situation that dramatizes and expresses *Atlas Shrugged's* abstract theme.

Rand presents a conflict in terms of action, thus creating a "purposeful progression of events" (2000a, 17). To do this, she portrays strong willful characters, the creators and the looters, who are in sharp moral conflict with one another. She thereby expresses the plot conflict in action. Dagny Taggart and Hank Rearden, the primary creators, philosophically are against the looters, but in action they support them. In addition, existentially Dagny and Rearden oppose Galt and the strikers but philosophically agree with them. The plot of *Atlas Shrugged* is a story of human action from which moral issues cannot be separated (Bernstein 1995).

The major plot of *Atlas Shrugged* is the story of the strike (Rand 1997, 399, 416–17, 428–33). In her 1994 audio course, Kirsti Minsaas explains that Rand gradually supplies hints and clues about the strike and that, through the use and emphasis of subsidiary surface plots, she is able to keep the events of the major plot hidden and to reveal the strike only in a step-by-step and retrospective manner. These secondary cover plots include (1) Dagny Taggart and Hank Rearden's struggle to save their respective companies and industries primarily through the construction of the John Galt Line and (2) Dagny's quests to find the inventor of the revolutionary motor and to find and stop the destroyer who is draining the brains of the world. Through the pursuit of the above objectives, the main plot is revealed, the mystery is solved, the question "Who is John Galt?" is answered, and the reasons for the collapse of the railroad and of industrial society are understood (Bernstein 1995). The plot of *Atlas Shrugged* has an inexorable internal logic in which the intellectual puzzle is acted out and solved by the heroes.

In his 1995 audio course, Andrew Bernstein observes that there are dual lines of action in *Atlas Shrugged* involving the observable and the unobservable. We perceive Dagny and Hank striving to construct the John Galt Line and searching for the inventor of the motor. We also see the looters, their policies, and the disastrous effects of their policies. What is not discernible is John Galt removing the men of the mind from the world and relocating them in Mulligan's Valley. The key link between these two spheres of action is Eddie Willers, who unknowingly feeds information to John Galt, disguised as a low-level worker with whom Eddie has lunch. The construction of the John Galt Line most directly depicts the mind's role in human existence. Much of the balance of the novel demonstrates the effects of the absence of the men of the mind (Rand 2000a, 12). *Atlas Shrugged* teaches that prosperity and productivity depend upon the mind by showing both the presence and absence of the producers in the world.

LITERARY INTEGRATION

Many articles could be devoted to the study of Ayn Rand's literary theory and practice as exemplified in *Atlas Shrugged*. Among the topics that could be studied are her controlled and consistent literary patterns, plot and plot-theme, dialogues, use of action, method of portraying values, use of symbolism and imagery, use of mythology, approach to characterization and character development, method of controlling perspective, descriptive style, rhetorical approaches, and use of literary forms such as utopia, dystopia, tragedy, comedy, chronicle, and epic (Saint-Andre 2006; Cox 1986). This section of this article serves as a brief introduction to the literary aspects of *Atlas Shrugged*.

The most crucial events in *Atlas Shrugged* are dramatized. The key events are shown to the reader as if they were occurring before the reader's eyes. Rand also uses flashbacks (e.g., Eddie Willers thinking back to his childhood) to convey important information. Less critical information is simply narrated (Rand 2000a, 145–58).

Rand applies her inductive theory of concept formation in writing *Atlas Shrugged*, as well as in her other works of fiction. Rand projects important abstractions dealing with values, virtues, emotions, and so on in specific concrete actions. She first presents a "visual description by means of essentials and then the symbolic and philosophic meaning of that description" (127).

Atlas Shrugged is primarily presented to the reader in a form that a person would perceive it in real life. Although Rand chooses the focus or perspective, she presents the reader with "direct sensory evidence" and does not tell him or her what to think or to feel. She provides information by giving the reader precise, "concrete, objective facts" and observational details. The reader is given the evidence in context, and it is up to him or her to make a reasoned judgment (97).

Andrew Bernstein (1995, 2007, 53–62) has examined four of the integrated literary techniques Rand employed to magnify the plot-theme of the great minds on strike and, as a result, the theme of the mind's role in human life. These techniques included symbolism, irony, recasting Greek myths, and what Bernstein has called the juxtaposition of philosophical opposites. Bernstein points out that these literary techniques are never employed as ends in themselves, but rather only in order to further integrate and embody *Atlas Shrugged*'s plot-theme and theme.

Rand mainly dramatizes the meaning of *Atlas Shrugged* in action, but still effectively uses some symbolism as a supplemental technique. She often, but not always, first illustrates an idea in action and then uses a symbol to bring abstract subject matter down to the observational level. Some symbols in *Atlas Shrugged* are introduced before they are supported by observational detail. But there are no "floating symbols" in *Atlas Shrugged*. Rand has the reader experience particular concrete actions in order to have enough information to inductively derive and understand the principle involved, and she employs a symbol to capture the essence of the abstraction (Bernstein 1995). The idea that a tangible symbol represents is something abstract. Key symbols in *Atlas Shrugged* include (1) the oak tree, (2) the calendar, (3) the bracelet of Rearden Metal (in the form of a chain), (4) Wyatt's torch, (5) the sign of the dollar, (6) Galt's motor, and (7) the cigarette.

The oak tree on the Taggart estate had represented greatness, permanence, and strength to Eddie Willers until lightning struck it, tearing it apart and revealing that it was hollow and had rotted away on the inside. This symbolizes both the deterioration of Taggart Transcontinental, as evidenced by the presidency of the incompetent James Taggart, and the disintegration of modern industrial civilization. The calendar ominously looking over the city evokes the phrase "your days are numbered" to Eddie, thus supplying another symbol of the decay and encroaching demise of the economy. The bracelet of Rearden Metal made from the first pouring of this metal is symbolic, at one level, of Hank Rearden's life work and of his accomplishments. When he gives it to his wife, this shows his pride in his achievements. Later, Lillian calls it "the chain by which he holds us all in bondage," inviting the question of who is in bondage to whom and by what means. This implies to the reader that it is the spiritual chain of altruistic ethics that has Rearden tethered to his family members. When Ellis Wyatt leaves the outside world, he sets fire to his oil fields. "Wyatt's torch" continues to burn long after he departs, symbolizing both defiance of the looters and the fact that the mind cannot be forced to work. The dollar sign stands for the currency of the United States as a free society, and for the belief in capitalism as the most moral and pro-ductive system. Galt's motor is symbolic of the power of the human mind and of how the producers are needed in the world. Both Galt's motor and the men of the mind are withdrawn from the market economy. Finally, given the time period during which the novel is written, the cigarette may have been intended as a symbol of pleasure (Merrill 1991, 60–61; Bernstein 1995).

Irony, as a literary device, involves the use of words to convey an actual meaning that is opposite of their literal meaning. Irony in literature involves incongruity between the actual meaning of a statement, character, or event and its apparent meaning. Irony in *Atlas Shrugged* is integrated into the conflict and has both aesthetic and epistemological value to the reader. As explained by Andrew Bernstein (2007),

> *Atlas Shrugged*, as a whole, is a single, integrated, sustained exercise in liter-ary irony. This is inevitable because of the multiple action levels, the duality between appearance and reality. Since Dagny and the other narrators know nothing of the strike, they interpret the disappearances, the collapse, and the haunting question as inimical to man's life on earth. But to those privy to the strike, the meaning of these events is positive, for the events actually establish cultural groundwork for the intellectual-moral-political renaissance that, for the first time, will make possible the full flourishing of human life on earth. The all-encompassing global irony integrated into the very essence of the plot produces a riveting stream of brilliantly ironic scenes and passages. (56)

Robert Bidinotto (2007) observes,

> Rand's subtlety extends to dialogue . . . where double and triple meanings are often embedded in what seems to be casual conversations. For example, there is a delightful irony in many of the early references to inventor-hero John Galt, but since they occur long before he appears in the story, most of them won't be apparent during a first reading. (52)

Rand also effectively alters and adapts some famous Greek myths in order to tell them from an Objectivist viewpoint. These myths include (1) Phaëton, (2) Prometheus, (3) Atlantis, (4) Atlas, (5) Odysseus and the Sirens (as alluded to in the story of Roger Marsh), and (6) King Midas. Ayn Rand's use and recasting of ancient Greek myths adds to the epic scope of *Atlas Shrugged*. By changing them, she challenges their traditional meaning and endorses them with new meaning reflecting a revolutionary worldview com-plete with a new moral philosophy.

In the original Greek myth Phaëton, the son of Helios, steals his father's chariot, tries to drive the sun across the sky, and perishes. However, in Richard Halley's opera of the same name he succeeds. Prometheus in the original version gives fire to man and Zeus punishes him by having a vulture eat his liver every night only to have the liver grow back each morning. In Rand's version Prometheus is not doomed. She writes that John Galt is Prometheus who changed his mind. He has broken his chains and has withdrawn his fire until the day when men withdraw their vultures. The Atlantis myth tells the story of an initially noble and partly divine race of people who become corrupt and are punished by the gods who sink their island. In *Atlas Shrugged*, Rand creates her valley of heroes (known as Galt's Gulch, Mulligan's Valley, and Atlantis) as a utopian society where rational people can enter and live. In the original myth, Atlas was condemned to carry the weight of the world on his shoulders. In *Atlas Shrugged*, the weight of the world is placed on the shoulders of the producers. Francisco tells Rearden that he would tell Atlas "to shrug." Atlas symbolizes the prime movers or creators who are asked to shrug by going on strike in order to shake off their burden and to show the world how desperately that it needs them. Odysseus has been warned about the lovely Sirens whom he will encounter on his voyage home. The Siren's beautiful singing lures sailors to their death by leaping overboard in their attempts to join the Sirens. Odysseus has his men plug their ears with beeswax and has them bind him to the mast of the ship. He alone hears their seductive song as he begs to be unchained. His faithful men follow his instructions and bind him even tighter. In *Atlas Shrugged*, Rand tells the story of Roger Marsh, of Marsh Electric, who told Ted Nielsen, of Nielson Motors, that he did not want to become one of the deserters. He said that he would have himself chained to his desk so that he would not be able to leave regardless of the temptation. He said that if he did vanish, he would leave a note explaining why. He departed to live in the valley and left no such letter (Bernstein 1995; Minsaas 1994, 2007, 141–50). In Greek mythology, Dionysus granted Midas, king of Phrygia, the power to turn everything into gold by touch. After he turned his daughter into gold through a hug, he begged to be relieved of the gift. In *Atlas Shrugged*, Midas Mulligan received his name because he had a great talent to make profitable investments. Unlike the legendary King Midas, Mulligan is happy with his gift and does not want to give it up.

Rand's frequent use of the literary technique of the juxtaposition of opposites involves the sequential presentation and contrasting in consecutive scenes of the universe of the irrational Kantian-Marxists and the universe of the rational men of the mind. By dramatizing the world of the emotional and inefficacious looters with that of the creative and life-promoting producers in side-by-side scenes, Rand successfully illustrates entire opposed philosophical systems in action and in conflict (Bernstein 1995, 2007, 60–63). Minsaas (1995) instructs the reader of Rand's novels to pay close attention to the author's "thematic interweaving of ideas through the causal patterning and organization of the events." This involves the use of analogical juxtaposition—the method of holding up parallels and contrasts in scenes, descriptions, events, characters, symbols, and so on.

Lester Hunt (2007, 57–62) has commented that *Atlas Shrugged* is a very intentional novel with every detail designed to mean something. Every aspect of the story has a "why" and a "what for." Hunt then describes the extraordinary meaning-saturation of this novel. Hunt terms one structural feature Rand's "twinning device." Such mirroring with a difference involves "meaning-bearing elements that are linked by salient similarities and at the same time opposed to one another in potentially significant ways" (59). For example, there are two steel magnates (Rearden and Orren Boyle), two major characters with mixed philosophical premises (Rearden and Dr. Robert Stadler), two dysfunctional marriages (Hank and Lillian Rearden's and James and Cherryl Taggart's), two scientists (Galt and Stadler), and so on. Hunt explains that one of the results of this twinning device is to guide the reader's attention toward making mental integrations based on perceiving real similarities and real differences. This reflects Rand's epistemological theory, which holds that the creation of human knowledge involves the finding of bona fide similarities and differences among things.

Atlas Shrugged is a story of human action on a monumental scale in which Rand skillfully ties physical actions to important human values. Values and value premises, especially those relating to productive work and romance, are both implicit and explicit in *Atlas Shrugged*. The creator of this integrated work of literature realized that it is important to dramatize values. People need to see values embodied in a concrete form in the world. *Atlas Shrugged* provides specific examples of what individuals' values are or ought to be (Plauché 2007, 25–36). It inductively demonstrates the values of a new moral philosophy of rational self-interest. As a result, it provides the emotional fuel to stimulate one's love of existence and to motivate a person toward his or her full flourishing as a human being. This joyous "sense of life" involves admiration for man's highest potential (Madden 2007, 167–75) and the disposition that achievement and happiness are normal and expected whereas suffering and disaster are merely exceptions in life. Such a sense of life depends upon the acceptance and consistent practice of rationality in every area of one's life.

Rand illustrates in *Atlas Shrugged* that rationality is the primary virtue and moral requirement. Holding that morality is not primarily social, she explains and illustrates that morality applies even and especially to man alone. A man must choose to think. Rand maintains that rationality, the primary virtue, requires the exercise of six derivative virtues that can be viewed as expressions of rationality: honesty, independence, justice, integrity, productiveness, and pride (i.e., moral ambitiousness).[2] The heroes of *Atlas Shrugged* are characterized as possessing all of these virtues.

CHARACTERIZATION AND
CHARACTER DEVELOPMENT

Rand adeptly presents the nature of the heroes and villains in *Atlas Shrugged* in terms of their motives. Her main means of characterization are actions and dialogue (i.e., "words in the context of a character's actions"; Salmieri 2007). By observing a Randian character's actions and hearing his conversations, a reader is able to grasp the character's motives and to discern what is at that character's philosophical root. Rand masterfully integrates a character's internally consistent actions, decisions, and words with his or her motives. The particular details she presents are related to wider fundamental abstractions and deeper motivations of the character presented. A man's basic values and premises form his character and inspire him to action (Rand 2000a, 59–63).

Rand's characters are formulated with reference to philosophical principles and premises. Her character development involves characters making their philosophical premises ever more explicit. They follow up and build upon the logic of true premises, continue to follow false premises, correct their false premises, or betray their formerly held true premises (Salmieri 2007).

In her stylized portraits of the characters in *Atlas Shrugged*, Rand's goal is to present no random details and to focus on the essentials to understanding each character. The challenge in characterization is to present that which is essential to a particular type of person. By eliminating irrelevant and trivial attributes and actions, her characters become moral projections. Rand's characters are persons in whom certain characteristics and patterns of behavior are pinpointed more constantly and distinctly than in typical persons (Gladstein 2000, 62–63; Rand [1971] 1975, 87–89). Her method of slanted realism focuses selectively on motives, traits, and especially actions that constitute character differences. Rand realizes that what a hero or villain in a novel does paints the character better than what he or she says and enormously better than whatever the author may say about him or her. A character's actions always reveal key aspects of his or her character. Of course, like any good novelist, Rand uses various approaches to providing information about her characters. For example, the speeches by Francisco, Rearden, and Galt are critical to the characterization of each of these Randian heroes. By excluding superficial or accidental facets of a character's personality, Rand makes certain that attention is not averted from essential purposes and motives. As a result, the reader is able to gain a clear and deep insight into her characters.

Each character in *Atlas Shrugged* serves a purpose, and each one is an integral part of the entire structure. Rand integrates the characters into the story through the creation of bonds between the various characters.

According to Bidinotto (2007),

> Good drama is built on conflict. But strong conflict requires extremely willful characters pursuing incompatible goals tied to the story's theme. Their conflicts build powerfully throughout the story, until they're finally resolved in a climax that demonstrates that theme. . . . Ayn Rand shared this view of good fiction writing. In Atlas, her theme is the importance of reason to human life. Her plot, characters, dialogue, and descriptions all reinforce and advance that theme. (53)

Rand is a master of orchestration, as evidenced by her matching different kinds of characters against one another. At the most general level, we have the looters and the nonlooters (i.e., the thinkers and producers). At a more micro-level, the reader is able to gain a clear and deep insight into characters such as the self-made martyred industrialist with mixed moral premises (Hank Rearden); the ideal epic heroine (Dagny Taggart); the supremely able man who enjoys an exalted life on earth (Francisco d'Anconia); the brilliant scientist turned moral traitor and looter-politician (Robert Stadler); the envious nihilist death worshiper (James Taggart); the vacuous power luster (Lillian Rearden); the pivotal rational character who forces the conflict from beginning to end (John Galt); the man of justice who takes from the parasitical looters to restore wealth to the creative and productive people (Ragnar Danneskjöld); the loyal, morally courageous common man of modest ability (Eddie Willers); the mistaken hero-worshipper (Cherryl Brooks); the cynical young Washington bureaucrat just out of college who begins as a moral relativist but comes to admire and emulate the industrialist, Hank Rearden, and dies as a man of reason (Tony, the Wet Nurse); the villainous politician (Wesley Mouch); the immoral businessman (Orren Boyle); and so on.

Salmieri contrasts the heroes (i.e., the producers) and the villains (i.e., the looters) with respect to their motivations and worldviews. The heroes are motivated by final causes and are rationally purposeful. Their lives have directionality and unity of purpose, and they recognize the role of the mind in man's life. In contrast, the villains are not finally caused—they are merely efficiently caused as they are moved by outside forces. They are unlike the heroes who, as prime movers, initiate courses of action in pursuit of their ultimate goals. Heroes, like Dagny, understand and follow causality and are focused on doing things better and on earning their profits. The villains are portrayed as malicious, purposeless (or at best having short-term irrational purposes), and as seeking the unearned. *Atlas Shrugged's* villainous characters manifest different forms of irrational thought, actions, and pronouncements as Rand skillfully has the various villains expound a variety of economic and other fallacies. This technique aids in developing their characterization.

The looters are proponents of high taxation, big labor, government ownership, government spending, government planning, regulation, and redistribution. They include politicians and their supporters, "intellectuals," government bureaucrats, scientists who sell their minds to the bureaucrats, and liberal businessmen who, afraid of honest competition, sell out their initiative, creative powers, and independence for the security of government regulation. The nonlooters—the thinkers and doers—are the competent and daring individualists who innovate and create new enterprises. These prime movers love their work, are dedicated to achievement through their thought and effort, and abhor the forces of collectivism and mediocrity. The battle is thus between nonearners who deal by force and "profit" through political power and earners who deal by trade and profit through productive ability and enterprise.

Darryl Wright (2007) explains that the looters are impervious to reason and always believe that the "prime movers" will come to their aid and save them.[3] The looters also want to reverse the order of cause and effect. They believe that by expropriating the wealth of the creators they will gain unearned moral status and self-esteem, but the world does not work that way. By being rational and productive, a man gains moral status and self-esteem, and as a consequence, creates truly earned wealth. It follows that wealth is the effect of one's moral status. The looters engage in self-deception in order to fake their moral status and self-esteem to themselves. They use the code of altruism in their efforts to transfer moral status and self-esteem from those who have earned them to those who have not. Rather than attempting to earn wealth, self-esteem, and the respect of others, the looters seek to obtain money, the result of production, through the use of altruism and/or government force.

Rand's *Atlas Shrugged* presents the virtuous businessman in a realistic, favorable, and heroic image by emphasizing the possibilities of life in a free society, the inherent ethical nature of capitalism and of the good businessman, the strength and self-sufficiency of the hardworking man of commerce, and the value of the entrepreneur as a wealth creator and promoter of human economic progress. *Atlas Shrugged* shows the legitimate businessman's role as potentially heroic by celebrating the energy and opportunity of life for men of talent and ability to make something of themselves. This great novel teaches that acts of courage and creativity consist in following one's sense of integrity rather than in blind obedience, and in inspiring others instead of following them. *Atlas Shrugged* portrays the business hero as a persistent, original, and independent thinker who pursues an idea to its fruition. Rand's

1957 masterpiece dramatizes the positive qualities of the businessman by showing the triumph of individualism over collectivism, depicting business heroes as noble, appealing, and larger than life, and by characterizing business careers as at least as honorable as careers in medicine, law, or education—if not more so.[4]

Rand, like Aristotle in his *Nicomachean Ethics*, holds an agent-centered approach to morality and concentrates on the character traits that constitute a good person. Reading *Atlas Shrugged* prompts people to reflect on what is constitutive of a good life. Rand's heroes are shown to hold proper principles and to develop appropriate character traits. The villains in the novel provide examples of what happens to people when they hold faulty principles (or compromise certain important principles) and fail to develop essential virtues.

Atlas Shrugged illustrates that there are good and bad businessmen and that businessmen don't always act virtuously. There are two kinds of businessmen—those who lobby government for special privileges, make deals, as well as engage in fraud and corrupt activities. Then there are the real producers who succeed or fail on their own.

Rand's business heroes are independent, rational, and committed to the facts of reality, to the judgment of their own minds, and to their own happiness. All of them think for themselves, actualize their potential, and view themselves as competent to deal with the challenges of life and as worthy of success and happiness (Locke 2000). *Atlas Shrugged* makes a great case that the businessman is the appropriate and best symbol of a free society. Rand shows that, because life requires the production of values, true businessmen's actions are morally proper. The heroes of *Atlas Shrugged* find joy in taking risks and bringing men and materials together to produce what people value.

Atlas Shrugged chronicles the rise of corrupt businessmen who pursue profit by dealing with dishonest politicians. They avoid rationality and productivity by using their political pull and pressure groups to loot the producers. Rand is scathing in her indictment of these villains who would rob the creative thinkers who are responsible for human progress and prosperity. Wright describes the looters as secondhanders who exploit the creators in both physical and spiritual concerns. They attack reason through government directives that supersede the rational judgment of the creators. They assault purpose by reducing the selection of attainable goals down to those dealing with crises. In addition, they attack the self-esteem of the producers by advocating the morality of altruism, which holds that the pursuit of happiness is a source of guilt. The looters employ need, weakness, and incompetence as a demand on the creators. They claim that it is permissible and desirable to receive altruistic "gifts" when a person is weak, suffering, or incompetent.

Onkar Ghate (2004, 335–55) explains that the unreason of the looters is exemplified by James Taggart. The looters as secondhanders exploit the creators both materially and spiritually. Taggart is anti-effort and has the need to feel superior. For him, abstract ideas are meaningful only as a tool to bring or keep people down. For example, ideas like "public interest" and "social responsibility" are used to destroy the Phoenix-Durango Railroad, Taggart's main competitor in Colorado. Feeling a deep sense of inferiority, Taggart desires the unearned when it comes to physical or spiritual concerns. He does not have any positive ambitions or purposes. He is aimless, wants political influence, and sees only the opportunity to destroy. He ultimately seeks to destroy value because it is value. Although he wants to get unearned money, he does not view money as a value. Operating from the death premise, his unacknowledged goal is to destroy the values required by life. Taggart rationalizes, evades, and disregards his responsibility to think. As a whim-worshipper, he wants consciousness to control existence. He thinks that all he has to do is to "want" something. He wants to become rich without earning any wealth and wants to be loved and admired without earning the right to be loved and admired. Taggart desires a world in which reason and purpose are not required to survive and flourish in it. Rebelling against life and existence, he conceals his nihilism even from himself. He simulates concern with values that promote life. He is under the illusion that obtaining wealth and "success" without effort or rational thought will give him moral status and self-esteem. Ultimately, the self-deceived Taggart's desire to steal becomes a yearning to destroy values even though such destruction will result in the loss of his own life.

Minsaas (1995) has drawn attention to Rand's considerable use of analogy in her characterizations. The purpose of this device of presenting characters as parallels and contrasts is to allow the reader to perceive a character's distinctive nature through comparison with other characters. Her characters are presented contextually as she employs other characters as contrasts that draw out and emphasize each character's uniqueness. Minsaas explains that such analogical juxtapositions permeate Rand's novels. An awareness of this network of parallels and contrasts enhances the reader's understanding of the characters.

According to Minsaas, Rand's use of parallels and contrasts stems from her epistemology. Rand applies her theory of concept formation in portraying her characters, observing similarities and differences between them in order to comprehend their underlying motivations and conceptual and moral nature.

Rand's use of contrasts allows her to illustrate what it means for a human being to be a fully integrated person. At least three of her fictional heroes reflect mind-body integration through their total integrity and consistent loyalty to rational principles. These three are John Galt, Francisco d'Anconia, and Dagny Taggart. Dagny is the primary narrator of *Atlas Shrugged* (i.e., more is told from Dagny's point of view than from any other). Dagny is arguably the most developed character of these three and can be contrasted with two other characters who accept two different versions of the mind-body dichotomy—Hank Rearden and Robert Stadler.

Dagny, like Hank Rearden, is a self-initiator who goes by her own judgments and is the motive power of her own happiness. Unlike Rearden, she does not feel guilty for her achievements. She realizes that the world lives because of the work of the prime movers and then hates them for it. She also understands that sex is the supreme admiration of one human being for another and that the values of one's mind are connected to the actions of one's body.

Hank Rearden is a great productive industrialist and master of reality whose erroneous surface ideas do not corrupt his essential deeper character. Rearden's words and deeds initially sanction an unearned guilt. The doctrine of altruism held him guilty because of his greatest virtues. Similarly, in the beginning he also viewed his passion for Dagny as animalistic and degrading. Down deep he does not believe the notion of the mind-body split. Under the tutelage of Francisco and Dagny, Rearden awakens to the truth. By the end of the story, he understands the evil of the idea of the mind-body dichotomy both in economics and business and in romantic and other human relationships.

Robert Stadler is a Plato-like character who holds a theoretical versus applied science split. He is a cynical theorist and intellectual elitist who believes that most people are corrupt, stupid, and incapable of virtuous behavior. Stadler is contemptuous of applied science and material production. Thinking that his work must be sustained through government force, he resorts to extorting from citizens to finance his theoretical noncommercial projects. Stadler is doomed once he turns his mind over to force-wielders.[5]

THE PHILOSOPHICAL SPEECHES

The lengthy philosophical speeches in *Atlas Shrugged* are integrated components of the plot, make explicit the principles dramatized throughout the actions of the novel, and move the story onward. For example, Francisco's "money speech" attends to Rearden's moral turmoil, frees him from his feelings of guilt, aids him in his trial, and moves him toward joining the strike.

Salmieri observes that Francisco's money speech is an abstract summation of many points previously dramatized in the first part of the novel. Specifically, Francisco explains that reason is the root of production, that production is the root of money, that money is destroyed when detached from these roots, and that there is a moral difference between trade and force. This speech provides Rearden with new knowledge that will be important for his liberation from guilt (e.g., at his trial) as well as with gaining gratitude from

Francisco. He also learns to enjoy the wealth that he has earned from his production especially when he buys luxury items for Dagny—Rearden gains pleasure through such purchases.

Many readers skip or skim Galt's speech, at least on their first reading of *Atlas Shrugged*. They see it as a digression, as an interruption of the action, as a means to promulgate Rand's ideas, or as repetitive and redundant with respect to what has already been presented before in the story. Bennett Cerf, the head of Random House, begged Rand to cut Galt's speech because she had already made the same points numerous times earlier in the novel.

Although it may be true that people who skip Galt's speech do not totally miss Rand's message or lose the plot, reading the speech and comprehending its purpose certainly elicits a fuller understanding and appreciation of *Atlas Shrugged*. Ghate (2009, 363–74) maintains that Galt's speech is critical to the story and to its climax and that it is logically and inextricably connected to both the novel's theme and plot-theme. The theme is "the role of the mind in man's existence" and the plot-theme is "the men of the mind going on strike against an altruist-collectivist society." Ghate concludes,

> What an analysis of Galt's speech reveals—an analysis of its purpose, its content, its structure, its role in the story, and its contribution to the novel's theme—is that far from being "propaganda," a digression in the story's plot or even simply a pause in the action, the speech is integral to the novel. Without Galt's Speech, John Galt would not be John Galt—and *Atlas Shrugged* would not be *Atlas Shrugged*. (373)

Galt's speech on the radio ties together all the ideas previously dramatized in action in the novel, leads to Galt's capture and the story's climax, hastens the collapse, and makes the rebuilding of society easier. Galt's speech is necessary in order to understand the climax of the novel. When the looters hear his speech, they realize that he is the best thinker in the world and thus search for him in order to enlist his help in saving the deteriorating economy. It is the speech that moves Galt from mythical to concrete status in the novel. The events and actions prior to the speech provide the inductive evidence needed to derive the principle that "the mind is man's tool of survival." By then the reader and the American people in the novel have seen the men of the mind in the world, their gradual disappearance, the effects of the looters' policies, and the resulting crumbling of the world. It is a matter of justice for Galt to tell the people what he has done. It is through this speech that Galt demonstrates the value of the men of the mind. Galt's long speech is warranted because the detailed and complex events previously presented concretize the message given in his speech. The knowledge contained in Galt's speech is what convinced the strikers earlier in the novel to abandon their firms and to retreat to Galt's Gulch. The philosophy of the morality of life embodied in the speech is what the producers needed to hear and accept in order for them to realize their own greatness and to stand up against the looters. Galt's speech was not given until the American people were ready to hear it (Bernstein 1995; Ghate 2001, 2009, 363–74). In large part, his Objectivist statement is addressed to the common but rational listeners, many of whom are part victims and part supporters of the looter's creed, in an effort to gain their support by going on strike themselves. In his audio course, Ghate explains that after a brief introduction, Galt's speech is broken into three parts: (1) the Morality of Life (i.e., the Code of the Producers), (2) the Morality of Death (i.e., the Code of the Looters), and (3) the importance of choosing the morality of life (i.e., acting as a rational human being).

A national broadcast by Mr. Thompson, the head of the state, is interrupted by Galt, who, in a three-hour speech, spells out the tenets of his philosophy (Rand 1957, 923–79). Among his many provocative ideas is the notion that the doctrine of original sin, which holds man's nature as his sin, is absurd—a sin that is outside the possibility of choice is outside the realm of morality. The fall of Adam and Eve was actually a positive event since it enabled man to acquire a mind capable of judging good and evil—man became a rational moral being. Another provocative idea is that both forced and voluntary altruism are evil. Placing the welfare of others above an individual's own interests is wrong. The desire to give charity, compassion, and pleasure unconditionally to the undeserving is immoral.

Galt explains that reality is objective, absolute, and comprehensible and that man is a rational being who relies upon his mind as his only means to obtain objectively valid knowledge and as his "basic tool of survival." The concept of value presupposes an entity capable of acting to attain a goal in the face of an alternative. The one basic alternative in the world is existence versus nonexistence. "It is only the concept of 'Life' that makes the concept of 'Value' possible." An organism's life is its standard of value. Whatever furthers its life is good, and that which threatens it is evil. It is therefore the nature of a living entity that determines what is good or bad for it, and for those living things that can choose, it is the ultimate basis for how life is to be lived (and thus what ought or ought not to be done).

Galt identifies man's life as the proper standard of man's values and morality as the principles defining the actions necessary to maintain life as a man. Because life as a man is one's purpose, he has "a right to live as a rational being." To live, man must think, act, and create the values his life requires. In other words, since a man's life is sustained through thought and action, it follows that the individual must have the right to think and act and to keep the product of his thinking and acting (i.e., the right to life, liberty, and property).

He asserts that since men are creatures who think and act according to principles, a doctrine of rights that is enforced ensures that an individual's choice to live by those principles is not violated by other human beings. All individuals possess the same rights to freely pursue their own goals. These rights are innate and can be logically derived from man's nature and needs—government is not involved in the creation of rights and merely exists to protect an individual's natural rights. Because force is the means by which one's rights are violated, it follows that freedom is a basic good. Therefore, it follows that the role of government is to "protect man's rights," through the use of force, but "only in retaliation and only against those who initiate its use" (Ghate 2001, 2009, 363–74; Gladstein 2000, 98–106; Stolyarov 2007, 99–106; Gotthelf 2009, 375–95).

MIND-BODY INTEGRATION

Atlas Shrugged illustrates the inextricable linkage of the mind and the body. In it, Rand argues that the rational, purposeful, and creative character of the human person is reflected in the act of material production. The mind, humans' highest and noblest aspect, enables them to deal with physical reality in order to create wealth and abundance that sustain and promote their practical survival and flourishing on earth. Productivity involves the use of reason to adapt nature to humans' life requirements (Rand 1997, 549–51).

Likewise, *Atlas Shrugged* teaches, especially in the romance between Dagny and Rearden, that love is rooted in reason and that sexual choice is the result of a person's basic convictions and values. Sex is a "celebration of life," the ultimate form of admiration and respect of one person for another, and the physical expression of a person's spirit. Just as productive activity is the conversion of values into physical form, "sex is the means and form of translating spiritual admiration for a human being into physical action" (606–7). In an important way, the romance between Dagny and Hank ties the entire story together and shows that production and sex have a mutual essence that joins them (465). The same principles used in one's creative (i.e., productive) life are applied to one's personal life.

Atlas Shrugged demonstrates that man is an indivisible entity that can be separated only for purposes of discussion. There are inextricable linkages and correspondences among one's mind, body, and actions. It follows that the values of one's mind are not disconnected from the actions of one's body. Cartesian dualism of mind and matter is incompatible with true human existence. Man is an indivisible union of consciousness and matter (551).

Galt's speech embodies the principles of integration at the core of Objectivism. During the period in which she was working on this sixty-page speech, Rand commented,

> You had set every part of you to betray every other, you believed that your career bears no relation to your sex life, that your politics bear no relation to the choice of your friends, that your values bear no relation to your pleasures, and your heart bears no relation to your brain—you had chopped yourself into pieces which you struggled never to connect—but you see no reason why your life is in ruins and why you've lost the desire to live?. (Rand 1997, 661–62)

Rand's integrated worldview totally rejects the mind-body dichotomy and all of the additional mistaken dichotomies that are based on it. According to Sciabarra (2007, 26),

> By connecting reason and production, thought and action, theory and practice, fact and value, morality and prudence, Rand intended to uncover the "deeper, philosophical error" upon which these various dichotomies were based. As such, *Atlas Shrugged* was designed to "blast the separation of man into 'body' and 'soul,' the opposition of 'matter' and 'spirit'" (Rand 1997, 551). Rand rejected the metaphysical dualists who had bifurcated human existence. She proclaimed in her journal that "Man is an indivisible entity." Mind and body "can be considered separately only for purposes of discussion, not in actual fact," she explains. Thus, in the projection of her "ideal man," John Galt, there is "no intellectual contradiction and, therefore, no inner conflict" between mind and body. (June 29, 1946 in Rand 1997, 512)

It was this kind of "indivisible union" (663) that Rand glorified in her exalted conception of human sexuality as a response to values. She explained in her journals that she had wanted to concretize the "essential, unbreakable tie between sex and spirit—which is the tie between body and soul" (October 6, 1949 in Rand 1997, 609).

Sciabarra (2007) explains,

> In Rand's view, the "spiritual" does not pertain to an other-worldly faculty. The "spiritual" refers to an activity of human consciousness. Reason, as "the highest kind of spiritual activity," is required "to conquer, control, and create in the material realm" (Rand 1997, 551). Rand does not limit material activities to purely industrial production. She wishes to "show that any original rational idea, in any sphere of man's activity, is an act of creation" (550). This applies equally to the activity of industrialists and artists, businessmen and intellectuals, scientists and philosophers. Each of these spheres is accorded epistemological significance—and supreme respect. (26)

Atlas Shrugged masterfully illustrates that the production of goods, services, and wealth metaphysically precedes their distribution and exchange. The primacy of production means that we must produce before we can consume. Production (i.e., supply) is the source of demand. This means that products are ultimately paid for with other products. It follows that the passionate producer is the prime mover and visible hand in markets (Salsman 1997). Production, like existence, is primary and rests on the laws of identity and causality. Recognizing the integration of mind and body, Rand illustrated in *Atlas Shrugged* that the rational, purposeful, and creative character of human creation is manifested in the act of material production.

From the beginning, Rand intended *Atlas Shrugged* to be a "much more social novel than The Fountainhead" (Rand 1997, 398). She wanted to write a novel that would mainly be a portrait of the whole focusing on the relationships that make up society (392). Viewing each social problem from a transdisciplinary and multidimensional perspective, Rand dismissed all suggested one-sided solutions as inadequate and fragmentary.

A FULLY INTEGRATED PHILOSOPHICAL NOVEL

Atlas Shrugged concretizes through hierarchical, progressive, and inductive demonstration Rand's systematic philosophy of Objectivism. In her novel, Rand dramatizes grand themes and presents an entire and integrated view of how people should live their lives. She does this by providing an abstract and holistic moral perspective on the concretes presented in the novel. Rand is able to both concretize abstractions and draw abstractions from a number of concretes. She is able to project in action what each abstraction means. Rand's great power comes from her ability to unify everything in the text to form an integrated whole. The major theme of *Atlas Shrugged*, the role of reason in man's life, is embodied in every event, character, and line of dialogue. As a great novel of romantic realism, *Atlas Shrugged* magnificently demonstrates that men can objectively and rationally know the good and can freely choose the good. The theme and plot are inextricably integrated. Rand is a superb practitioner of synthesis and unity whose literary style and subject are organically linked and fused to the content of her philosophy. She unifies the many aspects of *Atlas Shrugged* according to principles of reality. Rand made many revisions and changes in this novel to make certain that everything fit together.[6] Believing that a novel should be an end in itself, she created *Atlas Shrugged* as a remarkably integrated organic whole. *Atlas Shrugged* is a brilliantly integrated and unified philosophical novel.

ACKNOWLEDGMENTS

Several people have contributed importantly to this chapter by reading and commenting on earlier versions of it. I am grateful to the following individuals for their useful observations and suggestions: Roger Bissell, Walter Block, Douglas J. Den Uyl, Mimi Gladstein, Steven Horwitz, Spencer MacCallum, Russell Madden, Allen Mendenhall, Douglas B. Rasmussen, Jeff Riggenbach, Peter Saint-Andre, Chris Matthew Sciabarra, Larry Sechrest, and Gennady Stolyarov.

NOTES

This chapter was first published in *The Journal of Ayn Rand Studies* 14, no. 2 (December 2014): 124–47. This article is used by permission of The Pennsylvania State University Press.

1. Greg Salmieri's 2009 essay, in Mayhew (2009), is based on his 2007 lecture.

2. For an excellent discussion of the role of the virtues in human flourishing, see Smith (2006).

3. Much of the material found in Darryl Wright's (2007) audio course can also be found in his chapter in Mayhew (2009).

4. For invaluable discussions of businessmen as heroes and prime movers, see Locke (2000), Rand (2000b), Locke (2009), and Debi Ghate (2009).

5. Andrew Bernstein (1995, 1996, 2001) provides in-depth and detailed perceptive analyses of Dagny Taggart, Hank Rearden, Robert Stadler, and many more of *Atlas Shrugged*'s dramatic characters in his audio courses. Readers interested in gaining a greater understanding of Rand's characters and process of characterization are encouraged to listen to Bernstein's more thorough and systematic explanations along the same lines as the brief character descriptions provided above.

6. Milgram (1998) illustrates and describes in her original archival research that Rand was a disciplined artist who made many additions, subtractions, and other changes.

REFERENCES

Bernstein, Andrew. 1995. *Philosophic and Literary Integration in Ayn Rand's "Atlas Shrugged."* Seven Audio Lectures. New Milford, CT: Second Renaissance Books.

———. 1996. *Ayn Rand's Fictional Characters as Philosophical Archetypes. Part 1.* Four Audio Lectures. New Milford, CT: Second Renaissance Books.

———. 2001. *Ayn Rand's Fictional Characters as Philosophical Archetypes. Part 2.* Four Audio Lectures. New Milford, CT: Second Renaissance Books.

———. 2007. "Transfiguring the Novel: The Literary Revolution in *Atlas Shrugged*." *The Objective Standard* 2, no. 3 (Fall): 47–66.

Bidinotto, Robert James. 2007. *"Atlas Shrugged* as Literature." *New Individualist* (October): 50–55.

Brown, Susan Love. 2007. "Beyond the 'Stillborn Aspiration': Virtuous Sexuality in *Atlas Shrugged.*" In *Ayn Rand's "Atlas Shrugged": A Philosophical and Literary Companion*, edited by Edward W. Younkins, 279–91. Aldershot, England: Ashgate.

Cox, Stephen. 1986. "Ayn Rand: Theory Versus Creative Life." *Journal of Libertarian Studies* 8, no. 1 (Winter): 19–29.

Ghate, Debi. 2009. "The Businessman's Crucial Role: Material Men of the Mind." In *Essays on Ayn Rand's "We the Living*," edited by Robert Mayhew, 299–316. Lanham, MD: Lexington Books.

Ghate, Onkar. 2001. *A Study of Galt's Speech*. Five Audio Lectures. New Milford, CT: Second Renaissance Books.

———. 2004. "The Death Premise in We the Living and *Atlas Shrugged.*" In *Essays on Ayn Rand's '"We the Living,"* edited by Robert Mayhew, 335–56. Lanham, MD: Lexington Books.

———. 2009. "The Role of Galt's Speech in *Atlas Shrugged.*" In *Essays on Ayn Rand's "We the Living*," edited by Robert Mayhew, 363–74. Lanham, MD: Lexington Books.

Gladstein, Mimi Reisel. 2000. *"Atlas Shrugged": Manifesto of the Mind*. New York: Twayne.

Gotthelf, Allan. 2009. "Galt's Speech in Five Sentences (and Forty Questions)." In *Essays on Ayn Rand's "We the Living*," edited by Robert Mayhew, 375–95. Lanham, MD: Lexington Books.

Hunt, Lester. 2007. "Some Structural Aspects of *Atlas Shrugged.*" In *Ayn Rand's "Atlas Shrugged": A Philosophical and Literary Companion*, edited by Edward W. Younkins, 57–62. Aldershot, England: Ashgate.

Jackson, Candice E. 2005. "Our Unethical Constitution." *The Journal of Ayn Rand Studies* 6, no. 2 (Spring): 405–44.

Locke, Edwin A. 2000. *The Prime Movers*. New York: AMACOM.

———. 2009. "The Traits of Business Heroes." In *Essays on Ayn Rand's "We the Living*," edited by Robert Mayhew, 317–34. Lanham, MD: Lexington Books.

Long, Roderick T. 2007. "Forced to Rule: *Atlas Shrugged* as a Response to Plato's Republic." In *Ayn Rand's "Atlas Shrugged": A Philosophical and Literary Companion*, edited by Edward W. Younkins, 89–97. Aldershot, England: Ashgate.

Machan, Tibor R. 2007. *"Atlas Shrugged's* Moral Principle of the Sanction of the Victim." In *Ayn Rand's "Atlas Shrugged": A Philosophical and Literary Companion*, edited by Edward W. Younkins, 75–88. Aldershot, England: Ashgate.

Madden, Russell. 2007. "Fuel for the Soul." In *Ayn Rand's "Atlas Shrugged": A Philosophical and Literary Companion*, edited by Edward W. Younkins, 167–75. Aldershot, England: Ashgate.

Mayhew, Robert, ed. 2004. *Essays on Ayn Rand's "We the Living."* Lanham, MD: Lexington Books.

———, ed. 2009. *Essays on Ayn Rand's "Atlas Shrugged."* Lanham, MD: Lexington Books.

Merrill, Ronald E. 1991. *The Ideas of Ayn Rand.* Chicago: Open Court.

Milgram, Shoshana. 1998. *Ayn Rand's Drafts: The Labors of a Literary Genius.* Two Audio Lectures. New Milford, CT: Second Renaissance Books.

Minsaas, Kirsti. 1994. *Structure and Meaning in Ayn Rand's Novels.* Audio Lecture. Principal Source Audio.

———. 1995. *Concept Formation and the Fiction of Ayn Rand.* Lecture. Institute for Objectivist Studies. Summer Seminar.

———. 2007. "Ayn Rand's Recasting of Ancient Myths in *Atlas Shrugged.*" In *Ayn Rand's "Atlas Shrugged": A Philosophical and Literary Companion*, edited by Edward W. Younkins, 141–50. Aldershot, England: Ashgate.

Peikoff, Leonard. 1976. *The Philosophy of Objectivism.* 12 Audio Lectures.

———. 1997. *Unity in Epistemology and Ethics.* Eight Audio Lectures. New Milford, CT: Second Renaissance Books.

———. 2004. *The DIM Hypothesis: The Epistemological Mechanism by Which Philosophy Shapes Society.* Fifteen Audio Lectures. New Milford, CT: Second Renaissance Books.

Plauché, Geoffrey Allan. 2007. "On *Atlas Shrugged* and the Importance of Dramatizing Our Values." *Journal of Libertarian Studies* 21, no. 4 (Winter): 25–36.

Rand, Ayn. 1957. *Atlas Shrugged.* New York: Random House.

———. 1961. *For the New Intellectual.* New York: New American Library.

———. 1964. *The Virtue of Selfishness.* New York: New American Library.

———. [1971] 1975. *The Romantic Manifesto: A Philosophy of Literature.* 2nd revised edition. New York: Signet.

———. 1997. *Journals of Ayn Rand.* Edited by David Harriman. New York: Dutton.

———. 2000a. *The Art of Fiction.* Edited by Tore Boeckmann. New York: Plume.

———. 2000b. *Why Businessmen Need Philosophy.* Edited by Richard E. Ralston. Irvine, CA: Ayn Rand Institute Press.

Rasmussen, Douglas B. 2007. "The Aristotelian Significance of the Section Titles of *Atlas Shrugged.*" In *Ayn Rand's "Atlas Shrugged": A Philosophical and Literary Companion*, edited by Edward W. Younkins, 33–45. Aldershot, England: Ashgate.

Saint-Andre, Peter. 2006. "Image and Integration in Ayn Rand's Descriptive Style." *The Journal of Ayn Rand Studies* 7, no. 2 (Spring): 407–19.

Salmieri, Gregory. 2007. *Atlas Shrugged as a Work of Philosophy.* Four Audio Lectures. New Milford, CT: Second Renaissance Books.

———. 2009. "Discovering Atlantis: *Atlas Shrugged's* Demonstration of a New Moral Philosophy." In *Essays on Ayn Rand's "We the Living,"* edited by Robert Mayhew, 397–452. Lanham, MD: Lexington Books.

Salsman, Richard. 1997. *The Invisible Hand Comes to Life: Economics in 'Atlas Shrugged.'* Two Audio Lectures. New Milford, CT: Second Renaissance Books.

Sciabarra, Chris Matthew. 2007. "*Atlas Shrugged*: Manifesto for a New Radicalism." In *Ayn Rand's "Atlas Shrugged": A Philosophical and Literary Companion*, edited by Edward W. Younkins, 23–32. Aldershot, England: Ashgate.

Seddon, Fred. 2007. "Various Levels of Meaning in the Chapter Titles of *Atlas Shrugged.*" In *Ayn Rand's "Atlas Shrugged": A Philosophical and Literary Companion*, edited by Edward W. Younkins, 47–56. Aldershot, England: Ashgate.

Smith, Tara. 2006. *Ayn Rand's Normative Ethics: The Virtuous Egoist.* Cambridge: Cambridge University Press.

Stolyarov, Gennady, II. 2007. "The Role and Essence of John Galt's Speech in Ayn Rand's *Atlas Shrugged.*" In *Ayn Rand's "Atlas Shrugged": A Philosophical and Literary Companion*, edited by Edward W. Younkins, 99–106. Aldershot, England: Ashgate.

Wright, Darryl. 2007. *Ayn Rand's Ethics from The Fountainhead to Atlas Shrugged.* Two Audio Lectures. New Milford, CT: Second Renaissance Books.

———. 2009. "Ethics: From *The Fountainhead* to *Atlas Shrugged.*" In *Essays on Ayn Rand's "We the Living*," edited by Robert Mayhew, 253–73. Lanham, MD: Lexington Books.

Younkins, Edward W., ed. 2007. *Ayn Rand's "Atlas Shrugged": A Philosophical and Literary Companion.* Aldershot, England: Ashgate.

Chapter 3

Economics in *Atlas Shrugged*

Atlas Shrugged is an integrated masterpiece of philosophy, politics, and economics. It is an economically literate novel that provides economic enlightenment.[1] Based on an analysis of reality, it is well-informed on economics and can be viewed, in part, as a treatise on political economy providing a literary treatment of proper economic laws, principles, concepts, issues, and themes. This great novel portrays a growing crisis of interventionism and systematic government failure and presents a thorough defense of a totally unregulated market system. In her literary passages, Ayn Rand is able to teach the lessons of market-oriented economics in a far more memorable and engaging manner than can be found in most books and articles on economics. The goal of this chapter is to provide a summary of the types of economic issues found in *Atlas Shrugged.*

THE MIND IS THE SOURCE OF WEALTH

To begin with, *Atlas Shrugged* masterfully depicts the role of individual initiative and creativity in economic progress. Rand argues in her fictional world, especially through Galt's strike, that the mind is the fundamental source of wealth and profits. It is the thinkers who are the true creators of wealth and who are crucially responsible for prosperity. It is capitalists, industrialists, and entrepreneurs such as Hank Rearden, Dagny Taggart, Ken Danagger, Ellis Wyatt, and Midas Mulligan, who reshape the world by being prime movers in the marketplace. These top individuals on the pyramid of ability contribute much more to prosperity than those at lower levels in the hierarchy. It is the competent thinkers and doers who create wealth and promote human economic prosperity through innovation and the creation of new enterprises. It is these self-actuating rational valuers who propel Rand's fictional world and sustain it. Much of *Atlas Shrugged* is a study of the great producers who have the ability to see, to make connections, and to create what has not been seen before. *Atlas Shrugged* makes a convincing case that (1) the mind is at the root of the creation and maintenance of wealth; (2) the passionate producer is the prime mover and the visible hand in markets; and (3) the rational, purposeful, and creative character of the human person is reflected in the act of material production. As John Galt puts it in his speech:

> Physical labor as such can extend no further than the range of the moment. The man who does no more than physical labor consumes the material value-equivalent of his own contribution to the process of production, and leaves no further value, neither for himself nor others. But the man who produces an idea in any field of rational endeavor—the man who discovers new knowledge—is the permanent benefactor of humanity. Material products can't be shared, they belong to some ultimate consumer; it is only the value of an idea that can be shared with unlimited numbers of men, making all sharers richer at no one's sacrifice or loss, raising the productive capacity of whatever labor they perform. . . . In proportion to the mental energy he spent, the man who creates a new invention receives but a small percentage of his value in terms of material payment, no matter what fortune he makes, no matter what millions he earns. But the man who works as a janitor in the factory producing that invention, receives an enormous payment in proportion to the mental effort that his job requires of him. And the same is true of all men between, on all levels of ambition and ability. The man at the top of the intellectual pyramid contributes the most to all those below him, but gets nothing except his material payment, receiving no intellectual bonus from others to add to the value of his time. The man at the bottom who, left to himself, would starve in his hopeless ineptitude, contributes nothing to those above him, but receives the bonus of all of their brains. (Rand 1957, 1064–65)

Rand's view is that man has no innate ideas but does have the ability to reason. Man begins uninformed and becomes ever more knowledgeable about the world. Man has no innate knowledge and, therefore, must determine through thought the deeds, actions, and values upon which his life depends. Having free will, man is free to think or not to think. Rationality does not imply omniscience. A person's primary enterprise is to learn the causal connections among objects, actions, and the satisfaction of his needs in order to make rational decisions regarding his well-being. Economic life is constructed around the acquisition of knowledge. In *Atlas Shrugged*, Rand portrays a rational, economic man as a being who gradually gains the knowledge and resources necessary to attain his ends.

Rand depicts the entrepreneur as an economizing man who initiates and directs an uncertain causal process. The entrepreneur's activities include the set of functions essential for mobilizing the production process. His most important mission is to visualize and predict future wants and needs, gauge their relative importance, and attain knowledge of potential available means. The successful entrepreneur correctly anticipates consumer preferences and effectively uses reason to meet these preferences. His goal is to know the consumers' wants and needs before the consumers know them. An entrepreneurial insight is checked against reality through its incremental development as knowledge and experience are amassed. New ideas are refined, changed, refocused, improved, and expanded through incremental experimentation and the constant search for improvement. A wealth creator tends to be a person of superior ability who pursues his goals relentlessly in the face of obstacles, opposition, setbacks, and failures. He must persist in the face of adversity, confront the unknown, face challenges, risk and learn from failure, have confidence in his capacity to deal with the world, and take practical, rational steps in the pursuit of his goals.

In *Atlas Shrugged*, Hank Rearden is the prime example of a visionary, competent, independent, action-oriented, passionate, confident, and virtuous entrepreneur. By focusing on reality, he has the vision to see the potential future value of a new metal that will take him ten years to develop. The tenacious and purposeful Rearden is committed to taking the actions necessary to invent this new metal.

Rearden learned a great deal by holding a variety of jobs in a number of companies in steel-related industries ever since he was fourteen years old. Through his intellect and tireless efforts, he ultimately owned and managed ore, coal, limestone, and steel companies. On the evening that he finally pours the first heat of Rearden material, he reflects upon the obstacles, opposition, setbacks, failures, frustrations, and fatigue that he experienced in order to get to this day. He also remembers the moment that he realized all of his purposeful actions were motivated from within.

He saw an evening when he sat slumped across his desk in that office. It was late and his staff had left: so he could lie there alone, unwitnessed. He was tired. It was as if he had run a race against his own body, and all the exhaustion of years, which he had refused to acknowledge, had caught him at once and flattened him against the desktop. He felt nothing, except the desire not to move. He did not have the strength to feel—not even to suffer. He had burned everything there was to burn within him; he had scattered so many sparks to start so many things—and he wondered whether someone could give him now the spark he needed, now when he felt unable ever to rise again. He asked himself who had started him and kept him going. Then he raised his head. Slowly, with the greatest effort of his life, he made his body rise until he was able to sit upright with only one hand pressed to the desk and trembling arm to support him. He never asked that question again. (30–31)

ECONOMIC JUSTICE

In *Atlas Shrugged*, Rand illustrates that justice, a form of adherence to the facts of reality, is the virtue of granting to each man that which he objectively deserves. Justice is shown to be the expression of a man's rationality in his dealings with other men, involving seeking and granting the earned. A trader, a man of justice, earns what he receives and does not give or take the undeserved. Just as he does not work except in exchange for something of economic value, he also does not give his love, friendship, or esteem except in trade for the pleasure he receives from the virtues of individuals he respects. The trader principle is a moral principle that involves the exchange of value for value through voluntary consent.

Rearden defends voluntary exchange, the trader principle, and economic justice when on trial for failing to comply with a government directive (i.e., the Fair Share Law) ordering him to sell an "equal amount" of Rearden Metal to everyone who wants it. He addresses the court as follows:

> I work for nothing but my own profit—which I make by selling a product they need to men who are willing and able to buy it. I do not produce it for their benefit at the expense of mine, and they do not buy it for my benefit at the expense of theirs; I do not sacrifice my interests to them nor do they sacrifice theirs to me; we deal as equals by mutual consent to mutual advantage—and I am proud of every penny that I have earned in this manner. I am rich and I am proud of every penny I own. I made my money by my own effort, in free exchange and through the voluntary consent of every man I dealt with—the voluntary consent of those who employed me when I started, the voluntary consent of those who work for me now, the voluntary consent of those who buy my product. (444)

Another character who promotes economic justice is Ragnar Danneskjöld, a philosopher turned pirate who raids only public, government cargo ships in order to return to the productive individuals what is rightly theirs. Robbing these ships prevents the government from redistributing wealth to failing foreign socialist countries. Danneskjöld converts the wealth that he has confiscated into gold and places it into accounts that he has set up for moral, productive, and competent businessmen in proportion to the income taxes that have been extracted from them.

In *Atlas Shrugged*, Rand illustrates how a tax is a compulsory payment by individuals to the government. Taxes are always coercive. Taxes can be used by the government to control citizens and to promote "social justice" through the redistribution of wealth. When taxes are used to redistribute wealth and to support social programs, they not only divert resources from other useful purposes, but also become a power contest between organized interest groups that pressure Congress to pass laws that are conducive to their perceived self-interest and that allow some people to "gain" at the expense of others.

Toward the end of the novel, the chief looter-politician, Mr. Thompson, offers John Galt the position of economic dictator of the nation. He tells Galt that he and the other government officials will obey any order he gives and Galt tells them to begin by abolishing all income taxes. This implies that Rand views income taxes as anti-productive, destructive, unjust, and immoral. This perspective invites a consideration of how the legitimate functions of the state (i.e., defense and protection of life, liberty, and property) would be funded. Where would the money come from to finance the armed forces, police, and law courts?

Is it possible to fund the functions of government without taxation? Even in a minimal state, police, the military, judges, and others have to be paid. One possible solution has been offered by Rand (1964) and elaborated upon by Tibor R. Machan (1982). They explain that a person could pay a user fee when he chooses to use a government service. For example, contract protection is a private good that the government supplies and national military defense is a public good that is provided by the government. Machan explains that the government could protect contracts and provide for national defense with voluntary payments for the contract services being used. He expands the case by observing that the government has overhead costs, including those needed to provide for the defense of the system of laws itself. This fees-for-services-plus-overhead plan is one possible way to finance the government in a free society.

The business heroes in *Atlas Shrugged* are just in their dealings with actual and potential employees, suppliers, customers, business partners, and competitors. They discriminate among all those they deal with based on competitive performance and character. They identify employees for what they accomplish and treat them accordingly. For example, at the end of chapter 1, Dagny wants to promote Owen Kellogg, a promising young engineer. Later, she hires a talented young scientist, Quentin Daniels, to work on reconstructing the motor that she found on the premises of the abandoned factory at the Twentieth Century Motor Company in Wisconsin. For contrast, consider the attempt by Hank's mother to get Hank to hire his worthless brother Philip. When Rearden refuses, his mother tells him that he only thinks of justice, is immoral, and that he never thinks of people and his moral duties. Rearden replies, "I don't know what it is you choose to call morality. No, I don't think of people—except that if I give a job to Philip, I wouldn't be able to face any competent man who needed work and deserved it" (Rand 1957, 209). Later, Hank is seen telling Tony the Wet Nurse, once one of the looters and now a man who shares Rearden's values, that he would hire him gladly and at once but the Unification Board won't allow it.

With respect to customers, we see Rearden choosing to deal with men who share his values such as Ken Danagger, a Pennsylvania coal producer, and Mr. Ward of the Ward Harvester Company, who needs Rearden Metal to keep his doors open. Hank justly takes Mr. Ward's order despite the fact that he is under a deadline to provide the metal needed for the construction of the Rio Norte Line. Our business heroes do not want to deal with "liberal" businessmen who, afraid of honest competition, sell out their initiative, creative powers, and independence for the security of government regulation. We see Dagny becoming enraged at the unjust elimination of her best competitor, Dan Conway's superb Phoenix-Durango Railroad, by a private body, through the National Alliance of Railroads' "Anti-dog-eat-dog Rule," which Dagny's incompetent brother James uses his political connections to get adopted by the alliance. Certainly, Dagny would like to put Conway out of business, but not this way. She wants to do it by outcompeting him by providing the best railroad service in the area. Dagny goes to see Conway and attempts to get him to fight this unjust rule, but to no avail.

Francisco d'Anconia's justice-oriented actions involve retribution against those who they think can rely on his business judgments. When the looters hear about Francisco's San Sebastián Mines, they invest in them. The San Sebastián Mines are revealed to be worthless and a fraud. Francisco intentionally wanted to ruin investors such as James Taggart, Orren Boyle, and others who attempted to ride on his coattails. They failed to think and to investigate the facts about the mines. As a result, they justly got what they deserved. The San Sebastián Mines and Line are nationalized and then the mines turn out to be worthless.

WEALTH IS THE SOURCE OF MONEY

According to Horwitz (2007, 226–36), in his "Money Speech," Francisco explains that *money is made* possible only by men who produce. Money is a tool of exchange that presumes productive men and the results of their activities. Wealth is thus the source of money. Money is the effect, rather than the cause, of wealth. The money that a person holds symbolizes production that has already occurred and that has been judged as valuable by other people. When an individual takes money as his reward for his work, he does so in order to exchange it for products and services made possible by other individuals.

> Money is a tool of exchange, which can't exist unless there are goods produced and men able to produce them. Money is the material shape of the principle that men who wish to deal with one another must deal by trade and give value for value. Money is not the tool of the moochers, who claim your product by tears, or of the looters, who take it from you by force. Money is made possible only by the men who produce. . . . When you accept money in payment for your effort, you do so only on the conviction that you will exchange it for the product of the effort of others. (Rand 1957, 410)

Money must be earned through the production of goods and/or services, and production requires the use of reason. This fact is recognized by the heroes of *Atlas Shrugged*. The villains, however, think that money is meaningful no matter how it is obtained. Ignoring the need to produce, the looters try to get money through the use of altruism and coercion. They attempt to evade the fact that life demands production.

Atlas Shrugged in general and Francisco's speech in particular emphasize that it is production that initiates demand for other products and services—production is the source of demand. *Atlas Shrugged* thus portrays and explains Say's Law of Markets, which states that supply constitutes demand. Production is primary and is a precondition to consumption. An individual can demand products and services from others only if he has previously successfully marketed his own products and/or services. People who consume need to produce in order to obtain money from someone who has produced that can be exchanged for other products and services (Salsman 1997, 2011).

In *Atlas Shrugged*, Rand skillfully dramatizes and concretizes the idea that productiveness is a virtue. Readers are shown characters who tend to be productive and successful when they are rational and self-interested. Rand explains that production requires individuals who are rational and self-interested. She illustrates that it is necessary for each person to voluntarily choose to think, plan, and produce if he wants to survive and flourish. The lesson is that it is only to the degree that people are rational and self-interested that they can produce. As Francisco puts it in his money speech,

> Those pieces of paper, which should have been gold, are a token of honor—your claim upon the energy of the men who produce. . . . Money is made—before it can be looted or mooched—made by the effort of every honest man, each to the extent of his ability. An honest man is one who knows that he can't consume more than he has produced. (Rand 1957, 410–11)

Francisco explains that money is, or should be, an objective standard of value tied to reality in order to act as an integrator of economic values. An objective standard tied to reality requires an objective commodity such as a quantity of gold. Gold is the means of preserving wealth and value. Money prices based on such an objective standard accurately express people's judgments regarding the value of goods and services. Francisco makes clear that this role of money is eroded by inflation. Inflation extinguishes the signaling function of money prices. He says that the debasement of money, through the substitution of paper for gold, is the road to the downfall of society.

> Money is the barometer of a society's virtue. . . . Whenever destroyers appear among men, they start by destroying money, for money is men's protection and the base of a moral existence. Destroyers seize gold and leave to its owners a counterfeit pile of paper. This kills all objective standards and delivers men into the arbitrary power of an arbitrary setter of values. Gold was an objective value, an equivalent of wealth produced. Paper is a mortgage on wealth that does not exist, backed by a gun aimed at those who are expected to produce it. Paper is a check drawn by legal looters upon an account which is not theirs: upon the virtue of the victims. Watch for the day when it bounces, marked, "Account overdrawn." (413)

PLANNING, REGULATION, AND REDISTRIBUTION IN A MIXED ECONOMY

Rejecting central social planning, Rand illustrates in *Atlas Shrugged* that there is no way for bureaucrats to make intelligent decisions to deliberately plan or design an economy because it is impossible for them to gain or possess sufficient knowledge. Centrally directed economies are bound to fail because they rely upon the limited knowledge of those who give the orders.

Rand agrees somewhat with such Austrian economists as F. A. Hayek, who argued that the proper role of the state is to create general rules that facilitate mutually beneficial interactions rather than to prescribe specific outcomes. For Rand, there is only one proper role of government and that is to protect individual rights through the use of force, but only in retaliation and only against those who initiate its use. Hayek is concerned with the hubris of reason that distinguishes what he calls "constructivist rationalism."[2]

Atlas Shrugged illustrates that the type and amount of knowledge needed to direct a whole economy are far different from what is required to run a business. Part Two of *Atlas Shrugged* portrays in great detail the inefficiencies and economic destruction that stem from centralized economic decision-making. In *Atlas Shrugged*, government officials try to regulate the economy through the Bureau of Economic Planning and Natural Resources, whose name is remindful of the real National Resources Planning Board that was part of the New Deal.

The intentional and rational planning on the part of industrialists like Dagny Taggart and Hank Rearden is in stark contrast to the efforts at comprehensive central planning of the economy by government bureaucrats. According to proponents of social engineering, there exist an elite who far exceed the general population in intellect, morality, and dedication to the "common good." They believe that their general superiority enables them to use their articulated rationality to function as decision-makers in governmental economic planning. Of course, the knowledge needed by these social architects is unattainable. For example, without market-based prices, decision-making by central planners would be irrational and arbitrary. *Atlas Shrugged* illustrates how economic interventionist policies tend to fail to obtain their objectives, generate unintended and undesirable results, and lead to further government controls. Unintended negative consequences result when social engineers try to direct an economy from the top down. In such an economy, interest groups lobby for special privileges that result in the redistribution of wealth rather than in the creation of wealth. Today's bailout plans and economic stimulus schemes are right out of *Atlas Shrugged*. The more incompetent that businesses are, the more handouts they will be given by politicians in Washington. For example, *Atlas Shrugged*'s Railroad Unification Plan and Steel Unification Plan are eerily similar to the contemporary notion of "too big to fail," which has been applied to distressed U.S. auto companies, banks, insurance companies, investment houses, and so on.

Atlas Shrugged demonstrates what occurs when government controls the distribution of resources. In a corporate state, crony capitalists (or political capitalists) turn to the government for special privileges in order to obtain protection from open competition. Crony capitalists curry favor with politicians to "defeat" competitors without having to perform better jobs. They gain their results outside the market process by receiving special privileges such as subsidies, grants of monopoly, tax breaks, legal permits, government grants, bailouts, price supports, subsidized loans, trade protections, resource privileges, and so on.

Sciabarra (2007) explains that in *Atlas Shrugged*, Rand examines a collapsing social order and its dysfunctional relations on three distinct analytical levels: Level 1: the Personal, Level 2: the Cultural, and Level 3: the Structural. According to Sciabarra,

A focus on the "structural" (what I've called "Level 3") provides Rand with an opportunity to portray, in frightening detail, the process by which a statist economy implodes. As the economic system careens from one disaster to another, as the "men of the mind" withdraw their sanction from a government that regulates, prohibits, and stifles trade, statist politicians attempt to exert more and more control over the machinery of production. To no avail. In the end, Directives are issued, like Number 10-289, which attach workers to their jobs, order businesses to remain open regardless of their level of "profit," nationalize all patents and copyrights, outlaw invention, and standardize the quantity of production and the quantity of consumer purchasers, thereby freezing wages and prices—and human creativity.

The "pyramid of ability" is supplanted by the "aristocracy of pull." What F. A. Hayek once called the "road to serfdom" is complete. A predatory neofascist social system, which had survived parasitically, must ultimately be destroyed by its own inner contradictions, incapacitating or driving underground the rational and productive Atlases who carry the world upon their shoulders. (Sciabarra 2007, 30)

Caplan (2007, 215–24) explains further that in *Atlas Shrugged* the reader is able to see how regulations in a mixed economy are actually made. Rather than to advance the so-called public interest, in reality regulations generally further the private financial interests of political insiders at the expense of others. Political interest groups lobby for contradictory measures, and the government grants favors to those who have the most votes, political pull, or influence at any given moment. A good example in *Atlas Shrugged* is the "deal" through which the Anti-dog-eat-dog Rule and the Equalization of Opportunity Bill result. Rent seekers such as James Taggart and Orren Boyle exploit innovators and prime movers by obtaining favorable governmental legislation and regulations rather than by being innovative and efficient.

The Anti-dog-eat-dog Rule ostensibly imposes a ban on "destructive competition" by granting seniority to the oldest railroad operating in a given region of the country. Although the stated reasons for the rule are to recognize historical priority and to avoid a transportation shortage, its real purpose is to put Dan Conway's superb Phoenix-Durango Railroad, Taggart Transcontinental's competitor for the Colorado freight traffic, out of business. The result is the sacrifice of one of the most productive members of the National Alliance of Railroads (Conway) to further Taggart's less productive company. There is more than a slight resemblance to the "production codes" under the National Industrial Recovery Act.

As Rand puts it,

The Anti-dog-eat-dog Rule was described as a measure of "voluntary self-regu-lation" intended "the better to enforce" the laws long since passed by the coun-try's Legislature. The Rule provided that the members of the National Alliance of Railroads were forbidden to engage in practices defined as "destructive competition"; that in regions declared to be restricted, no more than one rail-road would be permitted to operate; that in such regions, seniority belonged to the oldest railroad now operating there, and that the newcomers, who had encroached unfairly upon its territory, would suspend operations within nine months after being so ordered; that the Executive Board of the National Alliance of Railroads was empowered to decide, at its sole discretion, which regions were to be restricted. (Rand 1957, 75)

James Taggart uses his political friendship with steel producer Orren Boyle to influence the National Alliance of Railroads to pass the Anti-dog-eat-dog Rule. In turn, Boyle employs Taggart to use his influence in Washington in order to strip Hank Rearden of his ore mines, delivering them in turn to Paul Larkin, who would provide Boyle with the first chance to obtain the ore.

Boyle agrees to provide the votes needed in the National Alliance of Railroads, and in exchange Taggart uses his Washington connections to pass the Equalization of Opportunity Bill, which forbids any one person or corporation from owning more than one type of business concern. This, of course, prevents Rearden from owning the mines that supply him with the resources that he needs. In order to preserve the steel industry "as a whole" (i.e., to save Boyle's company), Rearden is stripped of his ore mines, which are then placed in the hands of someone else (i.e., Paul Larkin) who will give Boyle first priority for the ore. Although the stated rationale for the Equalization of Opportunity Bill is that it is unfair to permit one individual to own several business enterprises, the hidden agenda is to allow Boyle's unproductive Associated Steel to compete with the more efficient Rearden Steel. The result is the sacrifice of Rearden's productive firm for Boyle's unproductive company.

> A newspaper . . . editorial . . . was entitled "Equalization of Opportunity." . . .
> The editorial said that at a time of dwindling production, shrinking markets, and vanishing opportunities to make a living, it was unfair to let one man hoard several business enterprises, while others had none; it was destructive to let a few corner all the resources, leaving others no chance; competition was essential to society, and it was society's duty to see that no competitor ever rose beyond the range of anybody who wanted to compete with him. The editorial predicted the passage of a bill which had been proposed, a bill forbidding any person or competitor to own more than one business concern. (130)

Throughout *Atlas Shrugged*, both the government and "liberal" or statist politicians say that people must sacrifice for the public welfare. *Atlas Shrugged* illustrates the tragic consequences of following the principle of need rather than the principle of productivity, of adhering to the communist slogan "From each according to his ability, to each according to his need." For example, the SSI does not want Rearden to put his new metal on the market because of the "social damage" it will cause to steel producers (like Orren Boyle) who can't compete with him. When Rearden says that he does not worry about other firms, the SSI attempts to bribe and eventually to threaten Rearden to keep his new metal off the market. Rearden understands that true corporate social responsibility is to make profits for the owners while respecting the natural rights of individuals.

Then there is the story of the destruction of the Twentieth Century Motor Company in the wake of the Starnes heirs' small-scale socialist experiment.[3] Illustrating the consequences of Communism in practice, the employees as a group vote to decide the needs of each worker as well as the expected production of each laborer based on an assessment of his ability. The story of this company shows that when earnings are not based on production, incentives diminish, productivity plummets, and bankruptcy results. It thus serves as a precursor for the ultimate fate of an entire country that is heading toward collectivism (Boettke 2005, 451–60, 2007, 179–87; Bostaph 2007, 207–14).

The Twentieth Century Motor Company has constructed its own "society" based on a combination of Marxian and Rawlsian principles of justice that assign priority to the poorest, weakest, and most needy (i.e., "from each according to his ability, to each according to his need"). This system, based on some vague standard of fairness and on the nonrecognition of individual rights, is an inevitable failure.

In addition, there are the Colorado Directives that are intended (at least officially) to help with the national emergency by forcing Colorado to share the suffering. These new mandates included (1) a maximum speed and number of cars for all trains on the John Galt Line; (2) a prohibition on the number of trains to be run in Colorado exceeding the number of trains run in each of the neighboring states; (3) limits on the production of Rearden Metal so it will be no greater than the production of the steel mills of the same capacity; (4) a Fair Share Law that gives every desiring customer an equal amount of Rearden Metal; (5) a prohibition on business firms in the East moving to other states; (6) a five-year moratorium on the payment of railroad bonds; and (7) a 5 percent tax on gross sales made in Colorado in order to fund the administrative costs of the directives. These directives were due to the efforts of economic interest groups who wanted the industrially successful state of Colorado to force its profitable firms to redistribute their earnings. Of course, these laws prompted Ellis Wyatt to quit, put other firms out of business, and wiped out the Rio Norte Line. Ultimately, these destructive directives hastened the retirement and disappearance of many Colorado industrialists who had created enormously productive enterprises and who had been forced to carry less competent businessmen along with them. Ellis Wyatt and other

Colorado industrialists refuse to work under imposed conditions that would result in the destruction of any firms that attempted to abide by them.

We also encounter the Railroad Unification Plan and the Steel Unification Plan. The Railroad Unification Plan was James Taggart's desperate scheme to keep Taggart Transcontinental from going out of business by feeding off its competition. The plan provides that the total profits of all railroad companies be allocated according to the number of miles of track each owns and maintains instead of according to the amount of service that each supplies. Then there is the Steel Unification Plan, which would bankrupt Rearden. The Steel Unification Plan is patterned after the Railroad Unification Plan. All of the steel companies' earnings are to be rewarded according to the number of furnaces each owns. Because Boyle has a great many idle furnaces, he would be paid for almost double his actual output. In turn, Rearden would be paid for less than half of his actual output. Both the Railroad Unification Plan and the Steel Unification Plan require companies to produce "according to each one's ability" with the profits to be allocated "according to each firm's need."

Directive 10-289 provides the knockout punch to economic freedom in *Atlas Shrugged* (Boettke 2005, 2007; Caplan 2007; Bostaph 2007). Its purported purpose is to stop the country's economic decline by freezing the economy in its present state. The directive employs comprehensive central government planning to freeze everything at the status quo. It actually allows top government officials and politically connected businessmen to retain power and enhance their own control of the economy. This directive mandates that all workers remain at their current jobs, that no business close, and that all patents and copyrights be "voluntarily" turned over to the government. It also forbids the introduction of new products and innovations and requires firms to annually produce a quantity of goods identical to the quantity produced during the preceding year. In addition, the directive freezes all wages, prices, and profits, and requires every person to spend the same amount of money as he did in the preceding year. It prevents businesses from adjusting expenses and making other strategic and tactical decisions. Of course, given that appeals for exceptions can be made to the Unification Board, such government control inevitably leads to the buying and selling of economic favors.

GALT'S GULCH: MODEL OF A FREE SOCIETY

Galt's Gulch (also known as Mulligan's Valley and Atlantis) sharply contrasts with Directive 10-289 and with the mode of operation of the Twentieth Century Motor Company. Atlantis is a microcosm or model of a free society enshrouded by the collapsing interventionist one. This laissez-faire capitalist society is located in the heart of the United States. This paradigm of a free society consists of a voluntary association of men held together by nothing except every man's self-interest. Here productive men who have gone on strike are free to produce and trade as long as they observe the valley's customs. In this secret free society, each individual is unencumbered in the pursuit of his own flourishing and happiness. In Galt's Gulch, justice is based on the recognition of individual rights and individual achievement.[4]

Bostaph (2007, 2011) has commented on the ambiguity of Ayn Rand's theory of price. In a conversation that takes place in Galt's Gulch between Ellis Wyatt and Dagny Taggart, Wyatt states that he reduces the price he charges for oil as he improves his process of extracting oil from shale and decreases the effort he expends in extracting it (Rand 1957, 722). Bostaph observes that in this scene Rand may have been assuming a real-cost theory of pricing. He goes on to say that one could also assume that the amount of production would correspondingly increase, thereby making a marginal unit less valuable to the producer.

Bostaph (2011, 39) also notes that bits and pieces of economic ideas can be found scattered throughout Galt's speech. For example, Rand identifies the idea that spending creates wealth as a reversal of the law of casualty (Rand 1957, 1038); the view of a factory as a natural resource as the willful denial of human agency (1043); the view of the production of goods as an anonymous and automatic process not connected to that of distribution as a denial of both causality and property rights; the view that industrial progress is instinctual as obscenely stupid (1044); and the assertion that those who create wealth through the use of their minds are the exploiters of those who do not, and that the former should be enslaved for the benefit of the latter, as a vestige of the morality of barbarism (1049).

CONCLUSION

As we have seen, *Atlas Shrugged* contains a great deal of economic content. In it, Rand provides a literary description of economic institutions and conditions within a particular context. She is able to explain the proper principles and workings of a free-market system. Rand skillfully illustrates the cause-and-effect relationships of events in a society's economy. As a lesson in economics,[5] *Atlas Shrugged* illustrates the necessity to analyze the immediate and long-term, direct and indirect, and intended and unintended consequences of a governmental action or policy. Rand explains that the mind is the source of well-being and that the mind must be free to invent and produce new products and services. *Atlas Shrugged* illustrates that government intervention discourages innovation and risk-taking and obstructs the process of wealth creation. It also demonstrates that wealth is not causeless and that by removing the cause (i.e., the mind) the strike removes the effect (i.e., wealth). Capitalism is thus shown to be the only moral economic system because it protects a man's mind, his primary means of survival and flourishing.

ACKNOWLEDGMENTS

This chapter is an expanded version of a talk delivered on October 6, 2007, in Washington, D.C., as part of a celebration of *Atlas Shrugged*'s fiftieth anniversary sponsored by the Atlas Society. I would like to acknowledge the helpful comments, observations, and suggestions of Walter Block, Samuel Bostaph, David Brat, Bryan Caplan, Steven Horwitz, Richard C. B. Johnsson, Brian Simpson, and Russell Sobel.

NOTES

This chapter was previously published in *The Journal of Ayn Rand Studies* 13, no. 2 (December 2017): 12–39. This article is used by permission of The Pennsylvania State University Press.

1. Another economically literate novel is Henry Hazlitt's *Time Will Run Back* ([1966] 2007), originally published as *The Great Idea* in 1951.

2. On the parallels between Hayek's and Rand's critique of rationalism (particularly of the "constructivist" sort), see Sciabarra ([1995] 2013, 208–14).

3. A thorough discussion of the details and consequences of the Starnes Plan at the Twentieth Century Motor Company is provided in *Atlas Shrugged* when Dagny encounters Jeff Allen, a former employee of the company when the plan was introduced (Rand 1957, 660–72).

4. For detailed analyses of the operation of Galt's Gulch, see Sechrest (2007) and Bostaph (2007, 2011).

5. Several recent articles have discussed how *Atlas Shrugged* can successfully be integrated into a college economics course. See Boettke (2005), Kent and Hamilton (2011), and Chamlee-Wright (2011).

REFERENCES

Boettke, Peter J. 2005. "Teaching Economics Through Ayn Rand: How the Economy Is Like a Novel and How the Novel Can Teach Us About Economics." *The Journal of Ayn Rand Studies* 6, no. 2 (Spring): 445–65.

———. 2007. "The Economics of *Atlas Shrugged*." In *Ayn Rand's "Atlas Shrugged": A Philosophical and Literary Companion*, edited by Edward W. Younkins, 179–87. Aldershot, England: Ashgate.

Bostaph, Sam. 2007. "Ayn Rand's Atlantis as a Free Market Economy." In *Ayn Rand's "Atlas Shrugged": A Philosophical and Literary Companion*, edited by Edward W. Younkins, 207–14. Aldershot, England: Ashgate.

———. 2011. "Ayn Rand's Economic Thought." *The Journal of Ayn Rand Studies* 11, no. 1 (July): 19–44.

Caplan, Bryan. 2007. "*Atlas Shrugged* and Public Choice: The Obvious Parallels." In *Ayn Rand's "Atlas Shrugged": A Philosophical and Literary Companion*, edited by Edward W. Younkins, 215–24. Aldershot, England: Ashgate.

Chamlee-Wright, Emily. 2011. "Cultivating the Economic Imagination with *Atlas Shrugged*." *Journal of Economics and Financial Education* 10, no. 2 (Fall): 41–53.

Hazlitt, Henry. [1966] 2007. *Time Will Run Back*. Auburn, Alabama: Ludwig von Mises Institute.

Horwitz, Steven. 2007. "Francisco d'Anconia on Money: A Socio-Economic Analysis." In *Ayn Rand's "Atlas Shrugged": A Philosophical and Literary Companion*, edited by Edward W. Younkins, 225–36. Aldershot, England: Ashgate.

Kent, Calvin A., and Paul Hamilton. 2011. "Inclusion of *Atlas Shrugged* in Economics Classes." *The Journal of Private Enterprise* 26, no. 2: 143–59.

Machan, Tibor R. 1982. "Dissolving the Problem of Public Goods: Financing Government Without Coercive Means." In *The Libertarian Reader*, edited by Tibor R. Machan, 201–9. Lanham, Maryland: Rowman & Littlefield.

Rand, Ayn. 1957. *Atlas Shrugged*. New York: New American Library.

———. 1964. "Government Financing in a Free Society." In *The Virtue of Selfishness: A New Concept of Egoism*, edited by Ayn Rand with additional articles by Nathaniel Branden, 135–41. New York: New American Library.

Salsman, Richard. 1997. *The Invisible Hand Comes to Life: Economics in "Atlas Shrugged."* Two Audio Lectures. New Milford, Connecticut: Second Renaissance Books.

———. 2011. "Economics in *Atlas Shrugged*." *The Objective Standard* 6, no. 1 (Spring): 49–88.

Sciabarra, Chris Matthew. [1995] 2013. *Ayn Rand: The Russian Radical*. 2nd edition. University Park: Pennsylvania State University Press.

———. 2007. "*Atlas Shrugged*: Manifesto for a New Radicalism." In *Ayn Rand's "Atlas Shrugged": A Philosophical and Literary Companion*, edited by Edward W. Younkins, 23–32. Aldershot, England: Ashgate.

Sechrest, Larry J. 2007. "Atlas, Ayn, and Anarchy: A is A is A." In *Ayn Rand's "Atlas Shrugged": A Philosophical and Literary Companion*, edited by Edward W. Younkins, 189–96. Aldershot, England: Ashgate.

Younkins, Edward W., ed. 2007. *Ayn Rand's "Atlas Shrugged": A Philosophical and Literary Companion*. Aldershot, England: Ashgate.

Chapter 4

Business in *Atlas Shrugged*

Atlas Shrugged is very much a novel about business and the individuals located in the world of business. Businesspeople have always been among *Atlas Shrugged*'s most ardent admirers. They are thrilled to find a novel that understands, respects, and recognizes the value of what they do. In *Atlas Shrugged*, Rand clearly celebrated businesses from the industrial era (such as railroads, steel mills, and coal mines) that were dominant in America during her lifetime. In addition to championing industrial processes and producers in the novel, she also embraces the potential of future new technologies such as Galt's motor, which would supply "the cleanest, swiftest, cheapest means of motion ever devised" (Rand 1957, 289).

Instead of heavy industries, today's leading-edge companies and emerging technologies include software and information technology, biotechnology, logistics, social networks, telecommunications, photonics, nanotechnology, and so on. Despite this, the fundamental principles and virtues for business success in today's industries are the same as the ones illustrated in *Atlas Shrugged*. Readers can learn these from Rand's business heroes and learn what not to do from her business villains. In *Atlas Shrugged*, Rand provides crucial insights into business and especially the connections between business and the virtues.

The purpose of this chapter is to provide a description of Rand's treatment of business and businesspeople in *Atlas Shrugged*. The first section of this chapter discusses how this novel illustrates that wealth and profit are products of the human mind and that they are created by adding value to the world through the production of desirable and needed products and services. The following section compares, at a general level, the worldviews, motivations, strategies, and tactics of the business heroes and villains in *Atlas Shrugged*. The next part takes a detailed look at the novel's main producer-protagonists

Dagny Taggart and Hank Rearden. This is followed by a section that provides snapshot portraits of other *Atlas Shrugged* characters embedded in the business world. The last part of this chapter is devoted to a discussion of how *Atlas Shrugged* is being used in college and university business courses.

WEALTH CREATION, PROFIT, AND THE MOTIVE POWER OF THE HUMAN MIND

Wealth, in the form of goods and services, is created when individuals recombine and rearrange the potential resources that comprise the world. Something does not become a resource until its possible uses are discovered and developed. Wealth increases when someone conceives of and produces a more valuable configuration of the earth's substances. Although abeyant resources or raw materials are finite, the human mind, through ingenuity and creativity, is able to continually increase the wealth of the world (Simon 1996). Profits are a person's reward for wealth creation. The core of business is wealth creation through the offering of desirable goods and services.

Entrepreneurs create wealth by offering what is perceived to be a more valuable combination of resources than the combination that existed previously. Profits are an entrepreneur's reward for increasing the wealth of individuals in society. The entrepreneur does not profit at the expense of others. Rather, he gains because the product of his actions is judged to be worth more than what existed before his undertaking. *Atlas Shrugged* portrays wealth creators as able, rational, and visionary individuals who pursue their goals persistently in the face of obstacles and adversities.

In the Valley, Ellis Wyatt says to Dagny:

> What's wealth but the means of expanding one's life? There's two ways one can do it: either by producing more or by producing it faster. And that's what I'm doing: I'm manufacturing time. . . . I'm producing everything I need. I'm working to improve my methods, and every hour I save is an hour added to my life. . . . That's the savings account I'm hoarding. . . . Wealth, Dagny? What greater wealth is there than to own your own life and to spend it on growing? (Rand 1957, 721–22)

To be successful, entrepreneurs must objectively perceive reality and rationally process and evaluate information. They must detect information gaps between consumer wants and needs and the potential of a new but as yet undeveloped product or service to meet those wants and needs. They must anticipate new markets and consumers' future wants and needs, learn from competitors' successes and failures, accumulate capital for their projects, acquire the needed resources, coordinate numerous activities and employee skills, and take risks by trading present and known values for resources that only promise a potential future value. Profit is payment for the entrepreneur's thought, vision, initiative, determination, efficiency, risk-taking, and effectiveness.

Atlas Shrugged illustrates that the profit-and-loss system in a voluntaristic society is just and moral. A person's wealth under capitalism depends upon his productive achievements and the choice of others to recognize them. When pursuing profits, one must appeal to the interests of others. Profits indicate that a businessperson has pleased his fellow consumers by using resources to produce a product or render a service at costs below the value that people place upon the product or service. The firm making profits is using resources in a manner that satisfies what people want and need. Losses indicate that a businessperson has failed to deal with his fellow consumers efficiently.

This exchange takes place at a press conference when Hank Rearden is asked about his profit motive for building the John Galt Line with Rearden Metal. Rearden states:

> Inasmuch as the formula of Rearden Metal is my own personal secret, and in view of the fact that the Metal costs much less to produce than you boys can imagine, I expect to skin the public to the tune of twenty-five per cent in the next few years.

> "What do you mean, skin the public, Mr. Rearden?" asked the boy. "If it's true, as I've read in your ads, that your Metal will last three times longer than any other and at half the price, wouldn't the public be getting a bargain?"

> "Oh, have you noticed that?" said Rearden. (235)

In *Discovery, Capitalism, and Distributive Justice* (1989), Israel Kirzner explains that before a profit opportunity is discovered, it cannot be said to have existed in any economically intelligible and meaningful sense. The discoverer, who creates an opportunity and brings something into existence, is justly entitled to it. The discovery of the possibility that a certain act would be worthwhile actually created the opportunity's existence. It follows that the discovering entrepreneur is entitled to the profit he has created. The following exchange between James Taggart and Cherryl Brooks reflects this insight. Jim says:

> Rearden. He didn't invent smelting and chemistry and air compression. He couldn't have invented his Metal but for thousands and thousands of other people. *His* Metal!

Why does he think that it's his? Why does he think that it's his invention? Everybody uses the work of everybody else. Nobody ever invents anything. (Rand 1957, 262)

The puzzled Cherryl responds: "But the iron ore and all those other things were there all the time. Why didn't anybody else make that Metal, but Mr. Rearden did?" (262).

When Eugene Lawson, past president of the Community National Board of Madison, boasts that he has never made a profit in his entire life, Dagny solemnly responds: "Mr. Lawson, I think that I should let you know that of all the statements a man can make, *that* is the one I consider most despicable" (313).

Hank Rearden tells the judges at his trial:

I work for nothing but my own profit—which I make by selling a product they need to men who are willing and able to buy it. I do not produce it for their benefit at the expense of mine, and they do not buy it for my benefit at the expense of theirs; I do not sacrifice my interests to them nor do they sacrifice theirs to me; we deal as equals by mutual consent to mutual advantage—and I am proud of every penny that I have earned in this manner. (480)

Rand illustrates in *Atlas Shrugged* that the mind is the root cause of wealth and profit. It is the skilled thinkers and doers who create and maintain wealth and promote prosperity. Even inherited wealth requires entrepreneurship for it to be retained. In *Atlas Shrugged*, the passionate and productive prime movers include Hank Rearden, Dagny Taggart, Ken Danagger, Ellis Wyatt, Midas Mulligan, Dan Conway, Andrew Stockton, among others.

For example, Hank Rearden has the vision to foresee the possible future value, uses, and benefits of a new metal alloy that will take him ten years to invent and bring to market. He wants to make real his dream of developing a revolutionary metal that is stronger and lighter than steel. He is well-prepared and motivated to take on this pursuit. Beginning as a teenager, Rearden held various jobs in steel-related businesses. Eventually, he owned and operated ore, coal, limestone, and steel businesses. Not only does Rearden Metal enable Hank to earn his desired profits, its use in railroad tracks enables the John Galt Line to earn more profits by running faster and hauling more freight at lower costs to Colorado's industrial shippers who themselves, as a result, also earn greater amounts of income. These industrialists are able to expand their operations, purchase more resources, hire more employees, build more products that benefit their customers, and make greater profits—the rewards for wealth creation.

Bradley (2011) has commented that energy is at the center of business life in *Atlas Shrugged*. To begin with, there are John Galt's revolutionary motor, Ellis Wyatt's oil fields, Ken Danagger's coal mines, Taggart Transcontinental and the Phoenix-Durango railroads, Hammond and Nielson's automobile factories, Roger Marsh's electrical appliance company, Andrew Stockton's foundry, Dwight Sanders's airplane factory, and so on. In addition, the book portrays an energy planning agency (i.e., the Bureau of Economic Planning and Natural Resources), government intervention with energy, oil shortages, gasoline shortages, electricity blackouts, energy rationing, conservation edicts, an Industrial Efficiency Award, public utility regulation, common carrier regulation, and so on.

In discussing the importance of locomotives, Eddie Willers says to John Galt who is disguised as a railroad worker: "Motive power—you can't imagine how important that is. That's the heart of everything. . . . What are you smiling at?" (Rand 1957, 63). The next paragraph, which begins a new chapter reads:

> Motive power—thought Dagny, looking up at the Taggart Building in the twilight—was its first need; motive power, to keep that building standing, to keep it immovable. It did not rest on piles driven into granite; it rested on the engines that rolled across a continent. (64)

Entering the motor room of the locomotive during the initial run of the John Galt Line, Dagny contemplates what the engines depend upon:

> They *are* alive she thought, because they are the physical shape of the action of a living power—of the mind that had been able to grasp the whole of this complexity, to set its purpose, to give it form. For an instant, it seemed to her that the motors were transparent and she was seeing the net of their nervous system. It was a net of connections, more intricate, more crucial than all of their wires and circuits: the rational connections made by that human mind which had fashioned any one part of them for the first time.

> They are alive, she thought, their soul operates them by remote control. Their soul is in every man who has the capacity to equal this achievement. Should the soul vanish from the earth, the motors would stop because *that* is the power which kept them going—the power of a living mind—the power of thought and choice and purpose. (246)

Through her characters, Rand illustrates that human reason, insight, choice, creativity, and motivated action are the keys to productivity and wealth creation. Human beings have the intelligence to discern new possibilities, to discover the earth's productive potential, and to realize their creative insights through their persistent efforts.

PRODUCERS VERSUS LOOTERS:
A CONFLICT OF VISIONS

Not only is *Atlas Shrugged* a novel about philosophy, politics, and economics, it is also very much a novel about business and businesspeople. Not
only does much of its action take place in commercial settings, many of its
protagonists and antagonists are situated in business establishments.[1] While
many of the novel's heroes run businesses, a number of its villains also do
so. Of course, Rand distinctly differentiates between businesspersons and
those who merely are referred to as such because they are associated with
a business. Not every person who is referred to as a businessperson is an
authentic businessperson. Many of the inauthentic businesspeople do not
understand that reality is an absolute and that rationality is needed to deal
with reality.[2]

At a general level, we have the producers and the looters. *Atlas Shrugged*
follows the effects of the battle of the thinkers and producers versus the pred-
ators and parasites across the entire economy and over a long period of time.
The clash is between those who do business by voluntary trade and profit
through their initiative and productive ability and those who operate through
force and fraud and "profit" by means of political power.

Atlas Shrugged illustrates that business *qua* business serves those who
wish to trade and does not make use of coercion. When a failed or falter-
ing business is rescued by a government handout, it is no longer a genuine
business. Likewise, when businesspersons obtain results outside the market
framework by receiving special privileges granted by the government, they
forfeit their status as legitimate businesspersons. These special privileges
include bailouts, price supports, subsidized loans, trade protection, resource
privileges, grants of monopoly, and so on.

The thinkers and doers are rationally purposeful, are dedicated to their
work, achieve their goals through their initiative, thought, and action, con-
centrate on continual improvement, innovation, and on earning their profits,
understand that earned wealth is the effect of an entrepreneur's moral status,
and despise mediocrity and collectivism. *Atlas Shrugged* makes clear that,
because life requires the production of values, legitimate entrepreneurial
actions are morally proper. Rand's heroes flourish and find happiness in producing what others value.[3]

In contrast, the looters attack reason, are reactive to outside forces, advocate the morality of altruism, profit by dealing with dishonest politicians,
avoid rationality and productivity by utilizing pressure groups and political
pull to exploit the wealth created by the prime movers, and wrongly believe
that they will gain moral status and self-esteem through such expropriation. The looter businessmen fear genuine competition and surrender their

independence, resourcefulness, and creativity for the protection of government regulation. These crony capitalists gain their results outside the marketplace by running to the government for special privileges that protect them
from open competition. They tend to be supporters of government planning,
spending, regulation, and redistribution.

Both the producers and the looters want to obtain money but there is a
critical difference between their methods for doing so. The prime movers
make money by creating products and offering services that their customers
need and want to make their lives better. The looters' goal is to gain money,
the result of production, via government force and/or altruism. They believe
that money is meaningful no matter how it is obtained. The noncreators are
content with money acquired through corruption, dishonesty, backhanded
deals, and altruism.

An example of crony capitalism or crony statism in *Atlas Shrugged* is the
arrangement between James Taggart and Orren Boyle through which the
"Anti-dog-eat-dog Rule" and the "Equalization of Opportunity Bill" come
about. Taggart employs Boyle to use his connections to get the National
Alliance of Railroads to adopt the Anti-dog-eat-dog Rule to destroy Taggart's
chief competitor in Colorado, Dan Conway's outstanding Phoenix-Durango
Railroad. In return, Boyle gets Taggart to use his political connections in
Washington to divest Hank Rearden of his ore mines through the passage of
the Equalization of Opportunity Bill. Rearden is forced to give up his iron
and coal businesses in order to provide business opportunities for his struggling competitors. Ideas such as "social responsibility" and "public interest"
are used to sell the propriety of both of these decrees to the public. Many
businesspeople in the real world operate in the same manner as rent-seekers,
James Taggart and Orren Boyle, running to their political connections rather
than by being productive, efficient, and innovative.

Dagny is angry and disgusted at the unethical and undeserved liquidation
of Dan Conway's Phoenix-Durango Railroad through a vote of the members
of the National Alliance of Railroads. Unlike her brother, she would never
consider making money through the unjust destruction of a competitor. She
runs to Conway and urges him to fight them, but he declines. The only way
that she would like to put the Phoenix-Durango Railroad out of business is
through honest competition by providing the best railroad service in Colorado.

While in Galt's Gulch, composer Richard Halley tells Dagny that legitimate entrepreneurs are examples of a human being's highest creative spirit:

> Whether it's a symphony or a coal mine, all work is an act of creating and
> comes from the same source: from an inviolate capacity to see through one's
> own eyes—which means: the capacity to see, to connect and to make what had
> not been seen, connected, and made before. That shinny vision which they talk

about as belonging to the authors of symphonies and novels—what do they think is the driving faculty of men who discover how to use oil, how to run a mine, how to build an electric motor? That sacred fire which is said to burn within musicians and poets—what do they suppose moves an industrialist to defy the whole world for the sake of his new metal, as the inventors of the airplane, the builders of the railroads, the discoverers of new germs or new continents have done through all the ages? (782–83)

In his speech, John Galt discusses the nature of authentic businesspeople:

I have called out on strike the kind of martyrs who had never deserted you before. I have given them the weapon they had lacked, the knowledge of their own moral value. I have taught them that the world is ours, whenever we choose to claim it, by virtue and grace of the fact that ours is the Morality of Life. They, the great victims who had produced are the wonder of humanity's brief summer, they, the industrialists, the conquerors of matter, had not discovered the nature of their right. They had known that theirs was the power. I taught them that theirs was the glory. (1051)

In his "Money Speech," Francisco states:

To the glory of mankind there was, for the first and only time in history, a *county of money*— and I have no higher, more reverent tribute to pay to America, for this means: a country of reason, justice, freedom, production, achievement. For the first time, man's mind and money were set free, and there were no fortunes-by-conquest, but only fortunes by work, and instead of swordsmen and slaves, there appeared the real maker of wealth, the greatest worker, the highest type of human being—this self-made man—the American industrialist. (414)

Atlas Shrugged offers profound insights regarding the virtues that lead to morality and success in business. A case can be made that virtues should serve as a foundation for achieving a firm's goals, values, and purposes. Virtues, as rational moral principles, need to be integrated with a company's vision, culture, and climate. Rand's novel demonstrates the presence or the absence of these principles in the lives of the various characters. They include rationality, honesty, justice, independence, integrity, productiveness, and pride.[4]

Morality in business entails objectively recognizing individual rights by treating customers, employees, creditors, shareholders, and others as autonomous rational individuals with their specific goals and desires. Justice is the virtue of granting to each individual that which he objectively deserves. A virtuous businessperson must make certain that customers get what they pay for and need to hire the most talented employees and reward them for what they achieve. In addition, specific contractual agreements with creditors and others must be respected. Also, managers are the employees of the stockholders and have a contractual, fiduciary, and moral responsibility to fulfill their wishes. They have the obligation to use the shareholders' money for specifically authorized projects that are in the shareholders' interest. In *Atlas Shrugged*, the business protagonists are just in their business relations with their actual and potential employees, suppliers, business partners, customers, competitors, and other parties. They discriminate based only on performance, ability, and character.

The notion advanced by the looters in *Atlas Shrugged* that the producers should have a social conscience and an obligation to produce for society is similar to today's expectation that businesses have a social responsibility. At his trial, Hank Rearden goes out of his way not to apologize for his income and his wealth. He recognizes that a firm's social responsibility is to respect the natural rights of individuals while earning profits for the owners of a business. There is no special morality for businesses. The pursuit and earning of profit does not require moral absolution through social responsibility. There is no justified reason for an honest entrepreneur to be ashamed of his profession, to feel guilty about his earnings, or to think that he needs to "give back" in order to earn respect.

Atlas Shrugged demonstrates that production metaphysically precedes consumption and that productiveness is a virtue. We must produce before we can consume. It is production that originates demand for other products and services. Rationality and self-interest are prerequisites of production. A legitimate entrepreneur's actions are morally proper because life requires the production of values. The self-actualizing rational producer in *Atlas Shrugged* is the visible hand in markets. It is businesspeople, entrepreneurs, and industrialists who are prime movers in the economy. In *Atlas Shrugged*, Hank Rearden is the exemplar of a virtuous and productive businessman.

THE PRIMARY PRODUCER-PROTAGONISTS: DAGNY TAGGART AND HANK REARDEN

Achiever and creator, Dagny Taggart, the intellectual equal of Ayn Rand's male heroes, is perhaps the strongest female protagonist in Western literature. Free of inner conflict, she is passionately creative and comfortable with respect to her fundamental relationship to existence. She is a model of synthesis, unity, and mind-body integration. Dagny personifies the values of independence, individualism, purpose, and self-actualization.

Dagny is an engineer and the operating vice-president of a transcontinental railroad, who deals with every industry and every policy of the looters.

Because of her integrating context, she has contact with every industry, thus permitting the reader to see the total scope of modern industrial civilization.

Dagny, like Hank Rearden, is a self-initiator who goes by her own judgments and is the motive power of her own happiness. Unlike Rearden, she does not feel guilty for her achievements. Dagny is a purposeful, strong, and passionately creative embodiment of mind-body unity. She understands that the world both lives because of the work of the prime movers and then hates them for it. The parasites both need the creators and despise them at the same time. They desire to exploit the creators and then make them take blame for their actions. Dagny realizes that it is because producers are concerned with nature and reason that they are able to create within the reality of an objective and knowable universe. According to Dagny, "the sight of an achievement was the greatest gift a human being could offer to others" (237). She knows that material production is an expression of man's highest aspect and defining characteristic—his reasoning and creative mind. It is the mind that enables individuals to deal with physical reality. Dagny recognizes that the creators are wrongly expected by many people to feel guilty for their virtues. Of course, the creators are guilty only of not claiming their moral values and virtues. Dagny chooses romantic partners who affirm her positive sense of life, which involves the integration of values, including love and sex. She understands that love is an emotional response, as are friendship and admiration, when one encounters a person who embodies his or her values.

Dagny's romances with Francisco, Rearden, and Galt exemplify what a relationship between two integrated and self-actualized persons can be. Her relationships illustrate that sex is the supreme form of admiration of one human being for another and that the values of one's mind are connected to the actions of one's body.

Although Dagny is a paragon of mind-body integration, she does not fully understand the world's situation and is conflicted because of this lack of knowledge. Salmieri (2007)[5] notes that Dagny thinks that the strikers are "giving up." Although she realizes that it is wrong to live and work under the rule of the looters, she also believes that it is immoral and dishonorable to surrender the world to them. She views quitting as a form of resignation or capitulation. Dagny does not want to give up Taggart Transcontinental but does not realize that by staying in the world she is giving the looters the means to enslave her. By remaining in the world, she is sanctioning her enemies' moral code. Her willingness to continue to fight the looters in the world indicates that she does not completely understand the full value of herself and of the other producers. Dagny also does not totally comprehend that it is at root a battle of very different philosophical premises.

At one point in the novel, Dagny is on a "mini-strike" of herself when Directive 10-289 is passed. The Taggart Tunnel disaster is an effect of this directive and of Dagny's absence. She is not there to advise regarding the situation. The disaster is the effect of the mind's absence and thus concretizes the novel's theme of the importance of the mind in human existence.

Salmieri explains that for most of the story Dagny wrongly believes that the looters love their lives and that they want to live. We could say that she is on the "wrong track." She thinks that she can make them see the truth and that she can win the battle. Dagny does not want to abandon the greatness of the world of the producers. Throughout Part Three of the novel, she progressively comes to realize that the irrational looters are indifferent, purposeless, and do not value their lives. This begins to become apparent to her when she meets with Mr. Thompson and the other looter-politicians. At that point, she is on the verge of understanding that the strike is required by the nature of existence and is thus the embodiment of rational egoism. She and the other heroes will ultimately realize that the looters' irrational doctrines are not errors of knowledge but instead are conscious breaches of morality.

Throughout most of the novel, Dagny believes she is right to go on in a world that she does not fully understand that is somehow stopping her from achieving her values. She needed to check her premises. She did not comprehend that Taggart Transcontinental and other great enterprises are only values in a certain context and that the required context of freedom no longer existed in the looters' world. She ultimately realizes that the looters do not value her products or those of the other producers. By the end of the story, she understands what motivates the looters. At the close of the novel she understands the contradictions in her principles and the need to go on strike. She realizes that there is no chance of winning by staying in the world of the looters. Dagny recognizes that justice cannot be attained by submitting to injustice.

Dagny has a fuller and more explicit conception of morality than Rearden does and is more morally consistent than he is. Her error is that she does not fully understand the looters' moral code and motives. Although she sees Rearden's moral error, she is blind to her own. She understands that the looters' policies have the effect of keeping the men of the mind from functioning at their best, but she does not grasp that such obstruction is, in fact, their intention. This is an intention that they desire to hide even from themselves. It is inconceivable to Dagny that the looters actually want to destroy the creators. Their motive becomes fully clear to her when they want to torture and/or kill Galt rather than to switch course and rescue themselves. It becomes apparent to her that she must quit when she realizes that the looters do not desire to live and that they are motivated by hatred for Galt and the other prime movers, for themselves, and for existence. Prior to this point, she believed that the looters would eventually comprehend the uselessness of their policies and would concede. Because she thought that they were rational and that they wanted to live, she fought to save Taggart Transcontinental and to force the looters to give up (Wright 2007).[6]

Hank Rearden, a great industrialist who, despite accepting the mind-body dichotomy, is the primary human instantiation of Atlas in *Atlas Shrugged*. He is a master of reality whose erroneous surface ideas do not corrupt his essential character and subconscious in terms of his psycho-epistemology. Although Rearden's words and ideas sanction an unearned guilt, his actions belie his words. Down deep he does not believe the notion of the mind-body split. His error is the inconsistent application of rational principles in different aspects of his life.

Rearden is a self-made man who is devoted to productive work and achievement. In the beginning of the novel his existence is schizophrenic and compartmentalized with a most satisfying work life and a bad family life. Hank works passionately and enthusiastically and then feels guilty about it.

His family members, especially his nihilist wife Lillian, desire to destroy his greatness and do all they can to make him feel guilty for his productivity, work ethic, and rational achievement. As a result, Rearden feels a guilty sense of obligation toward his family and attempts to atone, in an altruistic sense, to their many accusations.

Hank and the other industrialists are the worst victims of the conventionally accepted altruist-collectivist philosophy. It is the mistaken sanction by the men of ability that paves the way for the parasites and statist looters who want the creators to produce for the world and then to suffer for doing so. A moral code based on altruism and the idea of a mind-body split holds the creators guilty because of their greatest virtues. This moral code is used as a weapon against Rearden who does penance by sentencing himself to many years of selfless service to his family and to the looters. Once Rearden and the other producers gain an understanding of the looters' evil and of the importance of their own morality, they will attain the sense that life is about accomplishment and joy rather than about suffering and disaster.

Not only is he a constant victim of the looters, his relatives, and his associates, Hank also views his passion for Dagny Taggart as animalistic and degrading. When Rearden finds himself desiring Dagny, his split-self experiences a meltdown. Riddled with guilt, Hank is worried about his wife and his lack of virtue. He considers his forced love for his wife to be virtuous and thinks that his authentic love for Dagny is wrong and a guilty pleasure. Early in the novel, Hank has concluded that sex is purely physical, degrading, lustful, sinful, and of no spiritual meaning. Although Rearden himself is a very sexual being, he regards sex as a lower bodily urge.

For a great part of the novel, Rearden experiences an internal civil war between the principles of the creators in his work and the principles of the looters and moochers in the rest of his life. Hank desperately needs to import to his personal life the same principles that he uses in his productive life. It is under the tutelage of Francisco and Dagny that Rearden slowly awakens to the truth, understands the motives of the looters and of his family, and realizes his own virtues and values. They assist Hank in integrating his productivity and sexual desire with each other and with his self-worth.

Salmieri explains that throughout the novel Rearden comprehends more deeply and progressively the causes of, and interrelationships between, the various problems he faces in his personal life and work life. The story of his liberation from guilt is one in which many strands and threads of his new realizations are woven together. For example, he sees the connection between the guilt surrounding the sale of Rearden Metal to Ken Danagger and the guilt associated with his affair with Dagny. Throughout the novel, the connection between economics and romance becomes ever more explicit. By the end of the story, he understands the evil of the idea of the mind-body dichotomy. Rearden's discussion with Francisco at James and Cherryl's wedding reception aids in Rearden's liberation from guilt. Francisco introduces a more philosophical perspective to Rearden and to the readers when he tells Rearden that he is willing to bear too much suffering. This talk gives Rearden a moral sanction and leads him to realize that he has been guilty in accepting a wrong moral code and of giving the looters and his family a moral sanction based on that wrong code of morality. He comes to understand that he should not accept condemnation from a false moral code. Rearden learns from Francisco that the guilt is his own because he has been willing to bear punishment for what were really his virtues. Hank voices at his trial what he has learned:

> I am earning my own living, as every honest man must. I refuse to accept as guilt the fact of my own existence and the fact that I must work in order to support it. I refuse to accept as guilt the fact that I am able to do it and do it well. I refuse to accept as guilt the fact that I am able to do it better than most people—the fact that my work is of greater value than the work of my neighbors and that more men are willing to pay me. I refuse to apologize for my ability—I refuse to apologize for my success—I refuse to apologize for my money. (Rand 1957, 480)

Throughout much of the novel, Rearden needs to absolve himself of his unearned and undeserved moral guilt that had damaged his moral estimate of himself and of his capability for self-esteem. He needed to attain a belief in his own morality and in his right to self-esteem. His limited tacit approval of the ethics of altruism was behind his failure to comprehend the role and existence of moral values and ideals in his life (Wright 2007).

Hank Rearden's decision to go on strike takes a long time to develop. Until his discussion with Tinky Holloway and the other looters regarding the proposed Steel Unification Plan, Rearden had thought that the looters would ultimately be rational. During this encounter the looters make irrational claims on Rearden to produce for them.

Under the Steel Unification Plan, Rearden will go bankrupt no matter what his output happens to be and Orren Boyle's Associated Steel will receive the majority of Rearden's profits. After the confrontation, Rearden drives back to his mills, happens upon the dying Wet Nurse, is saved by Francisco (disguised as worker "Frank Adams"), and listens to Galt's logic as delivered to him by Francisco. In the next chapter, "The Concerto of Deliverance," Rearden disappears to Mulligan's Valley. Now seeing the truth, he recognizes that he must give up the world in order to save it.

By understanding morality and himself in terms of the metaphysical principle of mind-body integration, Hank is freed from the self-sacrifice ethics that underpin his servitude. It is Rearden's inner conflict that drives the plot, and it is his liberation from his mistaken premises and ultimate conscious acceptance of his subconscious Objectivist premises that resolve the conflict. In the end, he no longer feels guilty for his greatest virtues.

Wright (2007) explains that Dagny and Rearden's misjudgment is that they consider evil to be powerless and view the looters' policies as self-defeating. They do not understand for much of the story that these are impotent unless they are empowered by the good (i.e., by themselves and the other creators). It is only the producers' toleration and tacit acceptance of the looters' moral code that makes the devastating results possible. The producers had allowed their enemies to write the moral code. Before Dagny and Rearden can effectively battle their enemies, they must come to understand how they are complicit in their own victimization. Irrational (i.e., evil) people and their schemes can only succeed if they are helped and supported by rational (i.e., good) individuals. Actually, Rearden accepts this conflict only in his personal life and Dagny does not accept it at all. However, she believes that the looters have made an error, but will come around if only she can show them the invalidity of their beliefs through her productive achievements.

Atlas Shrugged demonstrates that the greater a person's productive ability, the greater are the penalties he endures in the form of regulations, controls, and the expropriation and redistribution of his earned wealth. This evil, however, is made possible only by the sanction of the victims. By accepting an unearned guilt—not for their vices but for their virtues—the achievers have acquiesced in the political theft of their minds' products. *Atlas Shrugged* shows the creators being sacrificed to the parasites and also dramatizes that the irrational looters need the assistance of rational people in order to "succeed." The moral code of self-sacrifice is used against and accepted by many of the creators who are made to feel guilty for their achievements and wealth. This is the "sanction of the victim" moral principle. The fact that Galt understands this principle and that Dagny and Rearden fail to comprehend it establishes the major plot conflict in the story. In order to fight the altruist foundation of statist political economy, the men of the mind will need to withdraw their sanction.

Rearden, Dagny, and the other prime movers suffer spiritually and begin to view life as a mental weight and weary load rather than as a joy. Rearden's spiritual suffering runs deeper than Dagny's. Rearden lacks an explicit awareness of objective morality that Dagny possesses. He is open to attack because in his conscious beliefs he is oblivious to correct morality. Whereas Dagny never questions her right to her own happiness and self-esteem, Rearden does question his right to them. This destroys him spiritually and produces the foundation for his material exploitation. His partial acceptance of altruism despiritualizes his pursuit of happiness and his capacity for self-esteem. Rearden does not explicitly realize that he is operating by a moral code in his work life. Of course, he does so implicitly. His work life epitomizes morality as it leads to production, life, and life-enhancing values. Although he was proud of his thinking and acting, he did not explicitly identify these as moral and virtuous. He failed to identify the source of his pride as a moral value and as morally justified (Wright 2007).

OTHER BUSINESS CHARACTERS

Francisco d'Anconia inherited the world's largest copper mining company that has been in his family since the days of the Spanish Empire. A man of tremendous ability and intelligence, he is purposeful, courageous, benevolent, and enthusiastic. Francisco admires productive work and money making and is dedicated to d'Anconia Copper. As a young man his stated goal was to be worthy of what he had inherited by expanding the already massive d'Anconia Copper empire. Francisco is the first person to join John Galt's strike when he sees that the majority of people had abandoned reason. Although he is connected to the strikers in Galt's Gulch, he remains in the outside world in order to recruit additional strikers and to accelerate the fall of the anti-reason and anti-life world. As the president of d'Anconia Copper, Francisco deliberately, gradually, and systematically destroys his own company that is under threat of nationalization. By doing so he also helps to bring down the looter American businessmen who invested in his company, contributes to the destruction of other industrial concerns, and deprives people of benefiting from the accomplishments of his ancestors. This ironic character poses as a profligate playboy in order to camouflage his real purposes and essential nature.

Eddie Willers is Dagny's dedicated, indispensable, competent, and diligent chief assistant. His title is Special Assistant to the Vice-President of Operations of Taggart Transcontinental. Attached to the company, he is loyal to it and to Dagny. Eddie admires the achievements of productive geniuses such as Hank Rearden, Ellis Wyatt, and others. He is not a genius but he is rational, realistic, and highly moral. He always wanted to do "Whatever is right" (Rand 1957, 6). Eddie is John Galt's unwitting accomplice revealing information to Galt who is disguised as a common track worker in the employee cafeteria.

Dan Conway is the middle-aged owner and president of the Phoenix-Durango Railroad in Colorado. He built what was once a tiny railroad into the dominant railroad in the Southwest and Taggart Transcontinental's chief competitor in Colorado. His railroad supplies superior freight service to his commercial customers. This prompts James Taggart to conspire to get the National Alliance of Railroads, a private association, to pass the Anti-dog-eat-dog Rule, which puts the Phoenix-Durango Railroad out of business. He does not want to fight, accepts his defeat, and retires to his ranch in Arizona. Although he loves what he does, he does not protest being sacrificed because of the majority vote of the association members. Dagny urges him to fight but he declines. Conway explains that, although he does not think that it is right that he be sacrificed, he promised to obey the majority and, therefore, has no right to object. He has been taught to obey a moral code that makes him a willing victim. He says:

> Dagny, the whole world's in a terrible state right now. I don't know what's wrong with it, but something's very wrong. Men have to get together and find a way out. But who's to decide which way to take unless it's the majority? I guess that's the only fair way of deciding; I don't see any other. I suppose somebody's got to be sacrificed. If it turns out to be me, I have no right to complain. (78)

Later, Conway does take somewhat of a stand when he refuses to sell his Colorado railroad to James Taggart.

Ellis Wyatt is the most productive of Colorado's industrialists. The young, quick-tempered, and innovative entrepreneur devises a method for extracting oil from shale rock, thus creating an economic boom in Colorado. His production of oil from shale is eerily similar to today's fracking. Wyatt's oil enables other industrialists to run their machinery effectively and efficiently. Wyatt's company is the pillar of Colorado's economy. When the destructive Colorado Directives force the state's profitable firms to share the suffering by redistributing their earnings, Ellis Wyatt is prompted to quit. In an act of defiance, Wyatt sets fire to his wells resulting in "Wyatt's Torch" and disappears. He left behind a board nailed to a post containing a hand-written note stating "I am leaving it as I found it. Take over. It's yours" (336). These directives also put other companies out of business and destroyed the Rio Norte Line. The Colorado Directives precipitated the retirement and disappearance of many productive and competent Colorado industrialists including Andrew Stockton (foundry), Laurence Hammond and Ted Nielsen (automobiles), Dwight Sanders (airplanes), and Roger Marsh (electrical appliances), among others. Of the above productive individuals, Stockton is the only one that does the same work in Mulligan's Valley as he did in the outside world.

Ken Danagger is a no-nonsense, prototypical self-made coal producer and friend of Hank Rearden. He began as a coal miner and advanced to become the owner of Danagger Coal in Pennsylvania. He and Hank make a private agreement to circumvent legal restrictions on the amount of Rearden Metal that could be sold to one individual. Danagger and Rearden are indicted and charged with subverting government orders when Rearden sells an illegal amount of his metal to Danagger. He joins the strike after listening to the logic of the "destroyer" (Galt) just before Rearden's trial.

Financier Midas Mulligan was the owner of Mulligan Bank and was the richest man in the world. As a realist, he only makes loans to people who he judges will pay them back with adequate interest. He can tell whether or not a person is a good risk or not by judging his character, productive ability, and record. Mulligan joins the strike when a court orders him to grant a loan to the undeserving president of Amalgamated Service Corporation, Lee Hunsacker. Mulligan purchases a remote valley in the Colorado Rockies. This valley becomes Galt's Gulch where the able and competent "men of the mind" gather. Midas runs a bank in Galt's Gulch where all transactions must be made in gold.

Tony, the Wet Nurse, is a young man just out of college who is assigned by Washington bureaucrats to be Deputy Director of Distribution at Rearden's mills to enforce government policies. He began as a cynic who was taught nothing except moral relativism by his professors. He does not believe that there are any absolutes. Throughout the novel, he learns about values, comes to admire and respect Hank Rearden for his morality and productiveness, and recognizes the looters' evil. He asks Hank for a job and Rearden tells him that he would hire him gladly and at once but that he cannot because of the looters' restrictions. Hearing that from Rearden is what really matters to the Wet Nurse. Ultimately, he loses his life while protecting Rearden's mills.

Mr. Ward is the decent, hardworking president of Ward Harvester Company, a small, solid firm that has been in his family for four generations. When Orren Boyle's Associated Steel fails to deliver the steel that he needs he goes to see Hank Rearden desperately in need of help. His company will go out of business if he does not get the required materials. He and Hank share the same values and virtues. Mr. Ward greatly needs to obtain some Rearden Metal to keep his business running. In order to do so, he is willing to sell at a loss and to pay Rearden anything that he asks. Rearden responds positively to Mr. Ward's request.

In the middle of Hank's quest to find the extra metal that Ward requires, Gwen Ives informs Rearden that the Equalization of Opportunity Bill had just passed. The shocked Mr. Ward gets up to leave and Rearden tells him to stay while they complete their deal. Rearden says: "We had business to transact, didn't we? . . . Mr. Ward what is it that the foulest bastards on earth denounce us for, among other things? Oh yes, for our motto of 'Business as usual.' Well—business as usual, Mr. Ward" (212).

Gwen Ives is Hank Rearden's efficient, professional, and loyal secretary. She and Dagny Taggart are the only two working women in business in *Atlas Shrugged* whom we see performing good work. She understands the evil of the looters' ideology and breaks down in tears when she learns about the passing of the Equalization of Opportunity Bill. When Rearden retires and disappears, he advises her to leave the firm and make a run for it, which she does.

Dick McNamara of Cleveland is the competent contractor who completed the San Sebastián Line for Taggart Transcontinental. Dagny initially lines up the reliable contractor to lay the new Rearden Metal track for the Rio Norte Line (i.e., John Galt Line). He is one of the best contractors in the country and gets his projects done right and on time.

Unfortunately, despite a thriving business, he walks out. He is the first one of Dagny's business associates to vanish mysteriously. Forced to find a replacement contractor, Dagny hires Ben Nealy. Nealy sees no role for intelligence in human accomplishments, does not exert much effort, is disorganized, is reluctant to make decisions, and requires constant instruction from Dagny. He expresses the erroneous Marxist belief that only physical labor creates value: "Muscles, Miss Taggart . . . muscles—that's all it takes to build anything in the world" (162).

James Taggart is the primary business villain in *Atlas Shrugged*. He epitomizes the looters' unreason, is reluctant to depend upon his own business judgments, and fears and dislikes businesspeople who do rely upon their own evaluations. James frequently takes credit for Dagny's decisions and relies on her to get him out of trouble. In addition, in his efforts to gain wealth, he tries to ride on Francisco's intelligence. He is anti-effort and wants the unearned. James is a parasite and a whim-worshipper who manipulates and deceives people in order to fake self-esteem to himself. Also, he is afraid that he will be held responsible for anything. Taggart has a strong sense of inferiority and needs to feel superior. Jim does not possess the skills, energy, and ability required for legitimate business success. Down deep he finds his self-deception ridiculed by the existence of individuals with real ability, values, and virtues. He obtains money by using his political connections to garner subsidies or to get regulations passed that stifle his competitors. He thinks that by gaining wealth in that manner he will achieve moral status and self-esteem. James spends most of his time on public relations, cultivating friendships, and knowing the people who make things possible rather than being concerned with facts and reality. He would rather deal with his friends than those who are best suited to produce the desired results. For example, Jim deals with Orren Boyle who will either deliver the product late or not at all. He rationalizes to others and to himself that he is motivated by his altruistic love for others and his dutiful concern for social justice. By the end of the novel, he realizes that he is actually a nihilist operating on a death premise and that he wants to destroy the good because it is good.

Orren Boyle is a friend of James Taggart and owner of Associated Steel. He started with $100,000 of his own and obtained government loans in the amount of $200,000,000 to purchase a number of struggling steel firms that he merged into Associated Steel. In *Atlas Shrugged*, he uses his political connections and a too-big-to-fail argument to obtain even more help from the government. Boyle runs his company badly; he is either late fulfilling his orders or does not deliver the product at all and measures his company's success based on its popularity. He is disdainful of efficiency monopolies and dominant producers, says that private property is a trusteeship for benefit of society as a whole, and contends that he wants everyone to have a fair chance of getting iron ore. He says that he wants to pass the Equalization of Opportunity Bill in order to preserve the steel industry "as a whole." The collectivist philosophy that he espouses portrays a world in which no one can survive at the same time that others fail.

This implies that all firms participate in a process that should yield equal benefits to all. Of course, his real goal is to divest Hank Rearden of his ore mines and have them turned over to Paul Larkin who would give Associated Steel the first opportunity to purchase the ore.

Both James Taggart and Orren Boyle are at war with reality. They are postmodern "businessmen" who think that they can create the reality that they desire merely by wanting it, thinking it, and persuading others to share in a narrative that supports their desires. They believe that social reality creates its own reality and that they can control reality by having the right political connections, the appropriate public relations strategies, and enough people having the desired opinion about them and their companies.

The Starnes heirs (Eric, Gerald, and Ivy) bankrupt the Twentieth Century Motor Company with their socialist scheme in which the employees as a group voted to determine the needs of each employee as well as the production expected of each worker based on an evaluation of his ability. They considered their father, Jed Starnes, to be an evil man who cared for nothing but money and business. Their plan was based on the principle of selflessness and required men to be motivated by love for their brothers rather than by personal gain. In effect, they put into practice the Marxist slogan "From each according to his ability, to each according to his need." They believed that the fulfillment of the needs of others is a person's greatest moral imperative. It follows that it is the inability to create value that merits rewards, rather than the ability to create value. When the plan failed, Ivy complained that it was defeated by greed and maintained that the plan was a noble idea but that human nature was not good enough for it.

Lee Hunsacker had been the incompetent president of Amalgamated Service Corporation which had taken over the Twentieth Century Motor Company. Midas Mulligan refused to grant Hunsacker a loan because of his past record of failures. Feeling that he was entitled, he brought suit against Mulligan under a law that said that people were not allowed to discriminate against anyone in a matter involving that person's livelihood. After Judge Narragansett instructed the jury to bring in a verdict for Mulligan, Hunsacker appealed the verdict, which was reversed by a higher court. Both Mulligan and Narragansett disappeared shortly thereafter. Eventually, Hunsacker was able to get a loan from the "banker with a heart," Eugene Lawson of the Community National Bank who had collectivist, humanitarian loan policies. Predictably, Amalgamated went bankrupt.

Paul Larkin is a weak, unsuccessful businessman who acts like he is Hank Rearden's friend. He is actually in on the deal that strips Hank of his iron ore and coal mines. In fact, when the Equalization of Opportunity Bill is passed, he takes possession of Rearden's ore mines and tells Hank that he will always consider the ore mines to belong to Rearden. Of course, this is untrue and Larkin gives Orren Boyle the initial opportunity to get the ore.

ATLAS SHRUGGED IN THE BUSINESS SCHOOL

Novels, as well as plays and films, are excellent teaching tools for communicating ideas to students. A well-constructed and compelling story can engage students and make a subject more vital to them. Fiction provides students with interesting material that does not seem like hard work. The result is that novels tend to have greater teaching power and more appeal to students than articles, textbooks, or case studies. Because students are apt to enjoy reading fiction, it is likely that they may grasp ideas quicker and better than when more conventional teaching methods are used. For many people, pure theory is not as exciting as a good story.

A compelling and relevant story stays in one's memory. Graduate and undergraduate business students have grounds for paying attention to novels concerning the business world. Many graduate business students are already in the world of entrepreneurship, manufacturing, and finance, and undergraduate business students aspire to soon be in the corporate world. Novels can provide examples of challenges that a student may one day confront. It is no wonder that business novels connect with such students and work their way into the students' thinking.

Novels can come close to mirroring reality and are able to illuminate the full context of a situation. Novels about business describe life as lived in the world of commerce. Situations in novels can be more realistic than the hypothetical examples postulated in articles, case studies, or lectures. A novel can provide a superb background from which to view business. A well-written novel about business can pose complex questions and deepen a student's capacity for critical thinking. Such a novel can bring management problems and issues of business ethics to life by contextualizing organizational and moral questions and dilemmas. Ultimately, one's character may be influenced by reading fiction. This pedagogical method may stimulate the moral cognition and insight of the reader. Some narratives have the potential to open one's eyes with respect to what is really important.

Unfortunately, most novels are not representative of the real business world. It can safely be said that businesspeople have not fared well in novels on the whole. The literary culture is often unflattering in its depictions of businesspeople and capitalism, has attacked business and industry for destroying an old communal order based on equality, laments the capitalist preoccupation with material success, and abhors the dominance of large organizations in people's lives. Many novels go so far as to portray the businesspeople with hostility and derision.

Fortunately, there is at least one novel—Rand's *Atlas Shrugged*—that portrays the entrepreneur in a positive manner by emphasizing the essential moral nature of business and the legitimacy of people engaged in business, showing us the energy and fortitude of the diligent men and women of commerce, and the value of the entrepreneur as a wealth creator and promoter of economic progress. *Atlas Shrugged* depicts the businessperson's role as potentially heroic. *Atlas Shrugged* shows the business hero as a determined, creative, and independent thinker who follows an idea to its accomplishment. Rand's novel dramatizes the positive qualities of the business by illustrating the victory of individualism over collectivism, portraying successful businesspeople as noble and attractive, and by characterizing business careers as at least as honorable as careers in other professions, if not more so.

Atlas Shrugged is now being taught in colleges and universities in a variety of courses. It is being used in the classroom to study the moral foundations of capitalism and commerce and related topics in philosophy, economics, free enterprise, management, business, and other areas.[7]

For example, due to the tireless efforts of John Allison, former CEO and chairman of BB&T Bank, there are now nearly seventy programs at institutions of higher learning that use *Atlas Shrugged* in their classes. This novel provides an excellent base for teaching issues in business, business ethics, economics, and political and economic philosophy. The use of *Atlas Shrugged* aids in moving between abstract principles and realistic business examples. The novel serves as a link between philosophical concepts and the practical aspects of business and illustrates that philosophy is accessible and important to people in general and to business people in particular.

Atlas Shrugged fosters a spirited exchange of ideas among students in the classroom as many students respond strongly and positively to this novel and its heroes. The novel presents the pursuit of profit as thoroughly moral, makes the discussion of capitalism intellectually legitimate, provides a powerful critique of socialism, and challenges the prevailing beliefs of our culture. Students are impressed with *Atlas Shrugged*'s prophetic nature. It portrays the United States economy collapsing due to government intervention and regulation, politicians placing the blame on capitalism and free market, and the government countering with ever more controls that further the crisis. Government intervention is shown to discourage innovation and risk-taking, and the novel portrays how regulations in a mixed economy are made with political interest groups lobbying the government, which grants favors to those who have the most votes, political pull, or influence.

I use *Atlas Shrugged* to help undergraduate business students better understand the philosophical, moral, and economic concepts underlying business and capitalism.

I incorporate Rand's novel into my "Conceptual Foundations of Business" course at Wheeling Jesuit University. In the class, students take turns leading discussions on all thirty chapters of Rand's 1,168-page novel.[8] During class discussions, students cite specific scenes and passages and their accompanying page numbers. During the last five class sessions, I deliver detailed and in-depth lectures on *Atlas Shrugged*. The final exam consists of an essay exam on the novel.

My book *Capitalism and Commerce* provides a discussion of the philosophical, moral, and economic foundations upon which a capitalistic society is constructed. Rand's novel becomes the vehicle for the incarnation of these ideas—bringing abstract philosophy to life through character and plot.

The novel shows students in this course that the only way for man to survive in society is through reason and voluntary trade. *Atlas Shrugged* focuses on the positive and shows students what it takes to achieve genuine business success and how to create value.

Like Aristotle, Rand maintains an agent-centered approach to morality and focuses on the character traits that distinguish a good person. Reading *Atlas Shrugged* prompts students to think about what makes up a good life. Rand's business protagonists are shown to live by correct principles and acquire pertinent character traits. The villains in the novel show what happens when people hold incorrect principles and fail to cultivate indispensable virtues.

Some discussions in class revolve around virtues such as rationality, independence, integrity, justice, honesty, productiveness, and pride. The novel's characters are analyzed to see if these are absent or present in them. The novel teaches students that there are traits that correlate with business success and success in life. These include independent vision or foresight, an active mind, competence, confidence, personal or egoistic passion, a drive to action, the love of ability in others, and, above all, having virtues.

Atlas Shrugged presents a thought-provoking portrait of entrepreneurs who won't allow politicians to kick them around anymore. The novel presents steelmakers, railroad tycoons, and bankers as heroes—the problem-solvers, producers, and thinkers. If Rand were writing today, she would likely be including software designers, builders of telecommunications networks, and those who work with photovoltaics, cryogenics, aerogels, biochips, radio-wave lighting, microelectromechanical systems, quantum chips, shape-memory metals, and so on.

The class discussion of heroes in *Atlas Shrugged* leads to comparisons with real-life business leaders such as Bill Gates, Ken Iverson, Jack Welch, Sam Walton, Steve Jobs, Thomas Edison, Michael Dell, Michael Eisner, Edwin Land, Henry Ford, Walt Disney, Roberto Goizueta, Fred Smith, Ginni Rommetti, Marissa Mayer, Meg Whitman, Denise Morrison, and Sheryl Sandberg. The class dialogue centers around the character traits, principles, decisions, and actions of these individuals.

In my course, I use the novel to show that there are good and bad businesspeople, and that they don't always act virtuously. There are two types of businesspeople. There are those who lobby the government for special privileges, make unethical deals, and engage in fraud and corrupt activities. In addition, there are the real producers who succeed or fail on their own. Rand's book illustrates what it takes to attain authentic business success and how to create value.

In a tribute article to the "money-making personality," Rand ([1963] 2011, 68–70) draws a contrast between mindful people of independent judgment who make money and the mindless socially dependent looters who appropriate it:

The Money-*Maker* is the discoverer who translates his discovery into material goods. In an industrial society with a complex division of labor, it may be one man or a partnership of two: the scientist who discovers new knowledge and the *entrepreneur*—the businessman—who discovers how to use that knowledge, how to organize material resources and human labor into an enterprise producing marketable goods.

The Money-*Appropriator* is an entirely different type of man. He is essentially non-Creative—and his basic goal is to acquire an unearned share of the wealth created by others. He seeks to get rich, not by conquering nature, but by manipulating men, not by intellectual effort, but by social maneuvering. He does not produce, he redistributes: he merely switches the wealth already in existence from the pockets of its owners to his own.

The Money-Appropriator may become a politician—or a businessman who "cuts corners"—or that destructive product of a "mixed economy": the businessman who grows rich by means of government favors, such as special privileges, subsidies, franchises; that is, grows rich by means of *legalized force* . . .

The Money-Maker, above all else, is the originator and innovator. The trait most signally absent from his character is *resignation*, the passive acceptance of the given, the known, the established, the *status quo*. He never says: "What was good enough for my grandfather is good enough for me." He says: "What was good enough for me yesterday will not be good enough tomorrow."

He does not sit waiting for "a break" or for somebody to give him a chance. He makes and takes his own chances. He never whines, "I couldn't help it!"—he can, and does . . .

The man who will never make money has an "employee mentality," even in an executive's job; he tries to get away with a minimum of effort, as if any exertion were an imposition; and when he fails to take the proper action, he cries: "But nobody told me to!"

The Money-Maker has an "employer mentality," even when he is only an office boy—which is why he does not remain an office boy for long. In any job he holds, he is committed to a maximum of effort; he learns everything he can about the business, much more than his job requires. He never needs to be told—even when confronting a situation outside his usual duties.

These are the reasons why he rises from office boy to company president . . .

It is only the Money-Appropriator who lives and acts short-range, never looking beyond the immediate moment. The Money-Maker lives, thinks and acts long-range. Having complete confidence in his own judgment, he has complete confidence in the future, and only long-range projects can hold his interest. To a Money-Maker, as well as to an artist, work is not a painful duty or a necessary evil, but a way of life; to him, productive activity is the essence, the meaning and the enjoyment of existence; it is the state of being alive.

Rand's business protagonists are independent, rational, and committed to the facts of reality, to the judgment of their own minds, and to attaining their own flourishing and happiness. Each one thinks for himself, actualizes his potential, and views himself as capable of dealing with life's challenges and as deserving of achieving success and happiness. *Atlas Shrugged* makes a case that the legitimate businessperson is a befitting symbol of a free society.

Atlas Shrugged also recounts the rise of "businessmen" who seek "profit" by currying favor with dishonest politicians. They refrain from rationality and productivity by using their political pull and pressure groups to rob the producers. Rand condemns those who would loot the individuals who create human progress and prosperity.

Government intervention discourages innovation and risk-taking and obstructs the process of wealth-creation. In *Atlas Shrugged*, the producers' minds are shackled by government policies. Lacking the freedom to create, compete, and earn wealth, the independent thinkers withdraw from society. This is Rand's recommended response to the bureaucratic assault of the entrepreneurial spirit.

Atlas Shrugged delineates government intervention as the great enemy of the entrepreneur. Rand details how government intervention into private markets produces costs and consequences more harmful than the targeted problem itself. Socialistic bureaucrats attempt to protect men from their own minds and tend to think only of intended, primary, and immediate results while ignoring unintended, ancillary, and long-term ones. Government-produced impediments to a free society are shown to include taxation, protectionism, antitrust laws, government regulation, social welfare programs, monetary inflation, and more.

Atlas Shrugged is a great story that helps students to understand the nature of the world in which they live. It illustrates that only a free society is compatible with human nature and the world and that capitalism works because it is in accordance with reality. Capitalism is shown to be the only moral social system because it protects the human mind, the primary means of human survival and flourishing. *Atlas Shrugged* is a powerful tool to educate, persuade, and convert people to a just and proper political and economic order that is a true reflection of human nature and the world properly understood.

ACKNOWLEDGMENTS

I would like to thank the following individuals for their useful comments and suggestions for improving and clarifying the ideas that appear in this chapter: Walter Block, Sam Bostaph, Rob Bradley, Stephen Cox, Eric Dent, Stephen Hicks, Jerry Kirkpatrick, William Kline, Allen Mendenhall, Jomana Papillo, John Parnell, Chris Matthew Sciabarra, Fred Seddon, Brian Simpson, Gennady Stolyarov, Michelle Vachris, and Gary Wolfram.

NOTES

This chapter was first published in *The Journal of Ayn Rand Studies* 15, no. 2 (December 2015): 157–84. This article is used by permission of The Pennsylvania State University Press.

1. In *Atlas Shrugged*, Ayn Rand assigns names of individual owners to companies operated by legitimate producer businesses and collectivist sounding names to companies run by inauthentic looter businessmen. Among those companies in the first category are Rearden Steel, Taggart Transcontinental, Wyatt Oil, d'Anconia Copper, Danagger Coal, and so on. Examples of firms in the second category are Associated Steel, Amalgamated Switch and Signal, and United Locomotive Works. The men who have attached their names to their companies ultimately became strikers during the course of the story.

2. Luskin and Greta (2011) introduce readers to real-life business heroes who have lived their lives like *Atlas Shrugged's* fictional heroes and the scoundrels who have lived like Rand's fictional villains. For example, on the business hero side, the book presents John Allison as John Galt, Bill Gates as Hank Rearden, and T. J. Rodgers as Francisco d'Anconia. On the business villain side, the authors cite Angelo Mozilo as Jim Taggart and Barney Frank as Wesley Mouch, who is a politician who meddles in the economy rather than actually working in the business world.

3. See Locke (2000), Rand in Ralston (2000), Locke (2009), and Ghate (2009) for excellent discussions of businesspeople as heroes and prime movers.

4. Ayn Rand's Objectivist virtues as a basis for morality and success in business are discussed in depth in Greiner and Kinni (2001), Woiceshyn (2012), and Younkins (2012).

5. Salmieri's (2009) essay in Mayhew (2009) is based on his 2007 audio course.

6. A great deal of the material found in Wright's (2007) audio course can also be found in his 2009 article in Mayhew (2009).

7. Several recent articles have discussed how *Atlas Shrugged* can be integrated into college economics courses. See Boettke (2005, 2007), Kent and Hamilton (2011), and Chamlee-Wright (2011).

8. I have my students read the entire text of *Atlas Shrugged* in my "Conceptual Foundations of Business" course. Some faculty members at various institutions choose to selectively assign portions of it to their students. For example, Michelle A. Vachris (2007) of Christopher Newport University assigns pages to be read and

typed answers to discussion questions to be brought to class and used as the basis for class discussions in her "The American Economy in Literature" course. Here is a summary of her page assignments and related discussion questions: (1) Who benefits and who is hurt by the Anti-dog-eat-dog Rule? What are some possible unintended consequences? (74–88); (2) Who benefits and who is hurt by the Equalization of Opportunity Bill? What are some possible unintended consequences? (130–36, 217–18, 270–71); (3) How does Galt's motor work? What would be the economic effects of such an invention? (287–91); (4) Who benefits and who is hurt by the Fair Share Law? What are some possible unintended consequences? (298–99, 360–67, 499–500); (5) In Francisco d'Anconia's "Money Speech": What are the roles of money and profit? Find examples that illustrate the differences between the voluntary nature of the market and the coercive nature of government (409–15); (6) Find examples of self-interest versus the public good (475–84); (7) Who benefits and who is hurt by Directive Number 10-289? What are some possible unintended consequences? (535–49); (8) Compare and contrast the two different views of why the Twentieth Century Motor Company failed (321–24; 660–72); (9) Explain the role that self-interest has in the market economy (701–61); and (10) Find examples of capitalism versus collectivism in terms of their views about prices, profit, and property rights (1009–69).

REFERENCES

Boettke, Peter J. 2005. "Teaching Economics Through Ayn Rand: How the Economy Is Like a Novel, and How the Novel Can Teach Us About Economics." *The Journal of Ayn Rand Studies* 6, no. 2 (Spring): 445–65.

———. 2007. "The Economics of *Atlas Shrugged*." In *Ayn Rand's "Atlas Shrugged": A Philosophical and Literary Companion*, 179–87, edited by Edward W. Younkins. Aldershot, England: Ashgate.

Bradley, Robert Jr. 2011. "*Atlas Shrugged*: Its Philosophy and Energy Implications." Online at: http://www.masterresource.org/2011/04/atlas-shrugged-and-energy-i/.

Chamlee-Wright, Emily. 2011. "Cultivating the Economic Imagination with *Atlas Shrugged*." *Journal of Economics and Financial Education* 10, no. 2 (Fall): 41–53.

Ghate, Debi. 2009. "The Businessmen's Crucial Role: Material Men of the Mind." In *Essays on Ayn Rand's "Atlas Shrugged*," 299–316, edited by Robert Mayhew. Lanham, Maryland: Lexington Books.

Ghate, Debi, and Richard E. Ralston, eds. 2011. *Why Businessmen Need Philosophy.* New York: New American Library.

Greiner, Donna, and Theodore Kinni. 2001. *Ayn Rand and Business.* New York: Texere.

Kent, Calvin A., and Paul Hamilton. 2011. "Inclusion of *Atlas Shrugged* in Economics Classes." *The Journal of Private Enterprise* 26, no. 2: 143–59.

Kirzner, Isiael M. 2009. *Discovery, Capitalism, and Distributive Justice.* Chicago: University of Chicago.

Locke, Edwin A. 2000. *The Prime Movers.* New York: AMACOM.

———. 2009. "The Traits of Business Heroes." In *Essays on Ayn Rand's "Atlas Shrugged,"* 317–34, edited by Robert Mayhew. Lanham, Maryland: Lexington Books.

Luskin, Donald L., and Andrew Greta. 2011. *I am John Galt*. Hoboken, New Jersey: John Wiley and Sons.

Mayhew, Robert, ed. 2009. *Essays on Ayn Rand's "Atlas Shrugged."* Lanham, Maryland: Lexington Books.

Rand, Ayn. 1957. *Atlas Shrugged*. New York: Random House.

———. [1963] 2011. "The Money-Making Personality." In *Why Businessmen Need Philosophy*, 67–74, edited by Debi Ghate and Richard E. Ralston. New York: New American Library.

Salmieri, Gregory. 2007. *Atlas Shrugged as a Work of Philosophy*. Four Audio Lectures. New Milford, Connecticut: Second Renaissance Books.

———. 2009. "Discovering Atlantis: *Atlas Shrugged's* Demonstration of a New Moral Philosophy." In *Essays on Ayn Rand's "Atlas Shrugged,"* 397–452, edited by Robert Mayhew. Lanham, Maryland: Lexington Books.

Simon, Julian 1996. *The Ultimate Resource 2*. Princeton: Princeton University Press.

Vachris, Michelle A. 2007. "Economics Lessons in Literature." *Virginia Economic Journal* 12, no. 1: 23–32.

Woiceshyn, Jaana. 2012. *How to be Profitable and Moral: A Rational Egoist Approach to Business*. Lanham, Maryland: Hamilton Books.

Wright, Darryl. 2007. *Ayn Rand's Ethics from "The Fountainhead" to "Atlas Shrugged."* Two Audio Lectures. New Milford, Connecticut: Second Renaissance Books.

———. 2009. "Ethics: From *The Fountainhead* to *Atlas Shrugged*." In *Essays on Ayn Rand's "Atlas Shrugged,"* 253–73, edited by Robert Mayhew. Lanham, Maryland: Lexington Books.

Younkins, Edward W. 2002. *Capitalism and Commerce: Conceptual Foundations of Free Enterprise*. Lanham, MD: Lexington Books.

———, ed. 2007. *Ayn Rand's "Atlas Shrugged": A Philosophical and Literary Companion*. Aldershot, England: Ashgate.

———. 2012. "Ayn Rand's Objectivist Virtues as the Foundation of Morality and Success in Business." *The Journal of Ayn Rand Studies* 12, no. 2 (December): 237–62.

Chapter 5

Atlas Shrugged and Social Change

Novels can provide a social message that can change people's outlooks and potentially contribute to social and cultural change. They can elicit intellectual and emotional responses that prompt readers to rethink their viewpoints. Novels can both entertain and lead individuals to think about the great moral questions of life. Novels are representations of reality that have human beings and society as their subject matter. The focus of attention on human problems and aspirations stimulates thought. When the creativity found in novels is added to the dynamics of society, then the potential for social change is inspired.

Throughout recent history, by examining and illuminating social problems and issues, novelists have offered a powerful medium, agent, and vehicle for fostering social change. The cultural power of social novels is illustrated in works such as Charles Dickens's *Oliver Twist* (1839) and *Hard Times* (1854), Victor Hugo's *Les Misérables* (1862), Émile Zola's *Germinal* (1885), Upton Sinclair's *The Jungle* (1906), John Dos Passos's *USA Trilogy* (1938), and John Steinbeck's *The Grapes of Wrath* (1939).

Ayn Rand's *Atlas Shrugged* is a novel of social change that differs radically from those listed above. Unlike those novels, *Atlas Shrugged* illustrates and explains that only a free society is compatible with the nature of man and the world and that capitalism works because it is in accordance with reality. Although Rand structured her cautionary tale much like a long Dickensian novel, she inverted the message while keeping the form. Capitalism is shown to be the only moral system because it protects a man's mind, his primary means of survival and flourishing. *Atlas Shrugged* presents a moral social system that makes it possible for individuals to exist and to function. A model for thoughtful social change is played out in the pages of this novel—both as a work of art and as a philosophical and educational tract. *Atlas Shrugged* has been frequently hailed for its enduring impact on individuals' minds and on culture.

This novel has sold more than eight million copies. In addition, respondents to a joint Library of Congress–Book of the Month Club survey in 1991 hailed the book as second only to the Bible in its significant impact on their lives (Fein 1991). *Atlas Shrugged* has also had a significant influence on a variety of people including writers, artists, and political figures.

Although *Atlas Shrugged* embodies Ayn Rand's advocacy of free-market capitalism, this support is related to the underlying purpose of her work. As she put it:

> The motive and purpose of my writing is the projection of an ideal man. The portrayal of a moral ideal, as my ultimate literary goal, as an end in itself—to which any didactic, intellectual, or philosophical values contained in a novel are only the means. (Rand 1971, 162)

Rand went on to say:

> Since my purpose is the presentation of an ideal man, I had to define and present the conditions which make him possible and which his existence requires. Since man's character is the product of his premises, I had to define and present the kind of premises and values that create the character of an ideal man and motivate his actions; which means that I had to define and present a rational code of ethics. Since man acts among and deals with other men, I had to present the kind of social system that makes it possible to exist and to function—a free, productive, rational system, which demands and rewards the best in every man, great or average, and which is, obviously, laissez-faire capitalism. (163–64)

Cowen (2008, 319–37) explains that some novels present informal models of reality and that individuals can profit from insights contained in novels that are full-length fictional stories intended to entertain, stimulate, and inspire readers. Such novels stand on their own as works of art while, at the same time, illuminating underpinning general principles and the implications of the author's underlying worldview. They tell memorable stories that elicit emotional responses and have models embedded in them that articulate the novelist's ideas about how the real world works. *Atlas Shrugged* is one of these novels. While the political, economic, and philosophical content of *Atlas Shrugged* fulfills Rand's goal, that content is not itself the goal of the novel. However, that content adds value to the novel with respect to its ability to stimulate social change.

The purpose of this chapter is to explain the various ways in which *Atlas Shrugged* is related to social change. This involves both how characters in the novel introduce change in the fictional world and how *Atlas Shrugged* itself can be a vehicle for change in the real world. The first of eight sections provides an introduction to the basic concepts of social change theory. The second discusses capitalism as social change. This is followed by a discussion of how the message and impact of *Atlas Shrugged* have been viewed by several prominent scholars. The next two parts illustrate how the heroic characters in the novel were practical men of action. The entrepreneurs and strikers in the novel are shown to be agents of economic, social, and cultural change. The sixth and seventh sections examine the potential effects on readers of *Atlas Shrugged* and explain that getting individuals to read *Atlas Shrugged* is a good initial step toward the establishment of a free society even though many additional actions will also be necessary. The final section of this chapter surveys how some social movements have adopted or adapted the ideas found in *Atlas Shrugged* into, or as, their own philosophy.

SOCIAL CHANGE THEORY

Social change has been defined by Rogers (1973, 7) as the process by which alteration occurs in the structure and function of a social system. Lippitt (1973, 37) has defined change as "any planned or unplanned alteration in the status quo in an organism, situation, or process." An innovation is "an idea, practice, or object perceived as new by the individual" (Rogers and Shoemaker 1971, 19). Zaltman and Duncan (1977, 10) have modified this definition and have commented on the distinction between change and innovation as follows:

> An innovation is any idea, practice, or material artifact perceived to be new by the relevant unit of adoption. The innovation is the change object. A change is alteration in the structure of a system that requires or could be required by relearning on the part of the actor(s) in response to a given situation. Often too, an appropriate response to a new requirement is an inventive process producing an innovation. However, all innovations imply change, but not all change involves innovations, since not everything an individual or formal or informal group adopts is perceived as new.

The process of gaining acceptance and/or adoption of an innovation is generally known as the diffusion of innovation process. Diffusion theory concerns the propagation of a new concept or object, called an innovation, among members of a given social system. According to Katz, Levin, and Hamilton (1963, 240):

> The process of diffusion is defined as the (1) acceptance, (2) over time, (3) of some specific item—an idea or practice, (4) by individuals, groups, or other

adopting units, linked to specific (5) channels of communication, (6) to a social structure, and (7) to a given system of values or culture.

Rogers and Shoemaker (1971, 22–23) have defined five perceived character-istics of an innovation that may influence its adoption. They include relative advantage, compatibility, complexity, trialability, and observability. Ostlund (1974, 24) added perceived risk to this list. Zaltman and Wallendorf (1983, 251) expanded the list of perceived attributes of innovations by adding divisibility, reversibility, adaptability, cost, and realization. Other researchers have formu-lated their own lists of characteristics depending on the innovation under study.

The first of Rogers and Shoemaker's innovation characteristics is relative advantage, which is the degree to which an innovation is better than the idea that it is intended to displace. The next innovation attribute is compatibility with existing values and practices. This is the extent to which an innovation is consistent with the values, past experiences, and needs of potential users. Complexity, sometimes referred to as simplicity or ease of use, refers to the degree to which an innovation is easy or difficult to understand and use. Trialability is the extent to which an innovation can be experimented with or experienced on a limited basis. There is less risk involved with an innovation that can be tried on a limited basis. Observability, or communicability, is the degree to which the results of using an innovation are observable to others. The more observable the results of an innovation are to individuals, the more likely they are to adopt it.

The participants in the change process include the change agent, the change target, and the client system. Zaltman and Duncan (1977)

take a broad view of the change agent role to include people within as well as outside the client system who are attempting to create some change in that system whether it is sanctioned or not. Specifically, a change agent is any indi-vidual or group operating to change the status quo in a system such that the individual or individuals involved must relearn how to perform their role(s). The change target system is the unit in which the change agent(s) is trying to alter the status quo such that the individual, group, or organization must relearn how to perform its activities. The change client system is the individual or group requesting assistance from a change agent in altering the status quo. (17–18)

CAPITALISM AS SOCIAL CHANGE

Capitalism as defined in this article (i.e., laissez-faire capitalism) involves that set of economic arrangements that could exist in a society in which a state's only function would be to prevent one person from initiating force or fraud against another person. No one has ever witnessed such a totally unencumbered market economy. It is a theoretical innovation that Ayn Rand has referred to as "the unknown ideal." This is the innovation or social change that *Atlas Shrugged* can best be used to promote. Although Rand's unique philosophy of Objectivism can also be viewed as an innovation, it is not likely that many potential advocates for a free society will quickly accept her full philosophy with understanding and conviction. It follows that the innovation of free-market capitalism is the most relevant and marketable social change that *Atlas Shrugged* can be used to dramatize and explain. Advocates of capitalism differ in their arguments for a social system that maximizes individual freedom. However, these various proponents do agree that the appropriate social system is one in which the initiation of physical force or fraud is forbidden. That is the major idea that *Atlas Shrugged* can get across to a great many people. It can help to spread the desirability of capitalism and the philosophy of freedom to the general public. Because man has free will and survives by reason, the initiation of force must be banned.

Rogers and Shoemaker's innovation attributes can be applied to capitalism in general and to its depiction in *Atlas Shrugged* in particular. Capitalism has relative advantages over other political-economic systems with respect to productivity, efficiency, and especially morality. Capitalism is moral in its effects because it makes personal morality possible. Because it is based on freedom of choice, it allows for the character development of each individual. With respect to compatibility, capitalism is consistent with the nature of man and the world. Each person has the right to have the opportunity to develop his potential as a free, individual human being. Capitalism is moral because it protects each man's right to his own mind—his survival instrument—and therefore it enables human survival. For centuries, the values of freedom and individualism have underpinned the American way of life. During the past 100 years or so, people's values have been increasingly corrupted as they have become dependent on the government. With respect to ease of understanding, the conceptual and moral foundations of a free society can be expressed in clear, cogent, and nontechnical language. In addition, its use simply means respect for the individual rights of other human beings. Capitalism can be tried on a limited and incremental basis with the gradual elimination of government activities, regulations, and so on. Finally, the results of a move toward a free society will be observable and easily communicated throughout society. *Atlas Shrugged* is an accessible, interesting, and exciting work that dramatizes and presents the case for freedom and against collectivism.

ATLAS SHRUGGED: MESSAGE AND IMPACT

Ideas are the most powerful forces in the world and the motive power of human progress. Fortunately, there exists a novel that articulates a theoretically consistent, systematic, and intellectually sound defense of capitalism; expounds the principles of traditional liberalism, voluntary cooperation, and individual freedom; and exposes the errors of coercion and collectivism. That novel is *Atlas Shrugged*. As moral warriors for capitalism, people can use this profound novel to disseminate the conceptual and moral foundations of a free society. They can use the novel to introduce people to the idea of the free market as a moral institution and not solely as a means for efficient production. *Atlas Shrugged* is an excellent means to market these ideas. It is an accessible, interesting, and exciting work that presents an integrated case for freedom and against collectivism. It is a powerful tool to educate, persuade, and convert people to support a just and proper political and economic order that is a true reflection of human nature and the world properly understood.

Rand understood that the American Revolution had been partial and remained unfinished. This understanding was one of her reasons for writing *Atlas Shrugged*. In *Atlas Shrugged*, she demonstrated what was needed to complete the American Revolution. Rand saw that the Founders' political revolution was not accompanied by a much-needed revolution in moral philosophy. According to Mayer (2008, 191–219), the Founders had espoused an anti- individualistic moral code grounded in Judeo-Christian ethics based on altruism. The failure to derive a proper and coherent moral theory of individual rights resulted in the subordination of self-interest to the notions of the public interest and the common good. What was needed was a firm philosophical underpinning to finish the work of the American Revolution. Mayer argues that through the demonstration and explication of a new code of morality in *Atlas Shrugged*, Rand supplies the missing ingredient of the American Revolution.

Onkar Ghate (2007) has called *Atlas Shrugged* America's "second declaration of independence," which has the potential to bring about an intellectual change in the culture. He explains that each individual needs an explicit moral statement of his own self-worth. According to Ghate, the original Declaration of Independence did not fully provide this moral statement due to the mystical Christian altruistic morality revealed in the Founders' writings. *Atlas Shrugged* offers a new conception of the moral ideal and can be viewed as a "declaration of moral independence." Whereas the Founding Fathers taught people not to accept undeserved political serfdom, *Atlas Shrugged* teaches people not to accept an unearned guilt, not for their vices but for their virtues.

The Declaration of Independence was not methodologically committed to individualism—it spoke in collective terms such as the "rights of the people" and "one people." In turn, the Constitution did not define rights, give a principled explanation of them, or assign the government the limited and narrow role of protecting and enforcing their rights (Jackson 2005, 405–44).

From the beginning, Rand intended *Atlas Shrugged* to be a "much more 'social' novel than The Fountainhead" (Rand, journal entry, January 1, 1945, in Harriman 1997, 390). She wanted to write a novel that would mainly be a portrait of the whole focusing on the relationships that make up society (392). Viewing each social problem from a transdisciplinary and multidimensional perspective, Rand dismissed all suggested one-sided solutions as inadequate and fragmentary. According to Sciabarra (2007, 23):

> *Atlas Shrugged* explores these relations in every dimension of human life. It traces the links between political economy and sex, education and art, metaphysics and psychology, money and moral values. It concentrates on the union of spiritual and physical realms and on the specific, concrete means by which certain productive individuals move the world, and by which others live off of their creations. It shows the social importance of the creative act by documenting what would happen if the prime movers, the "men of the mind," go on strike.

Sciabarra continues:

> As I have suggested in my book *Ayn Rand: The Russian Radical*, Rand's mature analytical framework reaches its apex in *Atlas Shrugged*. In this work, it can be said that Rand examines a collapsing social order and its dysfunctional social relations on three distinct analytical levels:
>
> Level 1: The Personal. On this level, Rand explores the mystics' epistemological and psychological assault on reason and the human mind, as well as the altruistic ethical inversion that is required of each individual who submits to the edicts of statist politicians. Such submission entails the "sanction of the victim," without which the whole coercive edifice would be undermined.
>
> Level 2: The Cultural. On this level, Rand explores the utter cultural, educational, and artistic bankruptcy of a society at war with human creativity, as well as the linguistic use of euphemism as a legitimating ideological tool of the politically privileged.
>
> Level 3: The Structural. On this level, Rand is concerned with the devastation of economic and political structures wrought by statist regulations, prohibitions, and controls on production, which foster a tribalist war of all against all.
>
> The novel shows how each of these levels entails relations among entities— Rand's characters, who are individual human beings acting purposefully within their given social context. In Rand's conception, the relations on these three distinct levels of generality—the personal, the cultural, and the structural—can only be abstracted and isolated for the purposes of analysis, but never reified as wholes unto themselves. The levels are both

preconditions and effects of one another. This has vast strategic implications for social praxis, for the techniques of social change: A genuine
revolution against the structural corruptions of politics and economics cannot succeed without a corresponding personal and cultural transformation.
(24–25)

In *Total Freedom*, Sciabarra (2000) cautions us not to reduce the study and
defense of freedom to economics or politics with an inadequate understanding
of the interconnections between the philosophical, the historical, the personal,
and so forth. Sciabarra's message is that libertarians need an effective strategy that recognizes the dynamic relationships between the personal, political,
historical, psychological, ethical, cultural, economic, and so on, if they are
to be successful in their quest for a free society. He explains that attempts
to define and defend a nonaggression axiom in the absence of a broader
philosophical and cultural context are doomed to fail. Typical libertarian
opposition to state intervention is not enough. Libertarians must pay greater
attention to the broader context within which their goals and values can be
realized. The battle against statism is simultaneously structural (political and
economic), cultural (with implications for education, race, sex, language, and
art), and personal (with connections to individuals' tacit moral beliefs, and to
their psycho-epistemological processes). The crusade for freedom is multidimensional and takes place on a variety of levels, with each level influencing
and having reciprocal effects on the other levels.

It is possible to analyze society from different vantage points and on different levels of generality in order to develop an enriched picture of the many
relationships between the various different areas. It cannot just be dictated
from the political realm but must filter through all of the various levels and
areas. Any attempt to understand or change society must entail an analysis of
its interrelations from the perspective of any single aspect.

People need to understand both the necessity for objective conceptual
foundations and the need for cultural prerequisites in the fight for the free
society because some cultures promote, and others undermine, freedom.
Freedom cannot be defended successfully when severed from its broader
requisite conditions. We must attempt to grasp and address all of freedom's
prerequisites and implications. Rand's greatest legacy to mankind, *Atlas
Shrugged*, addresses all of these prerequisites and implications, serves as a
blueprint for the future, and is a potential source for social change. According
to Sciabarra (2007):

As a manifesto for a new radicalism, *Atlas Shrugged* dramatizes the poison-
ous nature of predatory, coercive power upon many social dimensions. Rand's
magnum opus celebrates as antidote a rational and heroic conception of human

freedom—and the unique constellation of psychological, moral, and cultural factors that nourish it. (31)

David Kelley (2007, 40–49) maintains that *Atlas Shrugged* is still relevant and no less important today than when it was published. He is convinced, as so many of us are, that its message will still matter in the coming years. As he puts it:

> *Atlas Shrugged* is a timeless work because it is a philosophical work. Much in the book is dated, to be sure, but not its philosophical core. Atlas is a ringing defense of capitalism as the only social system consistent with human nature and human values. It lays out in dramatic form the worldview on which a capitalist society depends; that human life in this world is the standard of value and morality; that reason is man's means of survival and the glory of his nature; that production, not sacrifice, is the most exalted form of human activity; that producers are the Atlases who carry our world on their shoulders; that thinking, creating, and producing are activities of individuals, who must be free to act on their own judgments, following their own visions; that the individual has the moral right to live for himself and to pursue his own happiness, and does not need to justify his existence by service to God or country. (41)

According to Yaron Brook (2007):

> Scores of business leaders, from CEOs of Fortune 500 companies to young entrepreneurs in Silicon Valley, say that they have derived great spiritual fuel from *Atlas Shrugged*. Many tell me that the novel has motivated them to make the most of their lives, inspiring them to be more ambitious, more productive, and more successful in their work. And many of American's politicians and intellectuals who claim to fight for economic freedom name *Atlas Shrugged* as the book that has most inspired them. I have no doubt that the novel has played a considerable role in discrediting socialism as an ideal and in making discussion of capitalism intellectually legitimate. . . . So while *Atlas Shrugged* has provided millions with inspiration and with some level of appreciation for the virtues of capitalism and the evils of statism, it has not had nearly the influence it could have had, had its underlying ideas gained wider understanding. Though it has changed individual lives, it has not changed the world. But I believe it could—and should. . . . But in order to get there, the novel's full philosophic meaning must be grasped.

ENTREPRENEURS AS CHANGE AGENTS

An entrepreneur's discovery of economic opportunities comes from leading a life of purposeful action. Entrepreneurs discover new ways of creating and combining resources to meet the needs of other people. They recognize and take advantage of previously unexploited profit opportunities. The art of selecting particular projects, while rejecting other ones, characterizes entrepreneurial behavior as essentially moral in nature. An entrepreneur is an active moral agent whose life is interconnected with the lives of others. By pursuing his own self-interest, the entrepreneur creates value for other people.

In addition to being an agent of economic change, the entrepreneur is also an agent of social and cultural change. The economy is an integral part of the culture. The actions of entrepreneurs are open-ended and can be imagined and realized independently of existing social arrangements. They act upon their visions to effect economic changes that can lead to social and cultural changes. Culture is not immutable or homogeneous. It can change and evolve through the introduction of economic innovations in the form of goods and services. The introduction of these innovations can supply the means for others to bring about additional changes in the economy, culture, and society. An innovative idea or product by one entrepreneur not only contributes to the progress of others but can also create conditions permitting people to advance even further. Ideas interact in unexpected ways and are frequently used in unforeseen applications. Innovations build upon innovations in a free society. For example, skyscrapers, automobiles, and farm technology all built upon Carnegie's mass production of inexpensive steel.

In their 2016 book, *The Perfectionist Turn: From Metanorms to Metaethics*, Douglas Den Uyl and Douglas Rasmussen have a chapter titled "The Entrepreneur as Moral Hero." In this chapter, they discuss the creativity of human beings both in producing wealth and in making moral character, two activities that are parts of a flourishing life. Both of these projects require openness and alertness to new opportunities in the midst of changing circumstances across multiple dimensions of one's life. In general, it can be said that both entrepreneurship and ethics apply to virtually any type of human activity. Both entrepreneurship and moral action involve an insightful and evaluative approach to living one's life. The goal of both is integrity of action. Profit-making can be a legitimate form of ethical expression. As acting agents, entrepreneurs should be concerned with the universal ethical question of what type of life one should pursue for oneself. As ethical agents, they must decide how they should change the world to achieve that same goal. Discovery and evaluation are key concepts in both ethics and entrepreneurship. Success in the market can be related to success in living one's life. "Ethical wealth, like economic wealth, will be a function of the degree to which individuals take it upon themselves to produce good lives" (Den Uyl and Rasmussen 2016, 441).

Powell and Candela (2014, 258–72) observe that practical reason and entrepreneurship interact to enable a process of moral discovery. They explain that entrepreneurship is an innate potentiality of all human beings and that practical wisdom is an entrepreneurial moral discovery process, mainly of ourselves, but also of our possible relationships with other people.

The ascent of the sharing economy illustrates how entrepreneurs can create social change, make all parties better off, and improve the allocation of resources in the economy. For example, Uber and Airbnb create new marketplaces, prompt individuals both as consumers and property owners to change their behavior, and provide everyone who has property (i.e., capital) with opportunities to become entrepreneurs. People's views on capitalism, and themselves as capitalists, are likely to change as ideas in the structure of social change are embedded, intertwined, and distributed with other ideas and with new products, services, and marketplaces. As stated by McCloskey (2016, xii): "That is what mattered were two levels of ideas—the ideas of entrepreneurs for the betterments themselves (the electric motor, the airplane, the stock market); and the ideas in society about the businesspeople and their betterments (in a word, liberalism)." Munger and Netle (2013, 1–30) explain that such entrepreneurs (as middlemen) aid people in correcting errors by making exchanges that produce value for both parties. They contend that the profit motive can be consistent with virtue, that entrepreneurship is the habit of right action, and that efforts in facilitating positive-sum exchanges increase the division of labor, thereby expanding both the breadth and quality of resources available to everyone. Such a voluntary process of entrepreneurial discovery is both self-directed and dependent upon particular, specialized, and local knowledge.

Rand (1957) presents entrepreneurs in *Atlas Shrugged* as the moral heroes of our modern world. She has Francisco d'Anconia refer to the American industrialist as "the real maker of wealth, the greatest worker, the highest type of human being" (414). She illustrates this in characters such as Dagny Taggart, Ellis Wyatt, Ken Danagger, Dan Conway, Midas Mulligan, Andrew Stockton, and especially Hank Rearden. Rearden is an inventor, metallurgist, and agent of economic change who takes ten painstaking years to envision, invent, and market a revolutionary metal alloy that is stronger, lighter, and less expensive than steel. Rand's entrepreneurial heroes illustrate the mind's role in producing the practical requirements of human lives. Adapting nature to people's wants and needs creates material abundance for the purpose of surviving, flourishing, and enjoying life on earth.

Israel Kirzner (1973, 1989) has observed that certain people become alerted to the existence of opportunities that have been left unexploited simply because they have not been noticed by others. He explains that the act of discovering an opportunity can be viewed as a unique moral claim that confers property rights to the discoverer. In other words, the discovering entrepreneur is entitled to the profit that he has made.

A scene in *Atlas Shrugged* demonstrates this idea. When James Taggart tells Cherryl Brooks that Hank Rearden does not deserve to own his invention of Rearden Metal because he didn't invent all of the processes that led to its discovery, Cheryl answers: "But the iron ore and all those other things were there all the time. Why didn't anybody else make the Metal, but Mr. Rearden did?" (Rand 1957, 262).

In the real world, the entrepreneur in Silicon Valley can identify with the novel's emphasis on heroic individuals and their work ethic. To some extent, Silicon Valley is consistent with Rand's philosophy as depicted in *Atlas Shrugged*. The creative mindset of the independent innovators, inventors, investors, and founders in Silicon Valley is in accord with ideas found in *Atlas Shrugged*.

THE STRIKE AS A FORCE FOR CHANGE

Rand's epic is a story about a heroic group, led by John Galt, who rebel, struggle against, and defeat the state and its allied looter businessmen. Galt is a creative genius and brilliant inventor of a revolutionary motor powered by static electricity who secretly convinces the thinkers and producers to vanish mysteriously one after the other. He does this by educating and persuading them of the immorality of a culture that expropriates their talents. Galt's strategy is to "stop the motor of the world" by getting the creators to refuse to be exploited any longer by joining his slow-spreading strike and going to live in his secret utopian community founded on the philosophy of freedom. Knowing that the country will ultimately implode, Galt and the strikers will hasten its collapse by withdrawing the "sanction of the victims." At that point, they will return to the outside world. Galt is a rational man of action who pursues his goal despite obstacles, espouses a message of liberation through strategic withdrawal, and founds a community based on voluntarism, individuality, and self-interest.

The striker-heroes use the strategy and tactic of direct action against the state and its looter businessman allies. At the most general level, this occurs when the entrepreneurs, industrialists, inventors, and engineers altogether withdraw from society. By translating the theoretical products of reason into the practical requirements of individuals' lives, these producers, leaders, and wealth creators had been the foundation of the economy. When Galt announces and explains the strike in his radio speech, the American people come to understand the mind's role in material production and the mind's nonnegotiable need of freedom.

As change agents, the novel's heroes also take more specific steps and direct actions. For example, John Galt and Francisco d'Anconia, the strike's primary recruiters, meet with leading industrialists and engineers in order to educate and persuade them to join the strike. Galt's other direct actions include his unwillingness to introduce his revolutionary motor to the market economy and his takeover of public radio broadcasting for his three-hour speech in which he spells out the tenets of his philosophy. Francisco also deliberately destroys his copper mines methodically instead of allowing them to be taken over by the looters. Through this action and by his previous manipulations of the stock market, he contributes to the downfall of looter businessmen who invested in his company as well as to the disintegration of other businesses.

Other heroes employ a direct action in their efforts to change society. Here are a few examples. In an act of defiance in response to the destructive Colorado Directives, Wyatt sets fire to his oil wells and disappears. Banker Midas Mulligan withdraws from society when he is ordered to lend money to an incompetent and undeserving loan applicant. He liquidates his bank holdings, pays off his depositors, converts his wealth into gold, and purchases land that becomes Galt's Gulch, the hideaway of the striking entrepreneurs. An alternative currency, minted by Mulligan, is used in Galt's Gulch. The money supply in this hidden counter-economy consists of gold and silver coins. Then there is the pirate, Ragnar Danneskjöld, who raids state-owned cargo relief ships sent to Europe in order to return to the producers what is rightly their property.

In addition, we witness Ragnar leveling a factory of Orren Boyle's Associated Steel to the ground after giving his employees a ten-minute warning to leave the plant. Then toward the end of the novel, we see Dagny, Francisco, Ragnar, and Rearden invading the SSI in order to free John Galt, who is being held as a prisoner there.

THE EFFECTS OF *ATLAS SHRUGGED* ON READERS

Reading a novel is a private act and an individual undertaking that can have transformative effects. Its unpredictable effects are matters of individual rational discernment and emotional response. Ultimately, the impact of a work of literature depends upon the mind and heart of the particular reader. A meaningful reaction requires partnership between the author and the reader. There is a metadiscursive relationship between the novel and the individual reader. Each person must judge a work of imaginative literature for himself. Some people who read *Atlas Shrugged* will be turned off and others will be inspired by its vision. Of those motivated by the novel, some may embrace Rand's complete rethinking of philosophy based on the advocacy of a particular social system and a particular notion of human existence within a social context. However, it is more likely that the majority of those excited by her ideas will go no further than to embrace the idea of the desirability of free-market capitalism. Then there may be some individuals informed and excited by *Atlas Shrugged* who develop novel perspectives on Rand's ideas or take them into new directions. Ideas beget new ideas.

For some readers, *Atlas Shrugged* will be seen as the embodiment of the grandeur of human achievement in its heroic vision of individuals who do their work well and to the best of their ability, whatever that work and that ability may be. Such readers are likely to experience the joy of seeing other people doing their work extremely well. In Dagny Taggart's words: "The sight of an achievement was the greatest gift that one human being could offer to others" (237).

Many people process information in a narrative form and are therefore strongly influenced by stories. For such individuals, *Atlas Shrugged* can be a memorable and inspirational tale that can elicit an emotional response. It can make a difference to those who read it by providing a place to examine values, ethics, and morals. By projecting themselves into the story, readers can learn a great deal about reality. Through reading *Atlas Shrugged*, people may actually end up changing their own values, ideas, and actions.

Atlas Shrugged offers a total reformulation of philosophy and its function in the various dimensions of an individual's life. Its speeches lay out a new philosophy and moral code and the heroes' actions dramatize that philosophy and moral code. It supplies a number of specific insights into the nature of human beings and the actions required to live a flourishing life as a unique individual. The novel prompts its readers to consider the moral and ethical principles that they accept either explicitly or implicitly. It also disseminates and illustrates the principles and theories underpinning the freedom philosophy and promotes the values of the free-enterprise system in understandable language and depiction. *Atlas Shrugged* offers a vision of capitalism as a moral ideal. This novel has provided a gateway to many people to free-market ideas and will continue to do so. *Atlas Shrugged* can lead readers to discover works by other free-market-oriented philosophers and economists such as John Locke, Adam Smith, Jean-Baptiste Say, Herbert Spencer, Carl Menger, Ludwig von Mises, Murray Rothbard, Friedrich A. Hayek, Milton Friedman, James M. Buchanan, Robert Nozick, Thomas Sowell, and others. It has the power to convert beliefs and to elicit changes in a person's thinking.

A GOOD START, BUT NOT ENOUGH

At the end of *Atlas Shrugged*, the utopian entrepreneurs rescue Galt, the looters are vanquished, and the strikers return to the Valley. There we see Judge

Narragansett correcting contradictions in the Constitution and adding a new clause stating that "Congress shall make no law abridging the freedom of production and trade" (1167–68). Then we hear Galt pronouncing "The road is cleared, we are going back to the world" (1168).

This ending has always puzzled me. I wanted to see more. The strategy of the men of ability going on strike and moving to a remote valley where they could flourish in the absence of state regulation may be a good one, but it is not sufficient or realistic with respect to bringing about a long-term social change in the form of a free-market society. In the real world, attempts at achieving strategic withdrawal include the Free State Project in New Hampshire, Liberland in Europe, and seasteading and homesteading proposals in Central America and Somalia led by Werner Stiefel, Michiel van Notten, and others.

I have often wondered what would happen when Galt and the other heroes return to rebuild society. Yes, Galt explained the strike and the philosophy of life in a three-hour radio speech to the American people. In addition, the American people have seen the men of the mind in the world, their gradual disappearance, the effects of the looters' policies, and the resulting crumbling of the world. But have these events been enough to win their minds and hearts with respect to the need for a free society? The needed individual, cultural, and institutional changes require a lot of time and effort. The story of how the strikers rebuild America would be a great sequel to *Atlas Shrugged*, depicting them struggling through obstacles and opposition.

In the real world, there are a number of procedural and practical institutional steps that need to be taken in a disjointed incremental manner in order to move toward a society of laissez-faire capitalism. These steps include, but are not limited to, (1) privatizing government property, programs, and functions such as education; (2) reducing and ultimately abolishing income and inheritance taxes; (3) establishing freedom of production and trade by abolishing labor, licensure, antitrust, zoning, and other laws and regulations; (4) abolishing the central bank and instituting gold as money; (5) eliminating social security, medicare, public welfare, and public hospitals; (6) separating government and sciences because force and mind are not compatible; (7) ending business subsidies; (8) allowing free trade by eliminating tariffs, quotas, and other protectionist measures; (9) ceasing to be the world's policemen while maintaining a strong defensive military; and (10) eliminating government agencies and most cabinet departments, leaving a minimal state sufficient to protect contractual and property rights and provide for American's defense. Many intermediate, transitional, and incremental steps are needed to reach such a destination.

The institutions of a society can be affected by the ideas of the majority of the people in that society. If the goal is to create a capitalistic society, then it is important to get people to change their ideas. This will help to create a culture of liberty that would serve as a foundation for a free society. Intellectual, attitudinal, and behavioral changes are a function of culture and vice versa. There is a need to study the cognitive, cultural, and nonrational factors that affect people's attitudes and actions with respect to political, economic, and moral-cultural freedom. The key to going from our current interventionist political and economic system to a society of laissez-faire capitalism is long-term education aimed at rational persuasion and conversion.

As discussed by Sciabarra ([1995] 2013, 2000, 2007), attaining social change is a complex, nonlinear, interlocking process that occurs at the levels of (1) the perspectives of the cognitive, psychological, and moral dimensions of individual human beings; (2) the cultural traditions and ideologies that prevail in society; and (3) the political structures that define and protect individual rights and that make and enforce laws, regulations, taxation, and so on. These three levels are factors of social influence and change and they each have reciprocal effects on one another. Heterogeneous individual agents primarily working at different levels frequently interact when pursuing their activities. Respect for one another's metanormative rights and adherence to the rules of the game are crucial ingredients in this social change process.

Prospects for one monumental leap to a free-market society are not realistic. Many intermediate, transitional, and incremental steps are needed. It is necessary to disseminate the principles and theories of the freedom philosophy and promote the values of the free-enterprise system in understandable nontechnical terms in order to attain a shift of conventional wisdom. The institutions of any society stem from the ideas of the majority of the people in that society. It is important to get influential people to change their ideas. These ideas will then filter throughout society. The ideas of original thinkers like Rand need to be accepted by intellectuals and popularizers such as journalists, teachers, radio and TV commentators, writers, and so forth. In order to win the hearts and minds of a significant portion of the population, a multipronged educational approach is needed. This will require a long-time horizon and involves academic institutions, traditional and social media, popular culture, literature, and so on.

There are a great many coercive challenges, encroachments, and constraints that have inhibited the establishment of a society based on the natural liberty of the individual and the realities of the human condition. By nature, these barriers tend to be philosophical, economic, and political. Some of the strongest attacks on, and impediments to, a free society include collectivist philosophies, cultural relativism, communitarianism, environmentalism, public education, taxation, protectionism, antitrust laws, government regulation, and monetary inflation. These bureaucratic and socialistic ideologies and schemes tend to stem from various sources such as true human compassion, envy, the insecurity of people who want protection from life's uncertainties, categorical "solutions" proposed to solve social problems, idealism, and the tendency to think only of intended, primary, and immediate results while ignoring unintended, ancillary, and long-term ones.

Activists for freedom will not accomplish much unless they work to bring about a cultural renaissance to countermand the trends in today's culture that threaten individual liberty. They will have a difficult time making progress toward their goal of a free society unless they consider and analyze particular cultural, institutional, social, psycho-epistemological, and historical conditions of freedom and social order. It is essential for them to discover how these conditions can be changed in order to move toward the establishment of a free society. It will be easier to establish a minimal state in a culture in which people prize freedom, objectivity, responsibility, achievement, and personal happiness. To do so, they will need to evaluate various cultures and work to change individuals' cultural assumptions. There are reciprocal causes and effects between culture and the attitudinal and behavioral changes of individuals. It is essential for change agents to advance rational ideas throughout all aspects of our culture—education, commerce, science, art and music, media, politics, and so on. They need to promote a culture of reason and individualism and a sense of life oriented to production, innovation, material prosperity, great art and music, self-responsibility, happiness, and others. To reach their goal will require many small but meaningful changes in our culture.

There is a crucial need for cultural intellectuals who can help spread the philosophy of freedom to the general public. There are currently very few libertarians in the media and academia who advocate a free society. People must work to lessen the prevalent bias against capitalism in newspapers, magazines, novels, plays, television programs, philosophy and history books, and so on. For years, the media have consistently and persistently attacked capitalism, commerce, and the premises of classical liberalism. Change agents must cultivate a new generation of artists and reporters who will help to disseminate the ideas of liberty.

Individuals and private mediating institutions must take the lead in promoting a culture of liberty and virtue in which reason and independent thinking are highly valued. This can be done by example and through moral discourse, education, art and literature, praise and blame, and so on. All of this must be done without contradicting the nonaggression principle, which provides a metanormative foundational floor of basic morality for individual lives and societies.

A classical liberal social order allows people to be free to pursue their own ends and to associate with those they choose. Individuals are able to be self-directed and to express their diverse interests, values, and life goals once their rights are secured and protected. The desirability, legitimation, or justification of a minimal state that protects and secures freedom and diversity does not depend upon the existence of a particular type of moral-cultural order. Such a political order is objectively based on the nature of human beings who need a protected moral sphere for the possibility of self-directedness. It follows that a legitimate political order is not concerned with the culture, morals, values, and virtues of individuals. A political philosophy is not a philosophy of life.

Although a metanormative political order is not necessarily coincidental with, or dependent upon, a particular moral-cultural system, the establishment and support of such a political order would be easier to bring about if there were widely shared beliefs and articulations with respect to its underpinning political principles as well as with certain moral principles. It follows that people need to work as individuals, and in concert with others in civil society, to build a freedom-friendly culture of moral and virtuous people who strive to create a good life, to flourish, and to be happy.

ATLAS SHRUGGED IN SOCIAL MOVEMENTS

People join social movements because they want to manifest their beliefs in the world along with others who hold the same ideas. There are some social movements that have taken Rand's ideas as expressed in *Atlas Shrugged* and adapted or adopted them into, or as, their own philosophy. To some degree, *Atlas Shrugged* has inspired the Tea Party movement. Signs quoting characters from *Atlas Shrugged*, especially John Galt, proliferate at Tea Party rallies and protests. Tea Partiers resonate with the novel's messages of anti-big government, confidence in individual liberty, and the ethic of work and self-responsibility.

As a social movement, Objectivism is most strongly represented today by such organizations as the Ayn Rand Institute and the Atlas Society. The members of both of these organizations believe that *Atlas Shrugged* is a book that can aid in changing the world. Both organizations use Rand's novel in their efforts to bring about a cultural renaissance that will revise the anti-freedom, anti-reason, anti-individualist, and anti-capitalist concepts in modern culture. Whereas Objectivism is a closed system for the Ayn Rand Institute, it is an open system for The Atlas Society in which its ideas are susceptible to extension by individuals who accept its basic premises.

In 2017, the Ayn Rand Institute, under the general rubric of Objectivist Movement 2.0, began to place a greater emphasis on community building and cultural change. The idea is to bring together professional intellectuals—that is, scholars and advanced students—to discuss their work, to plan collaborative projects, and to exhibit and to increase the energy of the Objectivist community. Workshops brought together professional individuals from a variety of areas including philosophy, economics, business, education, science, psychology, law, and so on. In addition, the Ayn Rand Institute has held worldwide essay contests for students on Rand's novels (including *Atlas Shrugged*) for more than thirty years.

The Atlas Society, in keeping with its emphasis on reaching the next generation of leaders, has begun a new partnership with Turning Point USA. The Atlas Society and Turning Point screened the three *Atlas Shrugged* films on more than seventy-seven campuses in early 2017. The goal is to use *Atlas Shrugged* to introduce the next generation of citizens to the moral foundations of the free market. The Atlas Society is also working with Students for Liberty to provide an introductory course on Objectivism to their large following.

Atlas Shrugged is now being taught in colleges and universities in a variety of courses. These inroads have been largely made due to the tireless efforts of one man. Not only did John Allison, former president and CEO of BB&T Bank, require his managers to read *Atlas Shrugged*, he also funded nearly seventy programs at institutions of higher learning throughout the United States, which were required to use *Atlas Shrugged* in the classroom to study the moral foundations of capitalism and commerce. This is his strategy to spread free-market principles on U.S. campuses. This change agent is a man with a purpose. He is on a crusade to counteract the anti-capitalist orthodoxy and culture that are prevalent at most universities.

BB&T-funded institutions have offered a variety of classes in economics, the moral foundations of capitalism, business ethics, and so on. In addition, many have established centers or institutes, funded faculty chairs or professorships, held speaker's series, funded faculty research, and established Ayn Rand or capitalism reading rooms.

It is clear that Ayn Rand's *magnum opus Atlas Shrugged* is making advances into education and academia. It has already had various cultural effects that can only serve as the fuel for genuine institutional and social change.

ACKNOWLEDGMENTS

I wish to thank several people for their help in my efforts to clarify the ideas that appear in this article. I am extremely grateful to the following individuals for their useful comments, observations, and suggestions: Andrew Bernstein, Samuel Bostaph, Rosolino Candela, Emily Chamlee-Wright, Stephen Cox, Douglas J. Den Uyl, Mimi Gladstein, Carl Horner, Felix Livingston, Spencer MacCallum, Karen Michalson, Virginia Murr, Douglas B. Rasmussen, Richard M. Salsman, and Gennady Stolyarov II.

NOTES

This chapter was first published in The *Journal of Ayn Rand Studies* 17, no. 2 (December 2017): 285–305. This article is used by permission of The Pennsylvania State University Press.

REFERENCES

Brook, Yaron. 2007. "The Influence of *Atlas Shrugged.*" *Objectivism and Today's Issues* (9 October). Online at: https://ari.aynrand.org/issues/culture-and-society/more/The-Influence-of-Atlas-Shrugged.
Cowen, Tyler. 2008. "Is the Novel a Model?" In *The Street Porter and the Philosopher: Conversations on Analytical Egalitarianism*, 319–37, edited by S. J. Pert and D. M. Levy. Ann Arbor: University of Michigan.
Den Uyl, Douglas J., and Douglas B. Rasmussen. 2016. *The Perfectionist Turn: From Metanorms to Metaethics*. Edinburgh: Edinburgh University Press.
Fein, Ester B. 1991. "Book Notes." *New York Times* (20 November).
Ghate, Onkar. 2007. *Atlas Shrugged: America's Second Declaration of Independence*. Two Audio Lectures. New Milford, Connecticut: Second Renaissance Books.
Harriman, David, ed. 1997. *Journals of Ayn Rand*. New York: Dutton.
Jackson, Candice E. 2005. "Our Unethical Constitution." *The Journal of Ayn Rand Studies* 6, no. 2 (Spring): 404–45.
Katz, Elihu, Martin L. Levin, and Herbert Hamilton. 1963. "Traditions of Research on the Diffusion of Innovation." *American Sociological Review* 28, no. 2: 237–52.
Kelley, David. 2007. "A Philosophy for the 21st Century." *The New Individualist* (October): 40–49.
Kirzner, Israel. 1973. *Competition and Entrepreneurship*. Chicago: University of Chicago Press.
———. 1989. *Discovery, Capitalism, and Distributive Justice*. Oxford: Basil Blackwell.
Lippitt, Gordon. 1973. *Visualizing Change: Model Building and the Change Process*. Fairfax, Virginia: NTL Learning Resource Corporation.
Mayer, David N. 2008. "Completing the American Revolution: The Significance of Ayn Rand's *Atlas Shrugged* at its Fiftieth Anniversary." *The Journal of Ayn Rand Studies* 9, no. 2 (Spring): 191–219.
McCloskey, Deirdre N. 2016. *Bourgeois Equality: How Ideas, Not Capital or Institutions, Enriched the World*. Chicago: University of Chicago Press.
Munger, Michael C., and Juan Pablo Couyoumdjian Netle. 2013. "The "Character" of Profit and Loss: Entrepreneurial Virtues." Duke PPE Working Paper 13, 0306.
Ostlund, Lyman E. 1974. "Perceived Innovation Attributes as Predictors of Innovativeness." *Journal of Consumer Research* 1, no. 2 (September): 23–29.
Powell, Benjamin, and Rosolino Candela. 2014. "Markets as Processes of Moral Discovery." *Studies in Emergent Order* 7: 258–72.
Rand, Ayn. 1957. *Atlas Shrugged*. New York. New American Library.

————. 1971. *The Romantic Manifesto*. New York: Signet.

Rogers, Everett M. 1973. *Communication Strategies for Family Planning*. New York: Free Press.

Rogers, Everett M., and F. Floyd Shoemaker. 1971. *Communication of Innovations: A Cross-Cultural Approach*. New York: Free Press.

Sciabarra, Chris Matthew. [1995] 2013. *Ayn Rand: The Russian Radical*. Second Edition. University Park: Pennsylvania State University Press.

————. 2000. *Total Freedom: Toward a Dialectical Libertarianism*. University Park: Pennsylvania State University Press.

————. 2007. "*Atlas Shrugged*: Manifesto for a New Radicalism." In *Ayn Rand's "Atlas Shrugged": A Philosophical and Literary Companion*, 23–32, edited by Edward W. Younkins. Aldershot: Ashgate.

Zaltman, Gerald, and Melanie Wallendorf. 1983. *Consumer Behavior*. New York: John Wiley.

Zaltman, Gerald, and Robert Duncan. 1977. *Strategies for Planned Change*. New York: John Wiley.

Appendix

Ayn Rand's Philosophy of Objectivism

Capitalism demands the best of every man—his rationality—and rewards him accordingly. It leaves every man free to choose the work he likes, to specialize in it, to trade his product for the products of others, and to go as far on the road of achievement as his ability and ambition will carry him. His success depends on the objective value of his work and on the rationality of those who recognize that value. When men are free to trade, with reason and reality as their only arbiter, when no man may use physical force to extort the consent of another, it is the best product and the best judgment that win in every field of human endeavor, and raise the standard of living—and thought—ever higher for all those who take part in mankind's productive activity.

—Ayn Rand

Ayn Rand (1905–1982), the best-selling novelist and world-famous philosopher, developed a unique philosophical system called Objectivism, which has affected many lives over the last half century. This chapter represents an introduction to her systematic vision by presenting her essential ideas in a logical, accessible manner. This should contribute toward the appreciation of Rand's profoundly original philosophical system.

The specific purpose of this appendix is to introduce, summarize, logically rearrange, and clarify through rewording the ideas distributed throughout her books, essays, lectures, and novels (especially *Atlas Shrugged*), and as authoritatively described and systematically explained in Leonard Peikoff's monumental *Objectivism: The Philosophy of Ayn Rand*. Another fine but shorter source of much the same material as found in Peikoff's book is Allan Gotthelf's *On Ayn Rand*. Written from the viewpoint of a generalist in economics, philosophy, and the social sciences, this chapter is meant to provide a background for readers who wish to study specialized aspects of Rand's philosophy in greater detail.

Metaphysics is the subdivision of philosophy that studies the nature of the universe as a totality. Epistemology is concerned with the relationship between a man's mind (i.e., his consciousness) and reality (i.e., the nature of the universe) and with the operation of reason. In other words, epistemology investigates the fundamental nature of knowledge, including its sources and validation. One's theory of knowledge necessarily includes a theory of concepts, and one's theory of concepts determines one's theory or concept of value (and ethics). The key to understanding ethics is in the concept of value and thus ultimately is located in epistemology and metaphysics. The purpose of this chapter is to delineate the inextricable and well-argued linkages between the various components of Ayn Rand's philosophy of Objectivism. Rand's philosophy is a systematic and integrated unity, with every part depending upon every other part.

THE ESSENCE OF OBJECTIVISM

Hierarchically, philosophy, including its metaphysical, epistemological, and ethical dimensions, precedes and determines politics, which, in turn, precedes and determines economics. Rand bases her metaphysics on the idea that reality is objective and absolute. Epistemologically, the Objectivist view is that man's mind is competent to achieve objectively valid knowledge of that which exists. Rand's moral theory of self-interest is derived from man's nature as a rational being and end in himself, recognizes man's right to think and act according to his freely chosen principles, and reflects a man's potential to be the best person he can be in the context of his facticity. This leads to the notion of the complete separation of "political power" and "economic power"—the proper government should have no economic favors to convey. The role of the government is, thus, to "protect man's rights" through the use of force, but "only in retaliation and only against those who initiate its use." "Capitalism," the resulting economic system, "is based on the recognition of individual rights, including property rights, in which all property is privately owned." For Rand, capitalism, the system of laissez-faire, is the only moral system.

METAPHYSICS

Metaphysics is the first philosophical branch of knowledge. At the metaphysical level, Rand's Objectivism begins with "axioms"—fundamental truths or irreducible primaries that are self-evident by means of direct perception, the basis for all further knowledge, and undeniable without self-contradiction. Axioms cannot be reduced to other facts or broken down into component parts. They require no proofs or explanations. Objectivism's three basic philosophical axioms are "existence," "consciousness," and "identity"—presuppositions of every concept and every statement.

"Existence exists" and encompasses everything, including all states of consciousness. The world exists independently of the mind and is there to be discovered by the mind. In order to be conscious, we must be conscious of something. There can be no consciousness if nothing exists. Consciousness, "the faculty of perceiving that which exists," is the ability to discover, rather than to create, objects. Consciousness, a relational concept, presupposes the existence of something external to consciousness, something to be aware of. Initially, we become aware of something outside of our consciousness, and then we become aware of our consciousness by contemplating on the process through which we became aware.

The axiom of identity says that to be is to be "something" in particular. Identity means that a thing is "this" rather than "that." What exists are "entities" and entities have identity. The identity of an entity is the total of its features, including its potentialities for change. To have identity is to have specific characteristics and to act in specific ways. What an entity can do depends on what it is. A thing must be something and only what it is. In order for knowledge to exist, there must be something to know (existence), someone to know it (consciousness), and something to know about it (identity). That existence exists implies that entities of certain types exist and that a person is capable of perceiving that entities of various types exist. "Existence is identity" and "consciousness is identification."

All actions are caused by "entities." Rand connects "causality" to the law of identity and finds necessity in the nature of the entity involved in the causal process. She explains that "the law of causality is the law of identity applied to action" and that "the nature of an action is caused and determined by the natures of the entities that act; a thing cannot act in contradiction to its nature."

The concept of entity is presupposed by all subsequent human thinking because entities comprise the content of the world men perceive. Rand contends that the universe is not caused, but simply is, and that "cause and effect . . . is a universal law of reality." Knowledge of causality involves apprehending the relationship between the nature of an entity and its method of action.

Rand explains that the "metaphysically given (i.e., any fact inherent in existence apart from the human action) is absolute" and simply is. The metaphysically given includes scientific laws and events taking place outside of the control of men. The metaphysically given must be accepted and cannot be changed.

She explains, however, that man has the ability to adapt nature to meet his requirements. Man can creatively rearrange the combination of nature's elements by enacting the required cause, the one necessitated by the immutable laws of existence. The "man-made" includes any object, institution, procedure, or rule of conduct created by man. Man-made facts are products of choice and can be evaluated and judged and then "accepted or rejected and changed when necessary."

Rand explains that the existence of consciousness is obvious and fundamental, that consciousness is a characteristic of particular living creatures, that consciousness has causal ability, and that there is a basic consonance between mind and body. To deny consciousness is self-refuting. That consciousness can direct action is evident through extrospection (i.e., observation) and introspection. A man's consciousness is integrated with his body and is subject to his free will control. Rand contends that there is only one reality (not two opposing ones), that "consciousness is the faculty of awareness" (rather than of creation), and that the effects of consciousness are the caused outcomes of the interplay between a conscious person and the world.

EPISTEMOLOGY

Epistemology refers to the nature and starting point of knowledge, to the character and correct exercise of reason, to reason's connection to the senses and perception, to the possibility of other origins of knowledge, and to the constitution and attainability of certainty. Rand explains that reason is man's cognitive faculty for organizing perceptual data in conceptual terms through the use of the principles of logic. Knowledge exists when a person approaches the facts of reality through either perceptual observation or conceptualization.

Epistemology exists because man is a limited fallible being who learns in disjointed incremental steps and who therefore requires a proper procedure to acquire the knowledge necessary to act, survive, and flourish. A man does not have innate knowledge or instincts that will automatically and unerringly promote his well-being. He does not inevitably know what will help or hinder his life. He therefore needs to know how to acquire reliable and objective knowledge of reality. A man has to gain such knowledge in order to live. A person can only know from within the context of a human way of knowing. Because human beings are "neither infallible nor omniscient," all knowledge is contextual in nature.

"Sense perception" is man's initial and direct form of recognition of that which exists (i.e., of entities, including their characteristics, associations, and actions). Senses provide man with the start of the cognitive process. The senses neither err nor deceive a man. The senses do not judge, identify, or interpret, but simply respond to stimuli and report or present a "something" to one's consciousness. The evidence provided by the senses is an absolute, but a man must learn to use his mind to properly understand it. The task of identification belongs to reason operating with concepts. Man's senses only inform him that something is, but what it is must be learned by the mind which must discover the nature, the causes, the full context of his sensory material, and so on. It is only at the conceptual level, with respect to the "what," that the possibility of error occurs. At the conceptual level, awareness can lead to mistaken judgments about what we perceive. Conceptualization entails an interpretation that may differ from reality. However, man's reason can be used to correct wrong judgments and expand one's knowledge of the world.

A man's senses react to the "full context" of the facts. Sense perceptions are valid in that they are perceptions of entities which exist. Sensations are caused by objects in reality and by a person's organs of perception. It is the purpose of the mind to analyze the perceptual evidence and to identify the nature of what is and the causes in effect.

A difference in sensory form among various perceivers is merely a difference in the form of perceiving the same object in reality. As long as a person perceives the underlying objects and relationships in reality in some form, the rest is the mind's work, not the work of the senses.

Any perceptual mechanism is limited. It follows that the object as perceived is the result of an interaction between external entities and a person's limited perceptual apparatus. Forms of perceptions are circumscribed by a person's physical abilities to receive information interacting with external objects in connection with the laws of causality. In other words, perceptual awareness is the product of a causal interaction between sense organs and entities.

Perceptual awareness marks the beginning of human knowledge. In order to understand the world in a conceptual manner, man must integrate his percepts into concepts. A "concept" integrates and condenses a number of percepts into a single mental whole. Although based on sensory percepts, human knowledge, being conceptual in nature, can depart from reality. The mind is not infallible nor automatic and can distort and be mistaken. A man can only obtain knowledge if he adheres to certain methods of cognition. The validity of man's knowledge depends upon the validity of his concepts.

Whereas concepts are abstractions (i.e., universals), everything that man apprehends is specific and concrete. "Concept formation" is based on the recognition of "similarity" among the existents being conceptualized. Rand explains that an individual perceptually discriminates and distinguishes specific entities from their background and from one another. A person then groups objects according to their similarities, viewing each of them as a "unit." He then integrates a grouping of units into a distinct mental entity called a concept. "The ability to perceive entities or units is man's distinctive method of cognition" and the gateway to the conceptual level of man's consciousness. According to Rand, "a concept is a mental integration of two or more units which are isolated according to one or more characteristics and united by a specific definition." A definition is the condensation of a large body of observations.

Whereas a concept is assigned precise identity through the use of a definition, the integration (i.e., the concept) itself is kept in mind by referring to it by a perceptual concrete (i.e., a "word"). Words are concrete audiovisual representations of abstractions called concepts. "Words transfer concepts into (mental) entities" whenever definitions give them identity. Language makes this type of integration possible.

Concept formation is largely a mathematical process. There is a "connection between measurement and conceptualization." Similarity, an implicit form of measurement "is the relationship between two or more existents which possess the same characteristics but in different measure or degree." The mental process of concept formation consists in retaining the characteristics but omitting their measurements. The "relevant measurement" of a particular attribute "must exist in some quantity but may exist in any quantity." The "measurements exist, but they are not specified." A concept is a mental integration of units possessing the same differentiating characteristics with their specific measurements omitted.

Rand explains that a "conceptual common denominator" is made up of the attributes reducible to a unit of measurement by which a person distinguishes two or more existents from other existents possessing the attributes. In other words, the comprehension of similarity and difference is necessary for conceptualization.

Perceptual data lead to "first-level concepts." In turn, higher-level concepts are formed as "abstractions from abstractions" (i.e., from abstractions and subclassifications of previously formed concepts). Concepts differ from each other not only with regard to their referents but also in their distances from the perceptual level. Knowledge is hierarchical with respect to the order of concept formation. It consists of a set of concepts and conclusions ranked in order of logical dependence upon one another.

The last step in concept formation is "definition." A definition identifies a concept's units by particularizing their fundamental attributes. "A definition is a statement that identifies the nature of the units subsumed under a concept." A definition differentiates a given concept from all others and keeps its units distinguished in a person's mind from all other existents. The differentiation must be limited to the essential characteristics. Rand employs

Aristotle's "rule of fundamentality" when she explains that the essential characteristic is the one that is responsible for, and therefore can explain, the greatest number of the unit's other distinguishing characteristics.

She explains that concepts are instruments to save space and time and to attain "unit-economy" through the condensation of data. Concepts have a metaphysical basis since consciousness is the ability of comprehending that which exists. Concepts result from a particular type of relationship between consciousness and existence.

Definitions are statements of factual data as compressed by a human consciousness. Definitions involve the condensation of a multitude of observations of similarity and difference relationships. They are also "contextual" because they partly rely upon the definer's context of knowledge. A new or revised definition does not invalidate the objective content of the old definition. It simply encompasses the requirements of an expanding cognitive context—the sum of cognitive elements conditioning an item to knowledge. Full context is the sum of available knowledge.

According to Rand, the essential characteristics of a concept are epistemological (i.e., contextual and relational) rather than metaphysical. Rand explains that concepts are neither intrinsic abstract entities existing independently of a person's mind nor are they nominal products of a person's consciousness, unrelated to reality. Concepts are epistemologically "objective" in that they are produced by man's consciousness in accordance with the facts of reality. Concepts are mental integrations of factual data. They are "the products of a cognitive method of classification whose processes must be performed by a human being, but whose content is dictated by reality." For Rand, essences are epistemological instead of metaphysical.

Rand contends that, although concepts and definitions are in one's mind, they are not arbitrary because they reflect reality, which is objective. Both consciousness in metaphysics and concepts in epistemology are real and part of ordinary existence—the mind is part of reality. She views concepts as "open-ended constructs" which subsume all information about their referents, including the information not yet discerned. New facts and discoveries expand or extend a person's concepts, but they do not overthrow or invalidate them. Concepts must conform to the facts of reality.

In order to be objective in one's conceptual endeavors, a human being must fully adhere to reality by applying certain methodological rules based on facts and proper for man's form of cognition. For man, a being with rational consciousness, the appropriate method for conforming to objective reality is "reason" and "logic." In order to survive, man needs knowledge, and reason is his tool of knowledge.

Rand observes that human knowledge is limited and that humans are beings of bounded knowledge. It is because of this constraint that it is imperative for a man to identify the cognitive context of his analysis and conclusions. She points out that contextualism does not mean relativism and that context is what makes a properly specified conclusion objective. Certainty is a contextual evaluation.

Where do emotions fit in the Objectivist world? According to Rand, an emotion is an "automatic response" to a situation based on a person's perception, identification, and evaluation of the situation. Emotions are states of consciousness with bodily accompaniments and intellectual causes. Different from sensations, emotions are caused by what a person thinks. Emotions are the result of a man's value premises which stem from his thinking about, and in reaction to, situations he has met in life. After a person has made a range of value judgments, he makes them automatic. Present in one's unconscious, value judgments affect man's evaluative and affective experiences. Emotions are reactions to a person's perceptions and are the automatic results of a mind's previous conclusions. "Emotions are not tools of cognition"—they are not a substitute for reason. Truth cannot be attained through one's feelings. However, emotions do play a key role in one's life. They do provide the means for enjoying life. A person could not achieve happiness without them.

Rand contends that people are born both conceptually (i.e., cognitively) and emotionally "tabula rasa." For her, emotions are dependent phenomena and are the automatic products of man's value judgments. Rand believes that reason must "program" emotions properly if a person is to achieve happiness. She sees man with no inborn instincts and views reason as a person's only guide to knowledge. According to Rand, people do not have inborn emotions, temperaments, desires, personality characteristics, or ingrained behavior of any kind. She says that men's brains are not hardwired and that all human behavior is learned behavior.

ETHICS

Objectivism's ethical system rests upon the claim to have derived the "ought" from the "is." The defense of this claim starts by inquiring about the facts of existence and man's nature that result in value—"that which one acts to gain and/or keep." The concept of value "presupposes an entity capable of acting to attain a goal in the face of an alternative. Where no alternative exists, no goals and therefore no values are possible." The one "basic alternative" in the world is "existence vs. nonexistence." Since "the existence of inanimate matter is unconditional," "it is only a living organism that faces a constant alternative: the issue of life or death." Inanimate matter may change forms, but it cannot go out of existence. When a living organism dies, however, its basic physical elements remain, but its life ceases to exist. Life, "a process of self-sustaining and self-generated action," "makes the concept of 'Value' meaningful." "An organism's life is its standard of value." Whatever advances its life is good and that which endangers it is evil.

The nature of a living entity determines what it ought to do. All living entities, with the exception of man, are determined by their nature to undertake automatically the actions necessary to sustain their survival. Man, like an animal or a plant, must act in order to live and must gain the values that his life requires. Man's distinctive nature, however, is that he has no automatic means of survival. Man does not function by automatic sensory or chemical reactions. "Thinking," the process of abstraction and conceptualization, is necessary for man's survival. Thinking, man's basic virtue, is exercised "by choice"—"man is a being of volitional consciousness." Reason, "the faculty that perceives, identifies, and integrates the material provided by the senses," does not work automatically. Man is free to think or not to think. The tool of thought is logic—"the art of noncontradictory identification."

According to Rand, man has no innate knowledge and, therefore, must determine through thought the goals, actions, and values upon which his life depends. He must discover what will further his own unique and precious individual human life and what will harm it. Refusal to recognize and act according to the facts of reality will result in his destruction. The Objectivist view is that the senses enable man to perceive reality, that knowledge can only be gained through the senses, and that the senses are able to provide objectively valid knowledge of reality.

For man to survive, he must discern the "principles" of action necessary to direct him in his relationships with other men and with nature. Man's need for these principles is his need for a "code of morality." Men are essentially independent beings with free wills; therefore, it is up to each individual to choose his code of values using the standard that is required for the life of a human being. If "life as a man" is one's purpose, he has the right to live as a rational being. To live, man must think, act, and create the values his life requires.

Rand holds that morality (and ethics) depend upon a person's "pre-moral" choice to live. "To live is his basic act of choice. If he chooses to live, a rational ethics will tell him what principles of action are required to implement his choice."

Rand explains that moral values are neither subjective constructs nor intrinsic features of morality, but rather are objective. "The good is neither an attribute of things in themselves nor of a man's emotional state, but an evaluation made of the facts of reality by man's consciousness according to a rational standard of value." When one attributes moral value to something, he must address the questions of "to whom" and "for what." If something is a value, it must have a positive relationship to the end of a particular individual's life. Value is a function of the interaction between what is deemed valuable and the person to whom it is valuable. Value is neither totally internal nor completely external but is a function of a specific connection between external objects and an individual's ends.

Rand states that values reflect facts as evaluated by persons with respect to the goal of living. Whether or not a given object is a value depends upon its relationship to the end of a person's life. Life's "conditionality" is the basis of moral value. The thing in question must have certain attributes in order to further an individual's life, and the individual must seek his life, for that object to be valuable. The objectivity of value derives from the fact that particular kinds of action tend to promote human life. A specific object's value is a function of the factual relation between the object and a particular person's life. The valid attribution of value reflects a factual relationship. Rand's theory of objective value is both functional (i.e., directed toward certain ends) and naturalistic. It is naturalistic because values stem from certain facts about the nature of human life.

The requirements of a man's survival are determined by reality and the good is an aspect of reality that has a positive relationship to a man's life. An object's value thus depends on what the object is and on the way in which it affects a particular person. It follows that a variety of different things can be objectively valuable to different persons.

From an epistemological perspective, it is individuals who are objective (or are not objective) with respect to their judgments regarding value. A value's objectivity reflects the reality that values are the conclusions of a person's "volitional consciousness" and that individuals can be correct or can be mistaken in their judgments and choices. An authentic value must derive from a life-affirming relationship to a human being and must exist in a correct connection to his consciousness. A man's consciousness and elements of the external world must connect in order to properly judge particular things as objectively valuable.

For Rand, the designation, objective, refers to both the functioning of the cognitive process and to the output of that process when it is properly performed. A man's consciousness can acquire objective knowledge of reality by employing the proper means of reason in accordance with the rules of logic. When the mind conforms to mind-independent reality, the cognitive process being followed can be termed objective. In turn, when a correct cognitive process has been followed, it can be said that the output (i.e., the conclusion reached) of that process is objective.

Rand explains that all abstractions stem from facts, including the abstraction "value." All ideas, including the idea of value, are features of reality as they pertain to individuals. Values are metaphysically objective when their propriety and attainment require conformity to reality and are epistemologically objective when they are discovered via objective conceptual processes.

Rand asks what fact or facts of reality give rise to the concept of value. She reasons that there must be something in perceptual reality that results in the concept value. She argues that it is only from observing other living things (and one's self introspectively) in the pursuit of their own lives that a person can perceive the referents of the term "value." For example, people act to attain various material and other goods and determine their choices by reference to various goals, ends, standards, or principles.

For Rand, the concept of value depends upon and is derived from the antecedent concept of life. It is life that entails the possibility of something being good or bad for it. The normative aspect of reality arises with the appearance of life.

The fundamental fact of reality that gives rise to the concept of value is that living beings have to attain certain ends in order to sustain their lives. The facts regarding what enhances or hinders life are objective, founded on the facts of reality, and grounded in cognition. This should not be surprising because people do think, argue, and act as if normative issues can be decided by considering the facts of a situation.

Rand explains that the key to understanding ethics is found in the concept of value—it is thus located in epistemology. Her revolutionary theory of concepts is what directly leads her to innovations in the fields of value theory and ethics and moral philosophy.

Rand's theories of concepts, values, and ethics accurately reflect man's epistemic nature. Objectivism endorses a theory of objective value and an ethics that reflects the primacy of existence. Because Rand identifies and comprehends the epistemological nature of concepts and the nature of the concept of value itself, it is possible for us to understand them and to explain to others the logical steps that are included in their formulation.

Without self-value, no other values are possible. Self-value has to be earned by thinking. Morality, a practical, selfish necessity, requires the use of man's rational faculty and the freedom to act on his judgments. A code of values accepted by rational choice is a code of morality—choice is the foundation of virtue. "Happiness is the state of consciousness which proceeds from the achievement of one's values."

Because men are creatures who think and act according to principles, a doctrine of rights ensures that an individual's choice to live by those principles is not violated by other human beings. For Rand, all individuals possess the same rights to freely pursue their own goals. Since a free man chooses his own actions, he can be held responsible for them.

Ayn Rand defines value as "that which one acts to gain and/or keep." A value is an object of goal-directed action. In this sense, we can say that everyone pursues values. The term "value" thus can refer in a descriptive sense to what is observable. We see people going after things. Initially, we do not consider whether or not people are choosing properly when they pursue their values. As children, we first get the idea of value implicitly from observation and introspection. We then move from an initial descriptive idea of value toward a normative idea of value that includes the notion that a real value serves one's life.

Each derivative value exists in a value chain or network in which every value (except for the ultimate value) leads to other values and thus serves both as an end and as a means to other values. A biological ends-means process leads to the ultimate end of the chain, which, for a living entity, is its life. For a human individual, the end is survival and happiness, and the means are values and virtues that serve that end. Values and virtues are common to, and necessary for, the flourishing of every human person. However, each individual will require them to a different degree. Each man employs his individual judgments to determine the amount of time and effort that should go into the pursuit of various values and virtues. Finding the proper combination and proportion is the task for each person in view of his own talents, potentialities, and circumstances. Values and virtues are necessary for a flourishing life and are objectively discernable, but the exact weighting of them for a specific person is highly individualized.

In order for a chain of values to make sense, there must be some "end in itself" and "ultimate value" for which all other values are means. "An infinite progression" or chain of ends and means "toward a nonexistent end is a metaphysical and epistemological impossibility." All must converge on an ultimate value.

Each component of action of one's life (i.e., one's work life, love life, home life, social life, and so on) is an end in itself and a means to the end of one's life in total. "Man's life is a continuous whole." One's life in total is an end in itself and an ultimate value. An ultimate value is required for a person to rationally decide how to act. Evaluation necessitates teleological measurement in order to make our potential values comparable. When different values come into conflict, a person refers to a higher value in order to resolve the conflict.

An individual's task is to choose from among numerous values to find the most appropriate for himself. A person must make specific choices with respect to his career, his relationships, and so on. A "hierarchy of values" helps people make judgments regarding what to do or to pursue. To do this, an individual must assign a weight, either explicitly or implicitly, to his values. Values need to be weighted or ranked in terms of ordinal numbers. He must judge the ultimate contribution to the value of his life that exists at the apex of his hierarchy.

A value is an object of "goal-directed behavior." The fact that a person has values implies the existence of his goal-directed actions. Values are distinct from goals despite the fact that in general parlance goals and values are often used interchangeably. Actions are performed in response to one's values and are undertaken to achieve some goal or end.

To be a value means to be good for someone and for something. "Life" is one's "fundamental value" because life is conditional and requires a particular course of action to maintain it. Something can be good or bad only to a living organism, such as a human being, acting to survive. "Man's life" is the ultimate value and the "standard of value" for a human being.

A value exists in a chain of values and must have some ending point. There must be some "fundamental alternative" that marks the cessation of one's value chain. It is his life, "a process of self-sustaining and self-generated action," that is the fundamental alternative at the end of a person's value chain. One's life is the alternative that underpins all of his evaluative judgments.

Ethics, a code of values to rationally guide man's choices and actions, "is an objective, metaphysical necessity of man's survival." A proper ethics gives practical guidance to help people think and direct their lives. Ethics aids a man in defining and attaining his values, goals, and happiness. A man needs ethics because he requires values to survive. The *telos* of ethics is a person's own survival and happiness. The realm of ethics includes those matters that are potentially under a man's control. A man's uncoerced volition is necessary to have an objective theory of morality. He can discover values only through a volitional process of reason.

Rand's ethics identifies the good and bad according to the rational standard of value of "man's life qua man." Her Objectivist ethics focuses on what is, in reality, good or best for each unique individual human being. Such an ethics is rational, objective, and personal. Accordingly, a man's goal should be to become the best possible person in the context of who and what he is and of what is possible for him.

A person requires moral "knowledge" in the form of "abstractions" to guide his actions. Moral concepts necessarily come into play when one acts. A man needs an adequate set of general evaluative principles to provide basic guidance in living well. He must consciously identify the "principles" he wants to live by and must critically evaluate his values and principles.

Rational moral principles guide us toward values and are essential for achieving moral integrity, character, and happiness. When we habitually act on sound moral principles, we develop virtues and incorporate our moral orientation into our character. Rand connects virtues to the objective requirements of man's survival and flourishing. Moral principles are needed because the standard of survival and flourishing is too abstract. Acting on principles cultivates corresponding virtues which, in turn, leads to value attainment, flourishing, and happiness. According to Rand, "value is that which one acts to gain and/or keep—virtue is the act by which one gains and/or keeps it."

"Focus," a quality of alertness, involves a man's primary free will decision to activate his mind. It takes effort to stay in focus by using one's volition to activate his consciousness and mental resources. Although focus is not automatic and takes effort, it is rewarding and natural. Focus enters in the development of one's ideas, in the choice of his values, and in the selection of his moral principles. In addition, when one acts, he needs to focus in order to keep his ideas, values, and moral principles in his consciousness. A person must be alert for opportunities to form one's ideas, values, and principles and he must also use his free will to be in focus for his thinking to guide his actions. A person can be in focus, passively out of focus, or he can actively evade particular mental content. Rand says that "evasion is . . . the willful suspension of one's consciousness, the refusal to think . . . the refusal to know."

Moral principles are true or absolute in a given "context." A person needs to recognize the moral context of a situation. A man should not evade relevant knowledge or drop context when he acts. Some cases will fall outside the context in which they are defined and applicable. Thinking is needed in order to understand the facts of a situation and to apply appropriate principles to the circumstances. For example, "honesty," as a principle, states that it is immoral to misrepresent the truth in a context in which a person's goal is to "attain values" from others. It follows that in a different context in which someone is attempting to use deceit or force in order to gain values from an individual, it is appropriate for the wronged individual to choose self-defense (e.g., dishonesty) as the applicable principle instead of honesty. The context is different from one calling for honesty on his part. In this case, the person who is properly lying is not trying to gain a value. Instead, he is rationally acting in his own interest to protect a value that is being threatened.

Honesty is an essential principle because the proper end of a man's actions is his own objective flourishing. The moral appropriateness of honesty is grounded in metaphysics. A person must focus on what reality requires if he is to attain his ends. A person should tell the relevant truth. What the relevant truth is depends on the type of relationship a person has with the individual with whom he is dealing.

In Rand's biocentric ethics, moral behavior is judged in relation to achieving specific ends, with the final end being an individual's life or flourishing. The act of deciding necessitates the investigation of how an action pertains to what is best for one's own life. This is not done in a duty-based ethic that is limited to precepts and rules that are placed between a person and reality. In a biocentric ethics, what is moral is the understood and the chosen rather than the imposed and the obeyed. Principles are valuable ethical concepts that do not require imperatives or obligations as their justification.

Altruist moralities hold that morality is difficult and involves ideas such as self-abnegation and self-sacrifice. Contrariwise, an egoist morality, such as the one found in Objectivism, maintains that morality is natural and enjoyable. Of course, there is work involved in staying in focus, acquiring knowledge, formulating moral principles, and applying them in the appropriate contexts. Morality is demanding, but it is also indispensable and rewarding.

VALUES AND VIRTUES

Rand explains that to live, men must hold three ruling values—"reason, purpose, and self-esteem." These values imply all of the virtues required by a man's life. "Rationality," the primary virtue, is the recognition of objective reality, commitment to its perception, and the "acceptance of reason as one's source of knowledge, one's only judge of values, and one's only guide to action." "Independence," the acceptance of one's intellectual responsibility for one's own existence, requires that a man form his own judgments and that he support himself by the work of his own mind. "Honesty," the selfish refusal to seek values by faking reality, recognizes that the unreal can have no value. "Integrity," the refusal to permit a breach between thought and action, acknowledges the fact that man is an indivisible, integrated entity of mind and body. "Justice," a form of faithfulness to reality, is the virtue of granting to each man that which he objectively deserves. Justice is the expression of man's rationality in his dealings with other men and involves seeking and granting the earned. A trader, a man of justice, "earns what he gets and does not give or take the undeserved." Just as he does not work except in exchange for something of economic value, he also does not give his love, friendship, or esteem except in trade for the pleasure he receives from the virtues of individuals he respects. Love, friendship, and esteem, as moral tributes, are caused and must be earned. "Productiveness," the virtue of creating material values, is the art of translating one's thoughts and goals into reality. "Pride," the total of the preceding virtues, can be thought of as "moral ambitiousness."

CAPITALISM AND INDIVIDUAL RIGHTS

Rand's justification of capitalism is that it is a system based on the logically derived code of morality outlined above—a code of morality that recognizes man's metaphysical nature and the supremacy of reason, rationality, and individualism. The ruling principle of capitalism is justice. The overall social effect—the fact that individuals and groups who live under capitalism prosper—is simply a byproduct or secondary consequence. Political and economic systems and institutions which encourage and protect individual rights, freedom, and happiness are proper systems.

"A right is a moral principle defining and sanctioning a man's freedom of action in a social context." According to Rand, rights are innate and can be logically derived from man's nature and needs. The principle of man's rights, like every other Objectivist moral principle, is derived by way of ethical egoism. The state is not involved in the creation of rights and simply exists to protect an individual's natural rights. There are no group rights—only individual rights. Group rights are arbitrary and imply special interests.

Humans are material beings who require material goods to sustain their existence. If one's life is the standard, man has the right to live and pursue values as his survival requires. He has the right to work for and keep the fruits of his labor—the right of property. "Without property rights, no other rights are possible." A man who has no right to the product of his efforts is not free to pursue his happiness and has no means to sustain his life.

A violation of a man's property rights is an expression of force against the man himself. The purpose of the government is to "protect man's rights" (including property rights) and enforce contractual agreements—a breach of contract is an indirect use of force. The state's function is thus restricted to the "retaliatory use of force."

Under Randian capitalism, which historically has never existed, there is a complete separation of state and economics. Men deal with each other voluntarily by individual choice and free trade to their mutual benefit. The "profit motive" is just and moral. "Profit" is made through moral virtue and measures the creation of wealth by the profit-earner. The "market price" is objectively determined in the free market and represents the lowest price a buyer can discover and the highest price a seller can obtain. It is a socially objective value rather than a philosophically objective value. In a free market both parties expect to benefit—no one is willing to enter into a one-sided bargain to his anticipated detriment. A person's wealth under capitalism depends on his productive achievements and the choice of others to recognize them. Rewards are tied to production, ability, and merit. A producer can do with his wealth what he chooses as long as he does not infringe on the rights of another. However, Rand is against altruism, which involves giving up a higher value in favor of a lower one. Altruism is the moral doctrine that requires a man to live selflessly and disinterestedly for others and to place others above self. The essence of altruism is the demand for disinterested self-sacrifice instead of true concern for others. Altruism holds that self-sacrifice is the highest moral duty. Ayn Rand explains that it is not a self-sacrifice to help someone whose well-being is important to one's own life and happiness. Charity is rational, objective, and genuine when, rather than being offered indiscriminately, it is only offered voluntarily and only to valued individuals.

CONCLUSION

Despite inciting a number of vehement and critical commentaries, Rand's controversial, original, and systematic philosophical positions should be taken seriously and treated with respect. She persuasively expounds a fully integrated defense of capitalism and the component metaphysical, epistemological, psychological, ethical, social, political, cultural, and historical conditions necessary for its establishment and survival. Rand presents Objectivism as an integrated new system of thought with an organized, hierarchical structure. Whatever one's ultimate evaluation of her theories, Rand's unique vision should be considered worthy of comprehensive, scholarly examination.

Ayn Rand was a philosophical system-builder who consistently integrated the various aspects of her clearly written and compelling work. Rand's view of the world and of human possibility in the world is at the heart of her system. She sees a benevolent world that is open to man's achievement and success. Happiness and great accomplishment are possible in the world. To succeed, a man must comprehend the nature of the world and of man and must define, choose, and passionately pursue rational values. Moral greatness is possible for each of us if we rationally strive to live up to our potential, whatever that potential may be. A person who selects rational values and who chooses ends and means consonant with the nature of reality and with the integrity of his own consciousness exemplifies a moral ideal and can certainly be viewed as heroic. As a rational goal, Rand's ideal of moral greatness is available to every human being.

NOTE

This appendix is a chapter that appeared in my book, *Champions of a Free Society* (Lanham, MD: Lexington, 2008). It is a shortened and edited version of a chapter from my book, *Philosophers of Capitalism* (Lanham, MD: Lexington, 2005). All rights reserved and reprinted with permissions..

REFERENCES

Badhwar, Neera K. 2001. *Is Virtue Only a Means to Happiness? An Analysis of Virtue and Happiness in Ayn Rand's Writings*. Poughkeepsie, NY: The Objectivist Center.

Baker, James T. 1987. *Ayn Rand*. Boston: Twayne.

Binswanger, Harry. 1988. *The Ayn Rand Lexicon: Objectivism from A to Z*. New York: New American Library.

Branden, Barbara. 1986. *The Passion of Ayn Rand*. New York: Doubleday.

Branden, Nathaniel. 1989. *Judgment Day: My Years with Ayn Rand.* Boston: Houghton Mifflin Company.

———. 1999. *My Years with Ayn Rand.* San Francisco, California: Jossey-Bass Publishers.

Den Uyl, Douglas, and Douglas Rasmussen, eds. 1984. *The Philosophical Thought of Ayn Rand.* Chicago: University of Illinois Press.

Ellis, Albert. 1968. *Is Objectivism a Religion?* New York: Lyle Stuart.

Erickson, Peter. 1997. *The Stance of Atlas: An Examination of the Philosophy of Ayn Rand.* New York: Herakles Publishers.

Gladstein, Mimi. 1984. *The Ayn Rand Companion.* Westport, Connecticut: Greenwood.

———. 1999. *The New Ayn Rand Companion, Revised and Expanded Edition.* Westport, Connecticut: Greenwood Publishing Group.

Gotthelf, Allan. 2000. *On Ayn Rand.* Belmont, California: Wadsworth.

Greiner, Donna, and Theodore B. Kinni. 2001. *Ayn Rand and Business.* New York: W.W. Norton & Company.

Hamil, Virginia L. L. 1990. *In Defense of Ayn Rand.* Brookline, MA: New Beacon.

Kelley, David. 2000. *The Contested Legacy of Ayn Rand.* Poughkeepsie, New York: The Objectivist Center.

Long, Roderick T. 2000. *Reason and Value: Aristotle Versus Rand.* Poughkeepsie, New York: The Objectivist Center.

Machan, Tibor R. 1999. *Ayn Rand.* New York: Peter Lang.

Mayhew, Robert, ed. 2004. *Essays on Ayn Rand's 'We the Living.'* Lanham, Maryland: Rowman & Littlefield.

Merrill, Ronald E. 1991. *The Ideas of Ayn Rand.* Chicago: Open Court.

Nyquist, Greg S. 2001. *Ayn Rand Contra Human Nature.* Bloomington, Indiana: iUniverse, Inc.

O'Neill, William F. 1991. *With Charity Toward None.* New York: Philosophical Library.

Peikoff, Leonard. 1991. *Objectivism: The Philosophy of Ayn Rand.* New York: Dutton.

Porter, Tom. 1999. *Ayn Rand's Theory of Knowledge.* Reseda, California: Tom Porter.

Rand, Ayn. 1957. *Atlas Shrugged.* New York: Random House.

———. 1961. *For the New Intellectual.* New York: Random House.

———. 1963. *The New Left.* New York: Signet.

———. 1967a. *Capitalism: The Unknown Ideal.* New York: The New American Library.

———. 1967b. *Introduction to Objectivist Epistemology.* New York: The Objectivist.

———. 1971. *The Romantic Manifesto.* New York: The New American Library.

———. 1982. *Philosophy: Who Needs It.* Edited by Leonard Peikoff. New York: Bobbs-Merrill.

———. 1984. *The Early Ayn Rand.* Edited and annotated by Leonard Peikoff. New York: New American Library.

———. 1990. *The Voice of Reason.* Edited by Leonard Peikoff. New York: Penguin Books.

————. 1995. *Ayn Rand's Marginalia: Her Critical Comments on the Writings of Over 20 Authors.* Edited by Robert Mayhew. New Milford, Connecticut: Second Renaissance Books.

————. 1997a. *Journals of Ayn Rand.* Edited by David Harriman. New York: Plume.

————. 1997b. *Letters of Ayn Rand.* Edited by Michael S. Berliner, with an introduction by Leonard Peikoff. New York: Penguin.

————. 1997c. *Without a Prayer: Ayn Rand and the Close of Her System.* Unicoi, Tennessee: Trinity Foundation.

————. 1999. *Russian Writings on Hollywood.* Edited by Michael S. Berliner. Irvine, California: Ayn Rand Institute Press.

Robbins, John W. 1974. *Answer to Ayn Rand.* Washington, DC: Mount Vernon Publishing.

Ryan, Scott. 2003. *Objectivism and the Corruption of Rationality: A Critique of Ayn Rand's Epistemology.* Lincoln, Nebraska: Writers Club Press.

Sciabarra, Chris Matthew. 1995. *Ayn Rand: The Russian Radical.* University Park: Pennsylvania State University Press.

————. 1999. *Ayn Rand: Her Life and Thought.* Poughkeepsie, New York: The Objectivist Center.

Seddon, Fred. 2003. *Ayn Rand, Objectivists, and the History of Philosophy.* Lanham, Maryland: Rowman & Littlefield.

Smith, Tara. 2006. *Ayn Rand's Normative Ethics.* Cambridge: Cambridge University Press.

Valiant, James. 2001. *The Passion of Ayn Rand's Critics.* Dallas, Texas: Durban House Publishing.

Walker, Jeff. 1999. *The Ayn Rand Cult.* Chicago: Open Court.

Yang, Michael B. 2000. *Reconsidering Ayn Rand.* Cincinnati, Ohio: Enclair Publishing.

Index

About the Author

Edward W. Younkins is professor of accountancy and executive director of the Institute for the Study of Capitalism and Morality at Wheeling University. He is the founder of the university's undergraduate degree program in political and economic philosophy. He is also the founding director of the university's Master of Business Administration (MBA) and Master of Science in Accountancy (MSA) programs. In addition to earning state and national honors for his performances on the Certified Public Accountant (CPA) and Certified Management Accountant (CMA) exams, respectively, Dr. Younkins also received the Outstanding Educator Award for 1997 from the West Virginia Society of Certified Public Accountants. The author of numerous articles in accounting and business journals, his free-market-oriented articles and reviews have appeared in numerous publications. He is the author of *Capitalism and Commerce: Conceptual Foundations of Free Enterprise* (2002); *Champions of a Free Society: Ideas of Capitalism's Philosophers and Economists* (2008); *Flourishing and Happiness in a Free Society: Toward a Synthesis of Aristotelianism, Austrian Economics,* and *Ayn Rand's Objectivism* (2011); and *Exploring Capitalist Fiction: Business Through Literature and Film* (2014).

www.ingramcontent.com/pod-product-compliance
Lightning Source LLC
Chambersburg PA
CBHW032351280326
41935CB00008B/533